Utilitarianism as a Way of Life

Utilitarianism as a Way of Life

Re-envisioning Planetary Happiness

Bart Schultz

polity

First published in 2024 by Polity Press

Polity Press
65 Bridge Street
Cambridge CB2 1UR, UK

Polity Press
111 River Street
Hoboken, NJ 07030, USA

ISBN-13: 978-1-5095-5226-9
ISBN-13: 978-1-5095-5227-6 (pb)

A catalogue record for this book is available from the British Library.

Library of Congress Control Number: 2023950668

Typeset in 10.5 on 12 pt Times New Roman
by Fakenham Prepress Solutions, Fakenham, Norfolk NR21 8NL
Printed and bound in Great Britain by CPI Group (UK) Ltd, Croydon

For further information on Polity, visit our website:
politybooks.com

Contents

Acknowledgments

My deepest thanks to all the wonderful Polity people – Ian Malcolm, Ellen MacDonald-Kramer, Maddie Tyler, Glynis Baguley, and Leigh Mueller – for transforming the impossible into the possible, and the possible into the actual, when it came to this book. Their patience and guidance, along with that of the manuscript reviewers, Roger Crisp and Anonymous, made it happen. My family – Marty, Madeleine, and all our companion animals – make love possible, even in the "Anthropocene," and my expanded circle of Sidgwick enthusiasts, referred to throughout the text, know how much I owe them. I would like to dedicate this book to the memory of three of those enthusiasts, Placido Bucolo, J. B. Schneewind, and Derek Parfit, and to the memory of another philosophical friend, Timuel D. Black. They made my world a better place.

Introduction: Decolonizing Utilitarianism

> If the human is anything, it seems to be a double movement, one in which we assert moral norms at the same time as we question the authority by which we make that assertion. (Judith Butler, *Giving an Account of Oneself*)

Increasingly, as I look forward, I think back. And at times wonder, though not always. Other emotions crowd in.

No doubt age has something to do with that, but from my points of view, there is more to the story. After all, gazing at a dreadful future filled with existential and catastrophic threats – climate change and biodiversity loss, pandemics, nuclear war, and unaligned Artificial Intelligence, to name a few – makes many people wonder and worry about how we got here, about how, for example, various destructive forces of modernity took a sharp upward turn, like a hockey stick, around 1950 and have continued in that direction largely unabated.[1] The very processes of development trumpeted as marking the success of the "American century" – notably longer life expectancies, economic growth and reduced global poverty, and increasing democratization, amid a wealth of consumer goods – have increasingly taken on the appearance of short-term, unstable gains purchased at the expense of future generations and other vulnerable populations.[2]

There are many historical narratives here. The economic forces of a growth-obsessed capitalism and reckless industrialization, and the political and military forces of the neoliberal world order in the aftermath of the World Wars, figure in most. In longer perspective, these are often embedded in metanarratives about the formations of modern liberalism and individualism in modern nation-states, the legacies of the Renaissance, Reformation, Scientific Revolution, and Enlightenment. The glossings might vary, from Marxian laments about the birth of possessive individualism to liberal celebrations of the birth of tolerance and pluralism with liberty leading the people, but to a remarkable degree, and despite many challenges, the distinctively Eurocentric and/or Anglo-American stories about modernity have spread across the world like the disproportionate fossil fuel emissions from those locations. The "unfinished Enlightenment Project" manifests itself throughout the dominant rights-based frameworks informing the work of the United Nations and so many other national and international agencies.[3] No doubt the frameworks have improved in recent decades, recognizing for example the rights of Indigenous peoples, but the politics of such rights and recognition narratives mostly remains in the mold.[4]

But for many, certain critiques of such narratives, conjoined with resistance to them, must also be part of the story. The present work is written with those different framings in mind, in a spirit of alliance with the work of activists using critical race theory, critical race studies, and more or less recent decolonization and postcolonial scholarship to resist and rewrite the stories about liberalism and modernity that persist and harm, in both academic and popular political contexts. Standing with many such critics, from Cedric J. Robinson on racial capitalism to Edward Said on Orientalism, Lisa Lowe bluntly explains, "liberal philosophy, culture, economics, and government have been commensurate with, and deeply implicated in, colonialism, slavery, capitalism, and empire." As she elaborates on her project in *The Intimacies of Four Continents*,

> In examining state archives out of which these historical narratives emerge, I observe the ways in which the archive that mediates the imperatives of the state subsumes colonial violence within narratives of modern reason and progress. To make legible the forcible encounters, removals, and entanglements omitted in liberal accounts of abolition, emancipation, and independence, I devise other ways of reading so that we might understand the processes through which the forgetting of violent encounter is naturalized, both by the archive, and in the subsequent narrative histories. In a sense, one aim of my project is to be more specific about what I would term the economy of affirmation and forgetting that structures and formalizes the archives of liberalism, and liberal ways of understanding. This economy civilizes and develops freedoms for "man" in modern Europe and North America, while relegating others to geographical and temporal spaces that are constituted as backward, uncivilized, and unfree.

> Liberal forms of political economy, culture, government, and history propose a narrative of freedom overcoming enslavement that at once denies colonial slavery, erases the seizure of lands from native peoples, displaces migrations and connections across continents, and internalizes these processes in a national struggle of history and consciousness. The social inequalities of our time are a legacy of these processes through which "the human" is "freed" by liberal forms, while other subjects, practices, and geographies are placed at a distance from "the human."[5]

And, as Lowe observes, Marxian and Frankfurt School critical theory have a checkered history of buying into the same problematic Eurocentric erasures.[6]

Lowe allows that there is much valuable scholarly and activist work on one or another dimension of these issues, but for all that, there is "scarcely any that considers the connections, relations, and mixings among the histories of Asian, African, and indigenous peoples in the Americas."[7] In pursuing such research, as more are now doing, the archives are important, but so too are the literary forms of autobiography and the novel. "Commensurate with political philosophy's affirmation of the individual's passage to freedom through economic industry and political emancipation, the *autobiography* served as a particularly powerful genre for the individual achievement of liberty through ethical education and civilization. In a sense, the autobiography is the liberal genre par excellence."[8] Unsurprisingly, she pays careful attention to the autobiography of John Stuart Mill, perhaps the most influential liberal autobiography of all. The "intimacies" of the freedom-achieving modern self are fully on display there.

But the significance of Mill is larger still – indeed, emblematic of the logic of empire: "Like utilitarian thinkers Jeremy Bentham and Mill's father, James Mill, who were concerned with the 'governmental character' of liberalism, John Stuart Mill also emphasized that liberal freedom included discipline. In utilitarianism, additional freedoms necessarily required additional control and regulation; in this sense, 'education,' broadly understood, was the synthetic link between individual subjectivity and the state." Thus,

> it is not simply that Mill's thought merely accommodated colonial domination; rather his ideas provided the terms, logics, and powers through which older colonial domination was rationalized and new forms of imperial domination were innovated and executed. If we examine Mill's *Considerations on Representative*

> *Government* (1861), in relationship to his writing on the East India Company, we appreciate that he explained 'liberty' consistently through the division of those 'incapable of self-government' from those with the capacity for liberty. *Representative Government* begins and ends with explicit discussions of the need for authoritarian government in colonial India as a means of progress toward liberty and civilization.[9]

Lowe is not alone in arguing, correctly to my mind, that to understand Mill's philosophy and its significance, it is vital to consider both his life – notably his long-term employment at the British East India Company, which effectively ruled India – and his works, including a wider range of his works than that canonized in academic philosophy curricula.[10] And she is right to hold that his liberalism was grounded in his utilitarianism, a point that Mill himself always insisted upon. In *On Liberty*, after emphatically setting out his position that the "only purpose for which power can be rightly exercised over any member of a civilized community, against his will, is to prevent harm to others," he explains "that I forgo any advantage which could be derived to my argument from the ideal of abstract right, as a thing independent of utility. I regard utility as the ultimate appeal on all ethical questions; but it must be utility in the largest sense, grounded on the permanent interests of man as a progressive being."[11] That view was given powerful expression in his *Utilitarianism*, which first appeared as a series of three magazine articles in 1861, and laid it down that the "creed which accepts as the foundation of morals, Utility, or the Greatest Happiness Principle, holds that actions are right in proportion as they tend to promote happiness, wrong as they tend to produce the reverse of happiness. By happiness is intended pleasure, and the absence of pain; by unhappiness, pain, and the privation of pleasure."[12]

Are we to conclude, then, that the younger Mill, whose name is virtually synonymous with the term "utilitarianism" across much of the world, is a chief case in point for the claim that liberal philosophy grew in ways "commensurate with, and deeply implicated in, colonialism, slavery, capitalism, and empire"? Many, obviously including Lowe, would say yes, and some, including myself, would agree but go even further in detailing the type of racism that figured in Mill's ethics and politics (and historical context) when it came to the subjects colonized by the British Empire – a racism that was not as overtly offensive as that of, say, Thomas Carlyle, the influential historian of the French Revolution and "man of letters," but was nonetheless insidious enough.[13]

But then, to turn to the title of this book, if Mill is an emblematic case of utilitarianism as a way of life, and I am allying with his anti-colonialist and anti-imperialist critics, what could possibly be forthcoming here that could make good on my subtitle, “re-envisioning planetary happiness”? What, unless it is to the effect that a different and non-utilitarian way of life would be better, if there is to be any chance of addressing our global crises in ways informed by and in opposition to the harsh historical (and current) realities of colonialism, settler colonialism, and imperialism? What has historically marched under the banner of “the greatest happiness of the greatest number,” as the classical utilitarian slogan famously puts it, might appear rather to be the violent, even genocidal, policies and practices of domination, discipline, exclusion, marginalization, displacement, and eradication, the imperial heart of darkness making up stories about its beneficence.

My purpose is emphatically not to try to rehabilitate or legitimate Mill’s racist imperialism.[14] To the contrary, my primary aim, paradoxical as it may sound, is to consider how utilitarianism itself might be decolonized, might be de-centered and treated to an effort to unlearn and problematize many of the familiar, privileged Eurocentric historical stories featuring it as a lead player on the Enlightenment stage. A truly critical utilitarianism might even transcend itself, and help build solidarity with ways of life and philosophies that have allied with the very resistance movements opposing the deeply problematic Eurocentric realizations of utilitarianism and other ethical and political theories, which historically have often been worse.[15] Or at least fracture, taking any number of different and inconsistent forms. Arguably, it has often done just that.

Admittedly, utilitarianism against Mill is bound to sound like imperialism against empire or something equally absurd. The case is in the details and sources, and, in the end, I will only offer selective interventions, sketching various considerations in support of this critical effort. Still, these considerations are not to be reduced to the very tired exoneration to the effect that misapplications of utilitarian principles to, say, justify settler colonialism are merely that – misapplications, not bearing on the evident truth of the principles. Vindication is not that easy. If utilitarian principles were always and everywhere badly misapplied, one would have to wonder whether they were of any practical or theoretical use at all, since they would scarcely be fit for actual living and the problem-solving demands of human life. They would fail by their own standards.

While acknowledging the vast scholarly investments in the big polarities – say, between universalism and relativism, foundationalism and anti-foundationalism, or for that matter, structure and agency – what follows here is somewhat evasive with respect to them, and designedly so. What grounds critique and who is positioned to advance it are presented more as questions than as conclusions.

But for the purposes of this introductory chapter, and the rest of the book, some brief personal philosophical background might prove useful – some more thinking back, from what may admittedly be a problematic perspective, in light of the foregoing reservations about liberalism's autobiographies.

Unlike many who sympathize with utilitarianism, I have never held that either the "self" or the "interest" side of the notion of "self-interest" can be taken as a given. Indeed, the relationships that matter, for happiness and/or well-being, may be better for being less bounded by the apparent interests of some fictive personal identity over time, some supposed deep and weighty further fact that one is a unified individual person over a lifetime, like an enduring soul or a Cartesian Ego that has or owns conscious experiences but is not reducible to them. The philosopher Derek Parfit argued along those lines in his 1984 book *Reasons and Persons*, and in the process recognized that his "Reductionist" view of the individual person, as just so many selves woven from psychological connectedness in an ancestral chain of (non-branching) continuity, pointed up both how personal identity, defined in such terms, is not "what matters" and how views of that nature have a much wider and longer history than their rediscovery via Anglo-American analytical philosophy, particularly in various Buddhist practices.[16] They might even, Parfit suggested, supply some aid and comfort to utilitarianism, which some think of as virtually defined by a rejection of the moral significance of the separateness of persons.

My first published article in philosophy addressed Parfit's claims about personal identity and utilitarianism, claims that have never left me in peace, though I have not always pursued them via the standard approaches of analytical academic philosophy, even Parfit's own, which relied heavily on abstract thought experiments and puzzle cases.[17] Still, as I looked ahead to writing this particular book, I found myself increasingly looking back to his formative influence, and meditating on how it could take people in unexpected directions, as well as the expected ones.

Parfit's life and work have, after his untimely passing in 2017, lived on in both his own writings and such valuable books as Dave Edmunds's biography *Parfit: A Philosopher and His Mission to Save Morality* and various collections of essays, including Singer's *Does Anything Really*

Matter? Essays on Parfit on Objectivity and Jeff McMahan's volumes in the *Legacy of Derek Parfit* series, *Principles and Persons* and *Ethics and Existence*.[18] Such works represent the expected direction and are certainly important in many, many ways. But one of the unexpected directions is my direction, taken in this book, which takes a more critical and historical, and more biographical, approach, as evidenced in my books *The Happiness Philosophers: The Lives and Works of the Great Utilitarians*, *Henry Sidgwick, Eye of the Universe* and the edited volume *Utilitarianism and Empire*.[19] To be sure, in the years just before and after that early article on personal identity, much of my research concerned how Parfit's positions might bear on Bernard Williams's influential objections to utilitarianism for conflicting with individual integrity, on the liberal political philosophy of John Rawls and the Rawlsian critique of utilitarianism for supposedly ignoring the separateness of persons, and on Michael Sandel's communitarian construction of the self in opposition to Rawls's more neo-Kantian construction of the self. However, my attention soon shifted to seemingly more historical and biographical issues, especially related to the Victorian-era philosopher Henry Sidgwick, who was one of Parfit's heroes and a powerful influence on Rawls as well.[20] Sidgwick seemed to be a key source for both Parfit and Rawls, for both utilitarian sympathizers and their critics.

And what Parfit had mostly driven me to wonder about was just what the utilitarian self or selves might look like, or could look like, in fuller, concrete psychological and historical detail. His abstract, spare psychology of personal identity as continuity and connectedness, with less morally relevant "depth" than the Non-Reductionist alternatives, did not color in the lines with anything like a detailed personality theory, and, consequently, his arguments struck me as premature or hostage to facts about the realities of selfhood in all its messy relationality and complexity, all its affirmations, forgettings, projections, conflicts, identifications, roles, sexualizings, genderings, racializings, and so on and on. His account of personal identity was as devoid of living material as the Cartesian Ego it was set against. Better to look at real people, such as Sidgwick, and how they theorized and lived utilitarianism, insofar as they did, especially since, for me, the politics of experience has always looked more like that vividly described in Michael Pollan's *How to Change Your Mind*[21] than anything as oversimplified as the notion of psychological continuity.[22]

My shifting focus was in fact part of a wider recognition of the importance of philosophy as manifesting in certain ways of life, often a collective group or institutional life, beyond its formal bureaucratic definition as a modern academic discipline in the humanities. This recognition entailed a more reflexive, critical, and historical (perhaps genealogical) engagement with the ways in which philosophy's institutions and practices came to be in their current form, since their formative history seemed profoundly important but at times deeply troubling, and not simply for the reasons set out by such anti-philosophers as Michel Foucault and the neo-pragmatist Richard Rorty. Neither Foucault nor Rorty – famous for his 1970s debunking and dethroning of analytical philosophy, and depiction of philosophy as another genre of literature – ever went far enough.[23]

The importance of effecting this shift was driven home less by studying Foucault and Rorty, though there was plenty of that, and more by a series of events and encounters that heightened my sense of the problems of patriarchy, systemic structural racism, colonialism and settler colonialism, and their intersections, in the shaping of modern societies, including educational institutions, including academic philosophy.

There is a still longer, and relevant, personal history here reaching back to the politics of the 1960s and having to do with opposition to the US war of aggression in Vietnam. My interests in Daoism and Buddhism were in part the result of a countercultural allying with the cultures of the victims of American aggression and imperialism, and with such cogent activist critics of the war – and the institutions supporting it – as Bertrand Russell, Daniel Ellsberg, Thich Nhat Hanh, and Noam Chomsky, whose politics I continue to admire.[24] These brilliant dissenters knew first-hand how culpable Western institutions of higher education could be in facilitating injustices at home and abroad, and how the ethical and political responsibilities of academics went beyond anything in their job descriptions.[25] The violence of the Western Empires, the insanities of the supposedly "sane societies" (as detailed by Erich Fromm, R. D. Laing, Herbert Marcuse, Angela Davis, Frantz Fanon, Howard Zinn, Germaine Greer, Rudolf Dreikurs, Paul Goodman, and so many others, including those mentioned above), were never out of mind.

With that backstory, my later shift to a more critically distanced approach to academic philosophy, with greater attention to the power dynamics of the people, practices, and institutions responsible for the social production of "knowledge," may seem less puzzling.[26] For me, the "persons" and the "reasons" informed each other in ways untheorized by Parfit, and were mediated by forces and factors that he did not consider. His world was too small and took too much for granted about how "knowledge" production worked. Unfortunately, I had not, at that turning point, fully realized just how small my world was as well.

As it transpired, my subsequent decades of experience studying and teaching at the University of Chicago left me in little doubt about the limits of the Western canons, or the inertia of academics when it came to embracing in meaningful ways the demands for greater diversity, equity, and inclusion, or more ambitiously, decolonization.[27] Teaching courses in Gender Studies and the History of Sexuality spoke to my interests, including a growing interest in the life and work of Sidgwick's close friend John Addington Symonds, the extraordinary champion of "Greek Love" who led the way in scholarly research on the realities of ancient Greek same-sex love.[28] But few women and virtually no philosophers of color ever figured in the philosophy curricula.

Indeed, despite the seeming – but in fact tenuous – popularity of academic discourses of decolonization, there are very different degrees of ambition with respect to it. Historian Steven Mintz, for example, blogs in *Inside Higher Ed* that:

> It's fairly obvious what it means to decolonize a museum. It's a matter of making a museum more inclusive: expanding or dismantling the artistic canon, shedding or challenging Eurocentric aesthetic standards, and sharing authority for collecting and interpreting artworks with those whose voices and perspectives were previously marginalized.
>
> It's also pretty obvious how one might decolonize a scholarly journal like the *American Historical Review*. This requires the journal to correct the exclusionary practices that effectively silenced the voices of scholars of color and Indigenous and women scholars, slighted the historical experiences of nonelites, and snubbed facets of life that lay outside the privileged domains of politics, diplomacy and military and economic affairs.
>
> Decolonizing the *AHR* also means opening its pages more broadly, soliciting contributions aggressively from those whose work was previously ignored, evaluating submissions from a wider range of perspectives, reviewing more varied books, working more closely with authors asked to revise and resubmit, and making the journal more responsive to alternate points of view.[29]

Such steps are sensible enough, but, as Mintz allows, there is more to decolonizing the academy:

> At its most radical, decolonization means "resisting and actively unlearning the dangerous and harmful legacy of colonization, particularly the racist ideas that Black, Indigenous, and People of Color (BIPOC) people are inferior to White Europeans." It entails interrogating and dismantling "power structures that carry legacies of racism, imperialism, and colonialism." But more commonly, it calls on faculty to address a series of curricular, pedagogical and evaluative challenges.
>
> Professors have a responsibility as intellectuals to question established paradigms and hierarchies; combat the erasure (or mere ignorance) of knowledge produced by those outside established institutions; highlight the contributions, ideas and experiences of all people; and recognize the ways that power relations shape the production, dissemination and application of knowledge.[30]

Mintz does not pursue the political ramifications of the more radical perspective, though he does make some helpful suggestions about how faculty can decolonize their "curriculum, syllabi, classroom cultures, pedagogy and assessments." These suggestions deserve a wide audience.

Even so, such progress as has been made on these fronts has been very hard won and remains limited, hampered in no small part by – to voice the more radical line Mintz describes – the embedding of elite educational institutions (and others as well) in social contexts of deep inequality and vile, demented politics. Ultimately, "decolonizing" higher education is bound up with decolonizing society, an effort that, at this historical juncture and across much of the world, is challenged by a reemergence of white supremacism, overt, violent racism and authoritarian racist nationalism, and gender and anti-LGBTQ+ violence. "Culture wars" is not the right term for this, since the "wars" are wars of aggression against real people and on the basis not simply of their "culture," but of their race, gender identity, etc. The authoritarianism enabling and advancing these wars, on display in the chumminess of Trump, Putin, Modi, Orbán, and so many other aspiring autocrats, will opportunistically seize on any lie, the bigger the better, to erase history and promote its agenda, often doing so without fear of the courageous and brilliantly creative resistance of protesters such as Pussy Riot.[31] The cringy politics of it all has generated a supposedly "populist" reaction against elite academic institutions, though the resentment and fear animating such reactions can at times reflect legitimate (if misdirected) grievances about being left behind by societal elites, including the political elites who are scarcely responsive to popular demands.[32] In these times, whatever one may write or teach, it is too easy to be part of the problem, unthinkingly (or thinkingly) perpetuating a world order that in truth serves no one.[33]

Of course, even in the calmer moments of comparative neoliberal sanity (if it can be called that), such larger societal forces as racial capitalism, settler colonialism, and deep inequality can compromise the work and impact of the "best and the brightest." My long experience as Director of the University of Chicago Civic Knowledge Project, an entity founded by African American political philosopher Danielle Allen in 2003 with an eye to making the University a better neighbor to the largely low-income Black communities on Chicago's South Side, was an educational experience on a par with my graduate school education, albeit one that cast a harsh light on the limits of the latter.[34] Through the eyes of such figures as Timuel D. Black, the iconic Black civil rights activist and educator from Chicago's Bronzeville neighborhood, I came to grasp the unfortunate degree to which historically the University truly was an exclusive, largely white, predominantly male club, and had, without ever properly so much as apologizing for it, effectively created, enforced, and even funded policies of residential segregation in Chicago through such tools as "restrictive covenants" (agreements prohibiting the rental or sale of housing to people of color) and urban renewal policies of gentrification and displacement, not always announced as such.[35] And this while socializing students and faculty to, in effect (and out of fear), avert their eyes from the neighboring communities and ignore the University's historical role in creating some of the very social problems that students and faculty hoped their research would help them address. Far too many members of the University community were (and are) unaware that they were (and are) part of such a club, a case in point of systemic, structural racism. The Delphic mandate "Know Thyself" apparently has its limits, when considering the institutions enabling one's academic work. It is certainly not aided by college and university "News" offices. Given the University's highly publicized branding as a (very Millian) defender of academic free speech, and its long-proclaimed "Kalven Doctrine" supposedly prohibiting it from taking public political stances, there is an eerie way in which it can seem like a perfect microcosm of the Millian hypocrisies and complicities described by Lowe.[36]

The University of Chicago is of course scarcely unique in this respect, as shown by Davarian Baldwin's *In the Shadow of the Ivory Tower*, a cogent critique of the "Eds and Meds" approach to urban development and renewal that one finds in so many urban centers in the

US, and other countries as well.[37] Baldwin compares the University of Chicago (and its prominent Medical Center) to a range of other institutions, including Yale, with related profiles and problems. And, more generally, a slew of recent works chronicle the emerging and ongoing threats to institutions of higher education: Will Bunch's *After the Fall of the Ivory Tower*, Peter Fleming's *Dark Academia: How Universities Die*, Sara Ahmed's *Complaint!*, Lorgia García Peña's *Community as Rebellion: A Syllabus for Surviving Academia as a Woman of Color*, and Leigh Patel's *No Study without Struggle: Confronting Settler Colonialism in Higher Education*, and many additional books, essays, blogs, etc.[38] Of special note here is the moral philosopher Olúfẹ́mi Táíwò's compelling work on *Elite Capture*, pointing up how elites, including academic elites, can capture or co-opt identity politics and radical critiques of racial capitalism.[39]

The striking irony that so many of the above critiques were produced in and enabled by the very institutions being critiqued, and can be subject to elite capture and turned to the purpose of denying or downplaying the charges, should not be lost on the authors or their readers. Admittedly, it is hard to fully grasp the complexities of institutions of higher education, which have become such indispensable national resources that, at least with the most prestigious ones, they are in some respects "too big to fail," like certain banks or defense industries – though, unlike banks and defense industries, they do tend to attract a large number of clever, free-thinking societal critics committed to serious scholarly inquiry and contributing to society. The drawbacks and downsides do need to be kept in comparative perspective.[40] Academic clubs can vary greatly, and the freedom dreams of the 1960s, looking to institutions of higher education (rather than the working class) to galvanize and mobilize mass movements for social justice, endure in the perpetually paradoxical ways that they have always endured, as relatively marginal efforts that periodically incite vastly disproportionate, reactionary political blowback.[41]

At any rate, the problems the above works detail are often reflected or refracted in academic philosophy departments. Using highly selective and carefully curated canonical works such that the issues of race and racism, patriarchy, etc. loom small or vanish completely, and disembodied "arguments" that can be taught by departments in which faculty women of color are virtually non-existent and white men are never dislodged from the comfort zones of whatever they did in graduate school, academic philosophers have been very slow even to recognize the Experience Machine in which they exist. It is easily avoided bad form to dwell on the crude racism of Kant, and how it figured in his cosmopolitan view of history, or for that matter in the erasures wrought by Kant's many eminent successors, including Rawls. When, over 25 years ago, I first started teaching and writing candidly about the racisms to be found in the works of John Stuart Mill and Henry Sidgwick, I was stunned to find that hardly anyone who had written on Mill and absolutely no one who had written on Sidgwick acknowledged the issue, much less its importance – philosophical, political, and historical.[42] The transparent evasions of academic philosophers, who sought to downplay such matters as merely "personal" biographical problems characteristic of the "times," were offensive even then, and today, in the context of critical race theory and critical race studies, look increasingly desperate, the more so given the crude, naïve, and unhistorical conceptualizations of race and racism deployed by so many of those philosophers. Combating racism wherever one finds it should be more important than attempting philosophical cosmetic surgery on the "greats" of the canon. Critical race theory is *obviously* right to insist on the significance of race and racism, in their shifting historical constructions and systemic institutional incarnations.[43]

But, to return to the theme of this book, these fashionings of philosophical selves, embedded in and enabled by educational institutions, practices, and polities with histories too often as offensive as the statues to patriarchal slaveowners and imperialists dotting their campuses, and often masked in their academic publications, rendered the core issues of personal identity in all its textured varieties relevant in ways that they had not been in graduate school. As a result, I increasingly prioritized reading the utilitarians, especially Mill and Sidgwick, not only in the soft light of their academic philosophical followers and admirers, but also in the light of such critiques as Lowe's *The Intimacies of Four Continents*, Said's *Culture and Imperialism*, Ahmed's *The Promise of Happiness*, and many other works along such lines.[44] Some might deem this an effort to find a truly deep and wide (and interdisciplinary) Rawlsian reflective equilibrium among our considered convictions, but in this case, the "our" will be very different from the constructed audiences for the works of Rawls and Parfit.

Where does that leave Parfit? Oddly enough, it is hard to say. But as the following chapters will suggest, there is a lot to the idea that the better defenses of utilitarianism will indeed problematize the supposed "separateness of persons," not double down on it.[45]

In the chapters that follow, the various levels of decolonization that Mintz outlines will all figure, though with considerable critical emphasis on how the problems of decolonizing society impact the less ambitious, more local efforts to decolonize. The earlier chapters will look a lot like an effort to decolonize the familiar utilitarian canon and the institutions supporting it; the later ones, and some parts of the earlier ones, more like an eclectic critical theoretical exploration of the possibilities that emerge out of the cracks in the canonical narratives, albeit with an eye toward the dangers of the legacies and ongoing injustices of Anglo-American empire-building. The critical upshot is to find better ways to think about, teach, and apply a broadly utilitarian outlook.

Although some care must be taken with it, there is an interesting and not unrelated precedent and parallel for this project in Maia Ramnath's *Decolonizing Anarchism*, which is concerned

> not just with anarchism's role in decolonization but also with decolonizing our concept of anarchism itself. That means that instead of always trying to construct a strongly anarcha-centric cosmology – conceptually appropriating movements and voices from elsewhere in the world as part of "our" tradition, and then measuring them against how much or little we think they resemble our notion of our own values – we could locate the Western anarchist tradition as one contextually specific manifestation among a larger – indeed global – tradition of antiauthoritarian, egalitarian thought/praxis, of a universal human urge (if I dare say such a thing) toward emancipation, which also occurs in many other forms in many other contexts. Something else is then the reference point for us, instead of us being the reference point for everything else. This is a deeply decolonizing move.[46]

The phrase "universal human urge" is something of a red (and black) flag, but the emphasis on de-centering the stock Eurocentric narrative resonates with me.

But to add a little more summary, and a glimpse of the most important possibilities emerging out of all the critique. In a world of new and looming existential threats, most of the prominent Eurocentric ethical and political approaches seem inadequate to the task of facilitating the social change needed for survival on decent terms. It is alarming that not one of the more or less traditional, non-utilitarian Western alternatives has managed to formulate a compelling ecological ethic capable of underwriting genuine ethical concern for distant generations of both human and non-human entities in situations of ecosystemic integrity with a fainter human footprint.[47] The failures seem to reflect the limitations of the fundamental conceptual commitments of these frameworks, especially with respect to ethical standing – that is, who or what counts as worthy of ethical treatment.

In speculating on how a critical utilitarianism – as shared, lived relational practices, not merely a theoretical construction – might hold the potential for better addressing such challenges, this book will consider the canonical figures of classical utilitarianism and the work of prominent academic utilitarian (or congenially consequentialist) philosophers avowedly carrying on that legacy, especially Peter Singer, Dale Jamieson, Katarzyna de Lazari-Radek, Tim Mulgan, and Derek Parfit. But it will also invert and de-center these efforts, looking to and allying with other sources and strategies for a utilitarian outlook that can embrace a lifestyle more in line with deep green, ecocentric and ecofeminist perspectives. Beyond the familiar philosophical trajectory from Bentham to Singer, the case developed here will engage with alternatives to that Eurocentric story, exploring utilitarian filiations in forms of cultural resistance against the forces of colonialism, settler colonialism, imperialism, extractivist racial capitalism, and whatever utilitarianisms were bent into their service. Sources for this approach include Buddhist and Daoist philosophical practices, as well as the heroic work of Native American and other Indigenous peoples, particularly those involved in resurgence movements of political protest and non-anthropocentric (non-human-centered) approaches to environmental justice. Utilitarian sympathizers, with their legacy of going beyond anthropocentrism, might learn from, ally with, and defer to such movements.[48]

It is well known that the homes of Indigenous peoples, a small fraction of the world population, represent about 80 percent of global biodiversity.[49] The way forward for an ecological ethic capable of maintaining or restoring biodiversity, combating climate change, and meeting the challenges that threaten other planetary boundaries lies in part with meaningful collaboration with Indigenous peoples around the globe. If utilitarianism in some form cannot be part of this dialogue – if, as is so often the case, it is simply identified with racial capitalism and extractivism, with neoliberal missionary zeal – then it too will fail as a source for the needed change. That there is a chance that it need not fail is the suggestion of this book.

A Cautionary Note to the Reader

Please understand, as you read this book, that much of what follows here is from my own distinctive point or points of view, not an impersonal "Point of View of the Universe," the expression used by the Victorian-era philosopher Henry Sidgwick for the impartial and universal ethical point of view. This work seeks to bring together, update, refine, integrate, and repurpose interpretations and arguments that I have advanced over the course of my life, in previous writings, talks, and courses. So, some of the material will sound familiar to some readers, though there is much here that never found its way into my previous publications and everything here has been recast, rather than merely reproduced, and turned to the distinctive, creative purpose of decolonizing utilitarianism. Presenting the classical utilitarian philosophies from Bentham to Sidgwick to today in a more critically and historically responsible way might help the friends of that tradition better confront and come to terms with some of the most troubling aspects of it. These troubling aspects are not the (mostly) imaginary puzzle cases so beloved by many academic philosophers, but the more serious ones that have to do with how the utilitarians have often, in both theory and practice, been implicated in the horrific histories and ongoing atrocities of systemic racism, patriarchy, gender binarism, capitalism, colonialism, and imperialism. As utilitarianism is currently taught and canonized in many academic contexts, these matters are largely erased or avoided.

To reiterate: whatever defense of a utilitarian way of life one might find in these pages, it is clearly not one that will align with such -isms or avoid the problems they pose. It will rather seem like the thoughts that are left after all the radical critiques have run out, like the remnant of "happiness" that seems irrepressible even after the harshest critics of happiness studies have done their work exposing the perverse ideological, dystopian power dynamics to which happiness research has been turned. The result might be thought of as a form of critical utilitarianism that pushes its own de-centering, with a quasi-anarchist sense of the pervasive forms of violence and domination that need to be confronted, as the world burns its way into ever greater environmental disasters.

The emphasis here will be on the imperial designs of the UK and the US. Even so, the material presented is highly selective and meant to highlight key issues and problems, without pretending to serve as a comprehensive treatment of them. Too many issues are treated too lightly – indeed, more lightly than in some of my other works – and the points made are often more suggestive and speculative than definitive. The British Empire, for example, was so vast and figured in the works of the classical utilitarians in so many different ways that it would take an encyclopedic project to do justice to all the ways in which the philosophers considered here were entangled in it. From Hong Kong, to India, to New Zealand and Australia, to Kenya, to Jamaica, and on and on, there are materials and topics signaling that utilitarianism was one of the currents, sometimes a very important one, serving the cause of the "Expansion of England" and its "civilizing" mission, as the imperialist ideologue Sir John Seeley theorized it – a mission that was of a piece with certain "dreamworlds" of race and racism that still figure in world politics. Consequently, the chapters here present only a sampling of conspicuous cases, where the juxtaposition of the paternalism, racism, violence, and brutality of empire to the stock celebratory accounts of the utilitarians is especially illuminating – illuminating of the need for different and more responsible ways to teach utilitarianism to current and future generations, given the unprecedented challenges and crises confronting them. The future may well be "broken," a world in which not everyone's basic needs can be met. Utilitarianism today must orient itself to the different possible futures in relevant and meaningful ways – confronting its own broken history and neglected possibilities can help.

1

Utilitarianism Now and Then

As the Introduction implied, the possibilities for utilitarian selves and ways of living being tentatively defended in this work are critical of, not based on, the desiccated selves of formal utility theory and the hollow consumerist lifestyles associated with neoliberal notions of affluence and the good life. No one should admire "Davos Man" or the antics, both absurd and dangerous, of billionaires and aspiring billionaires described in *Survival of the Richest: Escape Fantasies of the Tech Billionaires*.[1] In the whirl of ever enhancing smartphones and big screens, the affluent world's sustained assault on kindness and meaningful relations is felt by many but tragically downplayed by elites and tech lords. Epidemics of loneliness, isolation, anxiety, depression, anger, resentment, dread, and nature-deficit disorder – masked by thin and uninformative measures of happiness and health – with so many people wondering why they should feel good about struggling just to keep up, working in "bullshit jobs" or being part of the "precariat," have produced widespread pain and deaths of despair.[2] As Angus Deaton puts it:

> Overall death rates in the United States have been rising, and even before the pandemic, adult life expectancy has fallen for ten years for those without a four-year college degree. We can legitimately argue about the measurement of material living standards, whether all sources of income are included in the data, how much the poorest spend, whether inflation is overstated and the rise in living standards understated, and whether schools are really that bad everywhere. But American deaths are hard to explain away – particularly the rising tide of suicides at a time when suicide rates are falling around the world.[3]

An insightful opinion piece in the *New York Times* adds: "Tens of millions of Americans are suffering pain. And chronic pain is not just a result of car accidents and workplace injuries but is also linked to troubled childhoods, loneliness, job insecurity and a hundred other pressures on working families."[4] Much of the pain has no identifiable physical cause, and the old, the middle-aged, and the young are all suffering.

And this is not to mention the more overt forms of violence, such as the gun violence that in the US is a telling symptom of how deeply disturbed society really is, making proclamations of societal "happiness" seem like a very sick joke. The same can, of course, be said of police violence and the prison-industrial complex; violence against women (as in the shocking numbers of missing and murdered Native American women); violence against migrants, Asian communities, LGBTQ+ peoples, and on and on, as described so vividly in *The Red Deal*. And, of course, there is the pervasive, inescapable background of violence against non-human animals, the painful and unnecessary deaths of billions of creatures through factory farms and other parts of the systems of food production and land "development" that have, with the complicity of governments, exacerbated environmental crises and generated any number of health problems – heart disease, cancer, diabetes, and more.[5]

It appears that all the genocidal depredations of colonialism, settler colonialism, and imperialism only succeeded in producing worlds that no one should want or admire, even in the metropoles of empire. Yes, indoor plumbing and antibiotics, etc., are wonderful, but they are clearly not enough of a bribe in a world of massive, structural, negative externalities. The legitimation crises, long overdue, dotting supposedly affluent countries around the world, from Japan and South Korea to Israel to the UK, France, and the US, sit uneasily with triumphalist rhetoric about national greatness. "Lying flat" or dropping out makes perfect sense to so many young people because it is so very unclear whether the strains of a consumerist modern life, in schools and workplaces, are truly worth it.[6] They probably are not. The "smart" society is too smart for its own good, a constant assault on the ordinary person's sense of adequacy:

> Tethered all our working hours to our devices, we've become subject to the manipulations of those who control the pipes, and their track record for enlightened despotism isn't good. We're anxious, overstressed, and hunched over our laptops. Friendship is dwindling – people report fewer close friends than they did

> thirty years ago, and 15% of men and 10% of women have no close friends at all. Our public and shared spaces risk decay – or privatization to become playgrounds for the wealthiest few.[7]

It is puzzling that such a world could ever be deemed a realization of the utilitarian dream, given the utilitarian theme of reducing pointless suffering and needless pain. Societal addiction to opioids, and to the lethal capitalism that pushed them, should not be taken as sound utilitarian policy. They are appalling even by the standards of "classical" Eurocentric utilitarianisms, and the century that produced the Opium Wars[8] – indeed, even by the standards of Adam Smith, who thought deference to the rich and powerful a delusion.[9]

Still, too many utilitarians, dead and living, have had trouble recognizing and owning up to damning problems and policies at home and abroad, and the "greatest happiness" principle should always come with a warning label and list of instructions for safe use. This chapter and the next two will tell some familiar stories about the development of modern utilitarianism, particularly in the work of the patriarchs Jeremy Bentham, John Stuart Mill, and Henry Sidgwick, but with some twists and more critical attention to their roles, often complicitous and oblivious, in the expansion of the British Empire. Illuminating the conflicting meanings of utilitarianism, even in its Eurocentric varieties, will help to facilitate the decolonizing project. So, there is a centering here, meant to facilitate the de-centering. It is in the tensions, reversals, and inversions of contending utilitarianisms that one can find some useful tools for at least escaping from, if not dismantling, the master's house, to adapt some words from Audre Lorde.

Another Cautionary Note

It is not easy to do justice to utilitarianism, even in its familiar Eurocentric and Anglo-American trajectory. The differences between such canonical figures as Jeremy Bentham and John Stuart Mill – or the latter and Henry Sidgwick – were deep and intractable. What, then, of the differences distinguishing such figures as Richard Cumberland, David Hume, Edmund Burke, William Paley, William Godwin, Harriet Taylor Mill, James Fitzjames Stephen, Herbert Spencer, G. E. Moore, and Bertrand Russell, all of whom have been classed as utilitarians? Realists, immaterialists, and idealists, empiricists, intuitionists, and rationalists, believers, agnostics, and atheists, socialists, liberals, conservatives, and anarchists have all at times adopted the label after their own fashions, or been awarded it by others, and often enough utilitarianism's better practitioners have not labeled themselves as such at all.

Admittedly, in the familiar narratives, and at a high level of abstraction, there are some unifying threads – primarily the notion that the top normative standard of individuals, social practices, and institutions should be to achieve the most ultimate good by somehow maximizing, or at least ambitiously promoting, the happiness (or well-being, or pleasure, or preference satisfaction, or beneficial life quality) of all beings or entities capable of experiencing it, present and yet to come (and perhaps past as well, if the belief system in question allows the possibility of making the ancestors or others in earlier generations better off).[10] Right and wrong are to be determined by the best (or better) and worst (or worse) consequences of actions, rules, social practices, institutions, or whatever the key foci are taken to be (acts versus rules being only one of the relevant controversies). A consequentialist, teleological framework defining right versus wrong in terms of maximizing the aggregate good (or optimizing, or satisficing), and rejecting the notion that anything – except perhaps violating the utilitarian principle itself – could be absolutely wrong, wrong "whatever the consequences," is perhaps the brightest thread. Broadly put, utilitarians are wary of dogmatic absolutism, in religion, ethics, economics, or politics, unless there are good consequentialist reasons to refrain from doubting. And bluntly put, they are given to pressing the question: what gain from the pain?

To be sure, some of the early English utilitarians assumed that decent ordinary people could best advance the general happiness by for the most part prudently tending to their own piece of the felicific calculus, their own individual happiness and that of their families and friends, given their superior knowledge of their own condition and the limited and uncertain means at their disposal for helping distant strangers. Arguably, in many times and places, people just do want to (or have to) get on with their lives without being in a state of perpetual anxiety and doubt about whether they are really doing the right thing. The interests of self and other, if not harmonized by God or theological considerations (as they were often taken to be by the religiously minded), were often supposed to be harmonized by the demands of social life, hopefully aided by the visible or invisible hands of sensible institutional design, guided by empirical evidence and with effective sanctions. Indeed, the impact of legal and political institutions – the 'thunders' of the commands of the law in Bentham's wording – was so important that utilitarians were well advised to devote most of their attention to those, rather than to the 'whispers' of private morality. There would be a steady egalitarian drift as societal institutions were reformed, and the accent would be not on retributive justice, exacting an eye for an eye, but on eliminating victimless crimes and the root causes of more serious crimes and other social problems – on reform, deterrence, and rehabilitation. The less pointless suffering, the better.

In recent decades, however, utilitarianism has often been presented in very different terms. Students in many introductory ethics courses treat utilitarianism as an easy sparring partner to batter before taking on the supposedly more serious alternatives, Kantian, Aristotelian, or whatever. Utilitarianism is condemned for holding that the end justifies the means; ignoring the separateness of persons and failing firmly to support basic rights and distributive justice; justifying the sacrifice of innocent persons for the greater good; calling for extreme, overly demanding self-sacrifice for the greater good; running roughshod over our defining attachments and life projects, our integrity, and so on through an endless array of puzzle cases, of which the "Trolley problems" – concerning the sacrifice of an overweight bystander to block a runaway trolley threatening to kill a group of people – are but one example.[11] The emphasis is often on individual ethical decision-making – what the classical utilitarians would have termed "private ethics."

Consequently, such students can be taken aback when exposed to the vast landscape of sophisticated, often highly technical, research on utilitarianism, and the endless theoretical refinements at issue – act versus rule versus motive/character versus global utilitarianism, utilitarianism as a decision procedure versus utilitarianism as a critical standard, direct versus indirect utilitarianism, total versus average utilitarianism, positive versus negative utilitarianism, welfarist versus non-welfarist utilitarianism, scalar versus non-scalar utilitarianism, quantitative versus qualitative utilitarianism, utilitarianism as a comprehensive ethical and political position versus utilitarianism as a political or institutional morality, person-affecting versus impartial or impersonal utilitarianism, expectational versus objective utilitarianism, cognitivist versus noncognitivist justifications for utilitarianism, and more. These are often elaborated via deep dilemmas challenging all schools of ethical and political theory, such as determining the shape of justice for future generations, or our obligations to non-human animals and the environment, or the basis for inter- or intra-personal comparisons of utility and utility theory in general, particularly when deployed for normative purposes.[12] In part because of shifts in early twentieth-century economics, including an account of welfare in terms of preference satisfaction (or, worse, simple monetary gain) and the related, positivist effort to avoid supposedly "unscientific" interpersonal comparisons of utility and instead emphasize optimization and Paretian or Kaldor–Hicks efficiency, there has been extensive debate about just what utilitarians should count as happiness, well-being, or the good – preference satisfaction, capabilities or objective quality-of-life factors, pleasurable consciousness, or some combination of these. The very meaning of the term "utility," as John Broome concisely shows, has shifted dramatically over time, adding to the confusion swirling around the label "utilitarian," a term that even the nineteenth-century utilitarians found wanting.[13]

How can one decolonize and de-center this amorphous blob of interdisciplinary, historically shifting theory and practice? Generalizations are risky, and at every turn there is some subfield of specialization and expertise, some pocket of researchers beavering away on some topic of indeterminate value. Not all of the refinements and innovations are reflected in the lives and works of the classical or nineteenth-century utilitarians, who were a very intellectually wide-ranging group that cannot be easily fitted within today's academic disciplinary boundaries. But whether that is a bad thing is very much up for debate. That not all of these refinements and innovations are recognized as intellectual progress is clear from the ways in which many eminent philosophical utilitarians of recent years have defended the classical perspective on key counts, notably in connection with the work of Henry Sidgwick. Some even regard the post-1900 economistic versions of utilitarianism as "but an amputated limb"[14] of the classical utilitarian body, a view perhaps reflecting the many waves of criticism washing over neoclassical economics and public policy analysis.

For the sake of providing a flexible terminology for present purposes, it is enough to go with the straightforward and accessible account given in Mulgan's *Utilitarianism*, which, in spelling out utilitarianism as requiring the "impartial promotion of well-being," helpfully isolates ten features frequently ascribed to hedonistic act utilitarianism: (1) consequentialism (or the promotion of valuable consequences – the outcomes of actions – as determining what is right); (2) welfarism (such that it is the welfare or well-being of individuals that figures in the value of outcomes); (3) hedonism (such that welfare or well-being is only a matter of the best balance of pleasure over pain); (4) totalism (so that it is total rather than average welfare that matters in outcome value); (5) temporal neutrality (time per se is ethically arbitrary to the value of outcomes); (6) expectation (the value "of an act is the sum of the value of each prospective outcome multiplied by the probability of that outcome occurring if the act is performed"); (7) maximization (the "right act is the one with the greatest (expected) value"); (8) act focus (the "primary focus of consequentialist evaluation is acts"); (9) direct evaluation (each act is evaluated "directly in terms of its consequences"); (10) individualism (the "primary focus of consequentialist evaluation is the particular acts of an individual agent").[15]

As Mulgan notes, every one of these components of hedonistic act utilitarianism is the subject of intense controversy, with the controversy often taking the form of debating whether utilitarianism might be better off without the component in question. Commonly enough, the first three, possibly four, are taken as the most important elements of classical utilitarianism in its most consistent forms – in, say, Bentham or Sidgwick, with later utilitarians being more agnostic or critical about 3 and 4, and the other components being even more negotiable as part of the core utilitarian position. Indeed, Mulgan himself does not take any such act utilitarianism as the default, central utilitarian perspective, but rather draws heavily on the possibilities for alternative foci of evaluation (not just acts), indirect evaluation, and collective evaluation – that is, he is concerned to explore utilitarian departures from act utilitarianism that mark "a shift from individual to collective evaluation; a shift from direct evaluation of acts to indirect evaluation of acts in terms of rules, motives, or outlooks, and a focus on the moral outlook that we should teach to future generations."[16] The first two shifts are well represented in the consequentialism of Parfit and the rule utilitarianism of Brad Hooker, but the third, "Ideal Outlook Utilitarianism," is Mulgan's own distinctive contribution:

> I dub my theory *Ideal Outlook Utilitarianism*. It begins by *directly collectively* evaluating moral outlooks, seeking the outlook that we should teach and encourage. But the resulting ideal outlook can play a variety of other roles. Once we identify it, we can use the ideal outlook for indirect evaluations. Individuals or groups could use the ideal outlook to guide their present deliberations about how to act.[17]

The emphasis on "outlooks" is distinctive in that it "leaves open whether the utilitarian ideal is a code of rules, a set of dispositions, a package of virtues, a set of priorities, a general moral outlook or (as seems most likely) some combination of these."[18] Outlook utilitarianism "captures a perennially attractive picture of morality as a collective human enterprise passed on from one generation to the next" and "is closer to the spirit of the classical utilitarians, especially

Jeremy Bentham and J. S. Mill." While other varieties of "collective utilitarianism often ask questions that could never relate to any possible practical situation … ideal outlook utilitarianism's question is practical." Indeed,

> if we interpret "moral teaching" broadly, then that question is inescapable. We *will* teach the next generation *some* moral outlook. Ideal outlook utilitarianism asks what we *should* teach. Even if we don't use the ideal outlook to judge individual actions, we surely want to know which moral outlook it would be best to teach. Moral philosophers, moral educators, and others who observe that moral outlooks have changed in the past all ask how those outlooks might change in the future. And this prompts the further question: how *should* moral outlooks change? If we could get the next generation to follow, adopt, or internalize any moral outlook, which outlook should it be?[19]

Another advantage of ideal outlook utilitarianism comes from the way it addresses problems about the demandingness of utilitarianism – the way, among other things, it asks "how much good would be produced overall if we tried to teach each competing outlook," allowing that less good might come from trying to teach more demanding forms of utilitarianism. But:

> The best argument for ideal outlook utilitarianism is that it represents the most compelling utilitarian response to the challenges of future ethics. We need a utilitarian question that counts distant future people equally without asking us to imagine or imitate their moral thinking, and one that also allows for moral change. My new ideal outlook utilitarianism fits the bill perfectly. It focuses directly on the next generation and only indirectly on the distant future.… Ideal outlook utilitarianism does not ask what outlook it would be best for the next generation to teach the third generation. It asks instead what would *actually* happen if we teach this outlook to the next generation. This includes also asking what outlook the next generation will actually teach – and what effects their teaching will have on later generations. After all, this is how moral education works. We teach the next generation. We cannot teach distant future people.[20]

As Mulgan implies, the fratricidal, internecine conflicts of utilitarianism are both synchronic and diachronic, contemporary and historical, even within the familiar Eurocentric and Anglo-American narratives. It is telling that Mulgan believes that ideal outlook utilitarianism is more in line with the legacy of the nineteenth-century utilitarians than the stick figure of hedonistic act utilitarianism, and regards this as a strength. Some such attitude characterizes many of the recent utilitarians featured in the following chapters. And Mulgan's central concern with education, broadly construed, is indeed deeply consonant with the lives and works of the classical utilitarians, though this concern is not characteristic enough of those today claiming their mantle, despite the fact that so much about the practices and moral psychology of utilitarianism gets spelled out in just this area.[21] Indeed, this orientation is a portal for the project of decolonizing utilitarianism, with the changes in utilitarian educational outlooks reflecting the changing affirmations and forgettings of the logic of empire and how the decolonization(s) of a shape-shifting utilitarianism might work against a shape-shifting set of empires.

Mulgan's case for ideal outlook utilitarianism is partly motivated by his recognition of the extraordinary challenges the broken future holds. But we must also take seriously the many ways in which the world has been and is broken, and this in profoundly inequitable ways. After all, do we really want to teach the next generation how to evade such issues, by pretending that utilitarianism and its history have only the cleanest of hands?

The Code of the Benthamites

The canonical story of utilitarianism, while recognizing its global ambitions and impact, is standardly cast as a very modern, very English, and very bourgeois one in its generation – narrow even by the standards of Eurocentric academic philosophy. Although there are usually nods in the direction of Epicureanism and the European – and Scottish – Enlightenment, to such modern figures as Cumberland, Helvétius, Beccaria, Montesquieu, Hume, and Smith, the accounts typically lift off with the exceedingly strange figure of Jeremy Bentham, the precocious London-based legal theorist, philosopher, and reformer who instructed that after his death his body should be publicly dissected, preserved, and displayed. This, he held, would serve the utilitarian cause both by supporting medical dissection for research purposes and by leaving his "Auto-Icon" as an inspirational relic. It is still on display, at University College London.[22]

There is something emblematic about the Auto-Icon, as a bold eccentricity challenging religious views of the afterlife in the name of science and happiness, but with a curious mix of methods. The body is just Bentham's padded-out skeleton wearing his clothes and holding his favorite walking stick, Dapple. But the head, at Bentham's instruction, was meant to be preserved in its entirety, after the fashion of the Maori of New Zealand. That attempt at cultural appropriation ended up failing grotesquely, and the repellent result was eventually locked away and replaced with a more lifelike wax replica. Bare bones, wax, and wire, all dressed up and ready to walk, with the actual head safely hidden away after an abortive attempt to turn Indigenous knowledge to a new purpose. Such is the course of empire. It does make one think.

Born in 1748, Bentham, who in fact coined the term 'utilitarianism' in 1781, came from a line of prosperous and well-connected London attorneys. He was only 12 when he went up to The Queen's College, Oxford, graduating when 16 with a BA and three years later with an MA and a lasting contempt for his alma maters. His time studying law at the Court of King's Bench, Westminster Hall (he was admitted to the bar in 1769), only strengthened his determination to reform the law rather than practice it, an outlook that was decisively molded by his return to Oxford to hear the lectures of the inaugural Vinerian Professor, William Blackstone – the lectures on English law that would become the influential treatise *Commentaries on the Law of England* (1765–79). It was also on a return visit to Oxford, in 1768, that Bentham claimed to have discovered the key utilitarian notion of promoting the greatest happiness of the greatest number in Joseph Priestley's "Essay on the First Principles of Government," a discovery that determined his "principles on the subject of morality, public and private together."[23] The expression "the greatest happiness of the greatest number" – which Bentham came to prefer to the term "utility" (which for Bentham mostly meant the property in objects or acts productive of happiness) – is not actually in Priestley's essay, and the likely source for it in Bentham's readings was Beccaria.

Bentham's writings, many unpublished during his lifetime, ranged widely, from his Panopticon prison scheme and his Chrestomathic schools for useful learning, to his elaborate rules of judicial evidence, to a vast scheme for the alleviation of poverty and indigence and guidelines on economic and financial regulation, to efforts at international (a term he coined) peace through a court of arbitration and ambitious proposals for constitutional codes for countries across the globe. Indeed, his biggest project was his never-completed Pannomion, a single comprehensive plan for legal systems on all fronts. His famous *Introduction to the Principles of Morals and Legislation* was mainly concerned with the penal branch of jurisprudence and did not reflect his comprehensive legal, political, economic, and philosophical positions. His other works often paint a much broader picture of his interests and demonstrate how his psychological theory could accommodate the force of human sympathy and devotion to the general happiness, as in his own life.[24] Whatever strategic, qualified, even hesitant, psychological egoism he favored, he allowed that people could act not only inconsistently and ignorantly, but from a pain-embracing asceticism, and, on the other side, that he himself was an example of someone who found their own happiness in promoting the greatest happiness. But most power elites, whether from State or Church, were not so beneficent and needed the tonic of democracy, or so Bentham came to think.

Bentham may be best known today for his Panopticon prison reform scheme, as depicted in Foucault's seminal work of social constructionism, *Discipline and Punish: The Birth of the Prison*. Elaborated in a collaboration with his brother Samuel and a series of letters to their father, the proposed prison reform scheme, with prison discipline and control through a central surveillance tower, was, for Foucault, a prescient template for biopower and the surveillance state. The Panopticon would

> induce in the inmate a state of conscious and permanent visibility that assures the automatic functioning of power. So to arrange things that the surveillance is permanent in its effect, even if it is discontinuous in its action; that the perfection of power should tend to render its actual exercise unnecessary; that this architectural apparatus should be a machine for creating and sustaining a power relation independent of the person who exercises it; in short that the inmates should be caught up in a power situation of which they are themselves the bearers.

Power must be "visible and unverifiable." But, for Bentham, as conservative commentators have complained, these institutional developments would have, if implemented, in effect produced a vast social safety net, a liberal welfare state, with a healthy representative democracy such that the watchers themselves would be surveilled by a critical and alert public, with a wide distribution of political power and the means to happiness.[25]

In any event, Bentham's early works, *A Fragment on Government* (1776) and *An Introduction to the Principles of Morals and Legislation* (1789, but long in the making and printed in part as early as 1781),[26] had him welding consequentialism to a hedonistic account of the good as pleasure and wielding it as a weapon for critiquing existing legal and political institutions (especially the penal code), which, he argued, were confused and cruel, steeped in the dogmatic superstitions of natural law, social contract theory, and, relatedly, Blackstone's *Commentaries*, a celebratory mapping of English law (including common law) and politics that Bentham deemed the perfect target for his "censorial" approach to those topics.[27] Over the course of his long life, he would devote himself to countering the *Commentaries* with clear codifications, spelling out a comprehensive, mutually supporting set of codes, from the constitutional to the civil to the penal, with much on judicial procedures and institutions as well.

Although in 1792 Bentham was made an honorary citizen of the new French Republic, and eventually had a notable global impact thanks to his Swiss follower Pierre Étienne Louis Dumont's translations and editions of some of his writings, he was not a friend to the notion of natural rights, famously dismissing it as "simple nonsense," and the notion of natural and imprescriptible rights as "rhetorical nonsense, nonsense upon stilts."[28] The concept of "rights," which relied on the concept of others being correlatively obligated to respect said rights, belonged for its substantial reality to the realm of positive law with its commands and sanctions for failing to meet the obligations in question, as justified by the felicific consequences – its this-worldly consequences, rather than appeal to theology, myth, and fantasies such as a social contract in a state of nature. By that standard, actually existing legal and political institutions failed badly, inflicting a great deal of pointless, unnecessary pain and death – Bentham was an emphatic critic of the death penalty – and doing so via an obfuscatory, often meaningless and absurd language that catered to sinister vested interests and cried out for critical dissection, for which Bentham ingeniously devised an analytical method. He is acknowledged as anticipating the work of such analytical philosophers as Russell and Quine with his method of "paraphrasis," such that a term can be explicated not by its referent or synonyms, but by translating or paraphrasing the sentences in which it is used, showing how it can be cashed out for more ontologically respectable wording.[29]

Indeed, throughout all his work, Bentham stressed the importance of reforming language to achieve maximal clarity, to distinguish the real, empirically evident entities from fictitious entities, and helpful fictitious entities (basically, abstractions) – that is, fictions that could be cashed out via paraphrasis for real entities, and about which there is no ontological confusion – from the pernicious fictions or falsehoods, especially the poisonous legal fictions that encouraged mendacity, corruption, and abuse. Bentham is to this day the (secular) patron saint of those who rebel against the turgidities of "legalese," and part of his long-standing antagonism toward the authority of Aristotle and things Aristotelian was related to his rejection of that influential model of classification, buoyed by his disdain for any superstitious worship of antiquity and dead languages. Interestingly, however, and against a common misconception, he did find value in poetry and works of the imagination, and even "called upon poets in his own day to correct 'the barbarous language that disgraces our statute book.'"[30]

But the basic normative grounding for all this reformist critique was always the "naturalistic" view that humanity and other sentient creatures are at bottom driven by the pursuit of pleasure and the avoidance of pain, with human psychology being a matter of conditioning by these forces – the association of ideas. Happiness equals pleasure (or the balance of pleasure over pain), which equals ultimate good (the only thing desirable for its own sake, according to philosophical hedonism), the maximization of which defines what is right, utility being simply the property in an object or act productive of benefit or happiness. In calculating this right-making maximal happiness, Bentham was surprisingly inclusive, as Lea Campos Boralevi demonstrated in her indispensable work *Bentham and the Oppressed*.[31] He was expressly anti-racism, anti-sexism, and anti-speciesism – not only urging that "the blackness of the skin is no reason why a human being should be abandoned without redress to the caprice of a tormentor," but also hoping that it "may one day come to be recognised that the number of the legs, the villosity of the skin, or the termination of the os sacrum are reasons equally insufficient for abandoning a sensitive being to the same fate."[32] Sentience is what makes for ethical standing, not reason, free will, possession of a soul, race, gender, species, or any of the other candidate criteria attempting to place humanity or some class of it at the crown of creation. In the history of "Western civilization," this was a bold, momentous step.

Yet as even Boralevi admits, Bentham was at times overly impressed by the possible risks of radical abolitionism with respect to, for example, slavery.[33] His too cautious reformism, and his largely indirect applications (or recommended applications) of the greatest happiness principle, came from his emphasis on security. His favored term for the primary task of government, along with securing subsistence and abundance, was "security" – security in one's life and possessions, more than equality and liberty, though both of these also had an important place and part of the latter was encompassed in security, the liberty to be free from harms, as distinct from the "anarchical" or negative liberty to do what one pleased. Security, for Bentham, was the crucial means to happiness for humanity. He was vividly aware of how human foresight and expectations affected pleasures and pains in ways not shared with most other animals. Indeed, he was given to extensively cataloging and classifying the various pleasures and pains, their sources, how they were modified by different sensibilities and circumstances, their intensity, duration, fecundity, and so on, and he appreciated the fact of declining marginal utility, in that accumulated units of wealth would be less productive of pleasure the more affluent was the recipient. But this largely reinforced his focus on security, on the vital importance of people's expectations of being secure in their lives and possessions, while he also urged that gradual, security-respecting reform should and would tend in a strongly egalitarian direction. He was, for example, a keen supporter of the reformist concern to enhance "aptitude" (competence rather than incompetence and corruption) in public administration, wryly noting that "aptitude, with relation to the exercise of political power, is inversely as the altitude of a man's place in the composite scale of political influence."[34] There were broad egalitarian distributive considerations built into hedonistic happiness and the means to it, but Bentham's sense that the cure to the ills of society should not be worse than the disease, and that it was better to, say, tax inheritance and expand free trade than to try to violently dispossess the aristocracy, reflected a cautionary politics, not revolutionary resistance. Educational reform, in a very broad and secular sense, was imperative.

Still, the more subversive egalitarian drift in Bentham's work, compromised as it was, grew stronger over the course of his life, despite his reliance on such aristocratic Whig patrons as Lord Shelburne. When various monarchs, notably George III, resisted or ignored his reformist efforts, he converted from enlightened monarchism to democracy, and the English Reform Act of 1832, extending the franchise to more of the middle class, owed much to the Benthamite influence. From around 1809 on, especially, he was a fierce advocate for parliamentary reform and greater representative democracy, endorsing nearly universal suffrage, a free press, and frequent elections, the secret ballot, and accountability from those in power.[35] And during his last two decades, his global reputation soared, across North and South America as well as various European countries, although it cannot be said that the recognition translated into the actual full implementation of his various codes and plans, even in England, where common law rather than codification endured. As he lamented in his *Constitutional Code*:

> In the here proposed code, of every proposed arrangement, from first to last, without any one exception, the end in view is the greatest happiness of the greatest number. Of the several arrangements in the English system, in no one instance has the greatest happiness of the greatest number been the end in view. At all times, – on every occasion, – in every instance, the end actually pursued by the several sets of rulers, has been the promotion of the particular, and hence sinister, interest of these same rulers.[36]

Thus, Bentham had both a sweeping vision and a wonkish obsession with policy detail – greatness and minuteness, as John Stuart Mill put it – when it came to envisioning utilitarian political, legal, and penal institutions effecting a junction of duty and interest. It was the scope and detail of his plans that distinguished him – as Mill wrote,

> he was the first who, keeping clear of the direct and indirect influences of all doctrines inconsistent with it, deduced a set of subordinate generalities from utility alone, and by these consistently tested all particular questions. This great service previously to which a scientific doctrine of ethics on the foundation of utility was impossible, has been performed by Bentham (though with a view to the exigencies of legislation more than to those of morals) in a manner, as far as it goes, eminently meritorious, and so as to indicate clearly the way to complete the scheme.[37]

Who else in England had dared to attack the British Constitution, the Church of England, and English common law in such pointed ways, breaking the spell of so many traditions? Who else had evinced such an aptitude for casting aspersions on their own home institutions, while also drawing up formidably detailed plans to replace them?

And there was even more to Bentham. What Foucault – and John Mill for that matter – missed was his creative, sensitive, and cruelty-averse side, a side that mostly came out in his unpublished works attacking the ascetic fixations of the Christian Church (particularly St. Paul) and other coercive anti-pleasure laws, institutions, and practices. His writings on sexual morality were far ahead of their time in calling for the decriminalization of same-sex behavior and mocking the very appeals to "natural" versus "unnatural" sexual practices that Foucault would later confront, albeit in different terms and contexts.[38] It is hard to imagine any nineteenth-century philosopher who could have been more welcoming of LGBTQ+ communities. Or one who could have sounded more like Foucault when celebrating the discovery of new pleasures. Addressing the "merit of novelty," Bentham wrote:

> For what is not, it is believed, as yet to be found in any book is any thing approaching to a compleat indication of the vast variety of acts by which from the source in question pleasure in various shapes may be said to flow. Let us then suppose a premium for him who shall have succeeded in shewing the greatest variety of shapes in which pleasure derived from this source may each of them in the greatest degree of magnitude – intensity, duration and extent taken together – be derived.[39]

The premium still holds.

Even Bentham's closest disciples could be clueless about his more unorthodox critical views. John Mill's father, James Mill, born in 1776 and author of the infamous, highly imperialistic *A History of British India*, was a very close disciple from around 1808 on, but remained at a considerable intellectual distance from Bentham on many matters. Mill senior knew nothing of Bentham's views on sex and sexuality, and he did not share Bentham's radical position on equality for women, though John Mill, with his wife Harriet Taylor Mill, would famously take on that cause. And on key questions of colonialism, settler colonialism, and imperialism, there is an ever growing literature devoted to determining just how and why Bentham and the Mills, both senior and junior, may not have been of one "utilitarian mind." Not many would claim of the Mills what Peter Cain claimed of Bentham – namely, that "it would be no exaggeration to say that Bentham made one of the greatest contributions to anti-colonial literature anywhere in the Western world, and one which in some ways was never improved upon in Britain."[40] But Cain is not alone in his praise of Bentham, and it is pleasant to think that perhaps even Bentham himself wanted to decolonize (literally) utilitarianism, at least in some ways. But the truth of the matter is messy.

Kathleen Blake also highlights Bentham's broader anti-colonialist statements, remarking of his "Emancipate your Colonies!" (addressed to the 1793 French National Assembly, and years later recycled to use against Spain): "Colonialism on the face of it fails to meet France's revolutionary ideals of liberty and equality, declares a vehement, radical Bentham. The French, though high-principled democrats in Europe, must look like sinister aristocrats in the foreign territories that they rule." Thus, drawing on arguments from Smith, Bentham "identifies monopoly as the first object of colonialism – a nation's effort to profit by ruling market conditions in foreign places – and he inveighs against it."[41] Colonialism only serves certain special interests, not the overall interests of the nations involved, which would have more mutually prosperous trade relations after independence, as proved to be the case, Bentham held, with Britain and the US. But practical policy may need to be accommodating in various ways, and thus "Utilitarian political economy does not maintain a firm anti-imperialist stance."[42]

Just what this means for the understanding of Bentham and Benthamism takes some spelling out. For critics such as Lisa Lowe, Bentham's utilitarianism contains the same contradictory mix of liberty and discipline or authority as the utilitarianism of James and John Stuart Mill, and it served the project of empire in similar ways.[43] Does Bentham's work call for much the same critique, or not?

There are many issues here, which is hardly surprising given that huge swaths of political and economic history are in question, from the American colonies and the West Indies, to transportation and settler colonialism in Australia, to the complex history of the British East India Company in its colonizations of Hong Kong, southeast Asia, and India, and more. And this is not to mention the fact that the Bentham Project has yet to finish the daunting task of producing the complete *Collected Works* and consequently some tentativeness is appropriate in describing Bentham's positions. Overall, however, a case can be made that neither of the Mills understood the details of Bentham's shifting and inconsistent, though frequently quite anti-colonial, stance (much less his views on sexuality). At the least, great care must be taken before lumping him together with his utilitarian heirs.

Possibly the best concise summary of Bentham's twists and turns on these issues comes from Philip Schofield, the Director of the Bentham Project at University College London, in his *Utility and Democracy: The Political Thought of Jeremy Bentham*:

> Bentham's underlying attitude towards colonies was captured in his phrase "Emancipate Your Colonies!", but not where the mother country was more likely than the colony itself to govern it beneficially. While the mother country (or at least its subjects) usually fared badly from the establishment of colonies, in certain economic and demographic circumstances colonization might on the whole be advantageous. As far as the constitutional dimension was concerned, once Bentham had discovered sinister interest and embraced political radicalism, he identified colony-holding as one of the sources of misrule. Hence, in his colonization society

> proposals, he was careful to ensure that no additional patronage would fall into the hands of government. It may have been for the same reason that he was relatively sympathetic to maintaining British rule over India in the hands of the East India Company, rather than transferring it to the government. Bentham's attitude to colonies was not so much "ambivalent", but rather, as Boralevi suggests, extremely sensitive to the particular circumstance of the case, within a general framework of economic and constitutional principles, but which themselves underwent modification as his thinking matured.[44]

This passage marks the takeaways from Schofield's review of contending interpretations of Bentham by Boralevi and by Donald Winch, who plays up Bentham's seeming inconsistencies, such as his end-of-life enthusiasm for Edward Gibbon Wakefield's influential plan for the colonization of Australia.[45] Schofield leans more toward Boralevi's defense of Bentham as consistent and simply being responsive to the different factual considerations in the different historical contexts.

Even conceding that there is something deeply correct about Schofield's synthesis, many questions remain about the degree of Bentham's flexibility and the how and why of it. A considerable literature has grown up around the East India Company, as it shifted from a trading company to an instrument of governance in India (replete with an extensive army) over the course of 1773 to 1858, before Crown rule. There is much peculiar paradox in the way that an enterprise that Adam Smith had disparaged as a conspicuous case of mercantilist corruption could become the very vehicle by which Bentham and the Mills envisioned the reform of India would take place, with them on board, albeit with many strange Evangelical bedfellows.

After all, James Mill worked in the East India Company Examiner's office from 1819 until his death in 1836 and was especially influential during the strongly Utilitarian Whig Governor-Generalship of Lord William Bentinck from 1828 to 1835; he also secured a position for John there, a position that the younger Mill would hold from 1823 until the East India Company had ceased to rule India, following the Sepoy Rebellion of 1857. Bentham was very much a presence and influence in their work until his death in 1832. As Jennifer Pitts notes,

> reformers directly or indirectly influenced by Bentham, men who believed they were carrying out the Benthamite projects, were powerful in Indian administration throughout the nineteenth century. Benthamites who felt they were too regularly thwarted

> in England, by entrenched powers and the recalcitrant body of common law, reveled in the opportunity that they believed despotic power provided for the establishment of a complete legal code.[46]

Indeed, much of the practical work of Benthamism was carried out, in distorted fashion, by his disciples, the two Mills and an extensive cast of other "Philosophical Radicals" – including the legal positivist John Austin, the economist David Ricardo, and the "radical tailor" Francis Place, and many political figures – who promoted utilitarianism in some form through such organs as the *Westminster Review*, the counter to both Whig and Tory publications. All agreed that Bentham was an inspiration in various ways. But how important was his role, and what did it involve, particularly with respect to India? What distinguished him from the two Mills and yet somehow allowed them to believe that they were in both theory and practice representing the best in Bentham?

Many Bentham scholars have defended Bentham by challenging the claims of Eric Stokes's *The English Utilitarians and India*, with its account of the authoritarian tendencies of utilitarianism in India stressing the culpability of both Bentham and Mill senior, rather than John Mill.[47] Against Stokes, Pitts builds an impressive case:

> A wide range of related considerations also cause his [Bentham's] views on colonialism to vary, including his fitful pacifism, his periodically expressed hopes that emigration might aid Europe's poor, and the differences between settler colonies such as Latin America and colonies such as British India that primarily involved the domination of a large indigenous population. Still, the concerns that Bentham brought to bear when considering colonial rule, in particular his belief that colonial rulers and administrators could never be trusted to rule well, and his suspicions of aspirations to civilize non-Europeans, stand in sharp contrast to the technocratic and cultural confidence of Bentham's successors. Several philosophical positions in particular stand out as introduced by Bentham's followers and largely alien to his own theory: their narrow and hierarchical understanding of progress; their belief that British rule of "backwards" peoples was both morally justified (even a moral duty) and good for the conquered nations; and their convictions that certain peoples were unfit for self-government.... I shall argue that Bentham did not regard utilitarianism as legitimating the sort of dictatorial imperial

> rule that characterized the hopes of many of his successors: the imposition from above without concern for the opinions of the ruled or their interests as they themselves understood them.[48]

Pitts urges that one of Bentham's texts on India, "Of the Influence of Time and Place in Matters of Legislation," although it has often been used to charge Bentham with imperialism, in fact "offers one of his most extensive and detailed critiques of British imperial practice in India" and "warns against the presumptions of legislators, particularly those who seek to transplant laws to distant and unfamiliar societies," expressing a "profound skepticism toward the motives and bona fides of colonial governors." The applications of British law in Bengal "were poisonous not only in their direct effects, but also because they were sure to undermine any sense of trust or goodwill that managed to emerge on the part of Indians toward their British governors." And worst of all, by Bentham's standards, was "the sense of insecurity felt by Britain's Indian subjects."[49]

The key point, for Pitts, is that, although "Bentham may have come by the end of his life to accept Britain's colonial vocation in India and to endorse an international hierarchy of metropoles and colonies, his lifelong engagement with colonial and international questions offers an instructive counterpoint to the imperial liberalism that regarded itself as an heir to and a refinement of his thought."[50] Such as the liberalism of the Mills. Thus, if "we are to understand how Bentham's views were transformed to become the foundation of one of the most self-confident and interventionist branches of British imperial practice … we must turn to the thought of James Mill."[51]

As his *History of British India* amply demonstrates, Mill senior was indeed committed to progressive narratives of the developmental stages of humanity from savagery to civilization, the sweeping, "conjectural" histories of civilizational progress popular in the Scottish Enlightenment. And this in contrast to Bentham:

> Bentham's sense of restraints and salutary self-doubt, a corollary of his belief in human fallibility, is particularly striking in his thought on empire and international politics. It is evident in his contempt for British and European pretensions to cultural superiority, in his lack of interest in triumphant narratives of progress and in ranking societies as barbarous or civilized, and in his resistance to the languages of character and national character that came to dominate Victorian political debate. He was alert to the dangers of hubris and complacency in the

> thought that people's interests could best be ascertained by others of supposedly more cultivated or more advanced judgment. Bentham also had a sense of political possibilities outside Europe that was distinctly more expansive than that of his followers, who saw Europeans as uniquely capable of self-government and as morally authorized to rule over other societies in the name of their improvement.[52]

Thus, "Bentham's perhaps surprising humility, and his insistence on both the reasonableness of diverse customs and the illegitimacy of imposing one's judgments on others, may serve as a helpful corrective to the persistent liberal temptation to liberate others by 'improving' them so that they are more like ourselves."[53]

And yet, for all that, Pitts admits that there are limits to her reading of Bentham. At best, she is claiming that "Bentham's global legislative ambitions might be seen as his own imperial project, though one very different in spirit from later liberal aspirations to use British despotism to civilize the backward." His "ambition to produce complete legislative codes for distant societies was undoubtedly presumptuous, but he was at least partly aware of its perils." And his late work:

> would seem to indicate a new acceptance of colonies as part of the European system. The international code and the postscript on India, then, indicate a new willingness by Bentham in his final years to conceive an international system divided into the civilized and barbarous and to accept colonial status as appropriate for the barbarous. At the same time, the writings on Tripoli and Egypt suggest that the boundary between these worlds remained more permeable for Bentham, even at the end of his life, than for many who followed.[54]

Consequently, the familiar charge that Bentham was often too quick to believe that he could devise legal, political, and economic codes and policies that could be adapted and applied anywhere in the world – that he was, in a famous phrase, the "Legislator to the World" – is difficult to shake. With appropriate adaptations, his censorial jurisprudence might be applied universally, as with his censorial educational philosophy. Clearly, Bentham was not, as he liked to claim, the "hermit" of the hermitage at Queen's Square Place in London – he brought to utilitarianism a missionary zeal that, as John Mill complained, too often reflected an inability to "derive light from other minds." Perhaps he was, ultimately, less "judgmental and more respectful of difference" than the Mills, as Pitts argues.[55] But his point of departure for recognizing and according significance to difference was always the codifications spun in his head, at home in the metropole.

It would seem, then, that even Bentham's warmest sympathizers allow that, whatever his consistency in principle and method, he was not consistently opposed to imperial domination. At different times during his life, notably the early 1800s, he struck very different notes. As Cain amplifies Bentham's twists and turns, noting the key differences between white settler colonialism, colonialism, and dependency status:

> His attitude to dependencies, where European settlement on any considerable scale was impossible, was somewhat different. In 1793, Bentham had argued that, although it could bring no economic benefit to the colonial power, it was in the long-term interests of India to be governed by a civilized nation like Britain. He reiterated that sentiment in 1829 and was ready also to apply it to China should that country fall under British control. At the turn of the century, he spoke of Egypt (recently invaded by France) in a similar manner. "It would be to Egypt an advantage beyond all price, to be under the government of Britain – that is, under a government of universal and perpetual security." Nonetheless, his was a more cautious Orientalism than that of his successors. In the case of India, he shared Burke's view that it was dangerous to leave a few Englishmen in charge of a country whose customs they understood little and sympathized with even less, especially when they were free of the critical eye of their peers in England. He understood that what the British brought with them had to be adapted imaginatively to the local scene if it were to be successful. Consequently, he was keen to see Indians actively involved in their own governance even if under overall British control.[56]

This explication implies that Bentham's caution was in some tension with his love of codification and bureaucratic efficiency devoid of the moral hazards of perverse incentives – that side of him that was reflective of the larger trend in governmentality described by Stokes, Foucault, and so many others. As Jon Wilson puts it:

> Many of the regimes that emerged across the globe in the nineteenth and twentieth centuries were different. They treated their subjects as unfamiliar beings who needed to be ruled using

> techniques of governance that did not presume prior familiarity. The inhabitants of those states were subject to grand strategies, objective forms of statistical knowledge and abstract codes of law. Though they often spoke of the need for rulers to be sympathetic to the welfare of the governed, few were concerned with the degree of affection existing between ruler and ruled.[57]

When subjects become strangers – Bentham cannot be wholly exonerated on this count, even if the stronger case is against James Mill. As Javed Majeed argues:

> Mill made clear the criteria he used to assess cultures. "Exactly in proportion as Utility is the object of every pursuit, may we regard a nation as civilized." The formulation of this scale was based on the Benthamite notion of the universal legislator, who compared and contrasted legal traditions through the principle of utility. It was also on this basis that Mill argued the legal systems of both Britain and India could be critiqued, and the different codes of law in India replaced by a single, comprehensive code, formulated in a similar manner. It was on these grounds that Mill argued that cultures and societies could be understood more comprehensively from a distance, when the sympathies of the commentator were not engaged in the detail of minute observations.[58]

Majeed's reading comports with Stokes's judgment that Mill senior's work "was principally an attempt to make a philosophic analysis of Indian society and assess its place in the 'scale of civilization'.... His astonishing arraignment of the entire populations of India and China shows the fantastic authority which he was prepared to grant to the philosophic intelligence."[59] The "scale of civilization" (or the "ladder of civilization") gauged by societal devotion to utilitarianism was of course one of the tools that pervaded the discourses of colonialism, settler colonialism, and imperialism, sometimes collapsing into rigid binary distinctions between civilized and uncivilized peoples.

Admittedly, there was some continuity between Bentham and James Mill on the economic arguments. As Majeed explains, Mill "argued that the expense of government, administration, and wars meant that Britain had not derived any economic benefits from India ... he denied the importance of colonies as markets and stressed that they did not yield any economic benefits ... colonies served as a source of power and patronage for the ruling elite and were used to perpetuate their position."[60]

But, as always, the economic arguments are problematic and raise more questions than they settle. As that great force in Indian affairs, the ambivalent sometimes-ally, sometimes-enemy, of utilitarianism, the Whig Thomas Babington Macaulay, put it, with revealing candor:

> It is scarcely possible to calculate the benefits which we might derive from the diffusion of European civilization among the vast populations of the East. It would be, on the most selfish view of the case, far better for us that the people of India were well-governed and independent of us, than ill-governed and subject to us; that they were ruled by their own kings, but wearing our broadcloth, and working with our cutlery, than that they were performing their salaams to English collectors and English magistrates, but were too ignorant to value, or too poor to buy, English manufactures. To trade with civilized men is infinitely more profitable than to govern savages. That would indeed be a doting wisdom, which, in order that India might remain a dependency, would make it an useless and costly dependency; which would keep a hundred millions of men from being our customers in order that they might continue to be our slaves.[61]

Neither the diffident Bentham nor the dogmatic James Mill were quite on board with Macaulay's vision of the culture war framing economic change, though Mill's view of Indian culture was just as dismissive. They stressed the power of law and government for effecting change – Mill, in the words of Stokes, "with the gesture of one demonstrating a geometrical theorem … had simplified the Indian question to three issues – the form of government, the nature of laws, and the mode of taxation."[62] Security and abundance had to come first, through light taxes and good government – in particular, a better-incentivized system of individual property rights to destroy aristocratic privilege and landed wealth. But Mill was not one to teach only by example, opting instead to use his influence to push hard for the forcible and quite undemocratic overhauling of the system of property rights and taxation to create the conditions for market-driven economic growth. This was, by Bentham's lights, trying to reform the moon.

History has not been kind to such pretensions.[63] In any event, even if Stokes was a little too quick to lump Bentham together with James Mill, one can see why he concluded that the "enduring influence of utilitarianism on India must be looked for in the administrative and judicial system, the 'steel frame', which, however obscured in its working by the political struggle, continued to supply the daily framework of State action to the end of British rule and beyond. It was in the realm of authority and not liberty that the Utilitarian work was done."[64]

No doubt Bentham and the Mills consistently took themselves to be working to promote beneficent reforms and experiments in living across the world, other parts of which were, they supposed, more promising in the long run than their home turf, where so many of the Benthamite reforms had fallen flat and the state of civilization was dismal by their own reckoning. But, as Bentham himself complained, their approaches to such experimentation were different, and it was hateful to think that the way to battle aristocratic hierarchy and corruption by sinister interests at home was through disparaging the peoples of India and the total, but often corrupt and uncomprehending, military and political domination of their country.[65] After all, these experiments were hardly being conducted with the informed consent of the experimental subjects.

Why did Bentham vacillate? In discussing Bentham's "Of the Influence of Time and Place in Matters of Legislation," Blake, like Pitts, concedes that the universalizing impulse is still there, and she makes it clear that Bentham "does not here question whether there should be such a transplantation. On balance, he expects good from it. In that sense he is a liberal imperialist."[66] As she drills down on this, she harks back to the foundational Benthamite sensibility, the "anti-hierarchical, individual-interest and freedom-promoting trends of Utilitarian political economy" that would later in the century be regarded as suspect by the more enthusiastic champions of "Greater Britain," while adding a complication:

> Each person's pleasure or pain counts equally into the sum of welfare ... The doctrine is disposed against distinction of persons for privilege or disability by group, especially by any group defined by inherited birthright, by blood or race.... Such a doctrine confirms and intensifies itself in the Indian context by antithesis. Thus Bentham backs off from the idea of emancipating an India that still binds and rank-orders her people by inherited caste. And some of the harshest passages in what has been judged to be a harsh treatment of India in James Mill's *History* concern caste, "the unfair and odious distinctions among men, created by the Hindus" (p. 81). The kinds of things that incite Mill's most vehement diatribes are, for instance, Brahmins' occupational advantages, lighter punishment under the law, exemption from

> taxes, preferential interest rates, and special legal protection in marriage (for husbands, that is) through severity of punishment for a wife's adultery in proportion to caste adulteration.[67]

She explains that, if Mill's tone "can be truly virulent on the Hindus," it can "also shift to a tone of admiration on the Muslims," who "were exempt from the institution of caste; that institution which stands as a more effectual barrier against the welfare of human nature than any other institution which the workings of caprice and of selfishness have ever produced."[68] However, that Mill was in part aiding the social construction of various stereotyped, Orientalizing identities and historical periods in seriously uninformed ways is difficult to deny. And Blake's account does not confront the issue of how in practical terms it is the "scale of civilization" rather than the issue of innate equality that raises the tough questions, how a contingent and racialized "inferiority" could serve for the disciplinary interventions emphasized by Lowe. Her defense of Bentham and the Mills is encased in a shell of concession: "I believe I do Mill justice. I demonstrate how his liberal tradition of Utilitarian political economy – with its wide reach in Victorian literature and culture – developed as liberalism even alongside and partly *through* imperialism."[69] Just so.

And in the end, whatever Bentham and the Mills may have supposed themselves to be doing, what they actually succeeded in doing was a different matter.[70] That they could have been as blind as they were to the economic despoliation of India wreaked by Britain and the East India Company, with all its violent physical and cultural accompaniments, is itself a condemnation of their vision, and not one limited to the case of India.

But, before devoting more attention to the Mills and their Empire, something must be said about how Bentham sought to establish his utilitarian influence not only by attacking the British Constitution, Monarchy, and Anglican Church, but also by displacing other forms of utilitarianism at home, including one that held great decolonizing potential.

Happy God, Happy Godwin – Two Alternatives

Bentham's influence eventually displaced the genuinely religious version of utilitarianism promulgated by William Paley, the Anglican clergyman whose *Principles of Moral and Political Philosophy* (1785) initially helped the utilitarian perspective to achieve wide influence and academic respectability, particularly at Cambridge University, where it was a favorite text well into the nineteenth century. But in his comprehensive study of Paley, *Utilitarianism in the Age of Enlightenment*, Niall O'Flaherty shows that Bentham had little understanding of how Paley was the heir to and apogee of the theological utilitarianism of John Gay, Edmund Law, and Abraham Tucker from earlier in the eighteenth century.[71] Bentham and company failed to appreciate Paley's theological lineage and instead treated him as an unwelcome competitor who might even have stolen his ideas from early unpublished versions of Bentham's *Introduction*.

It was not only the religious side of Paley that bothered Bentham. It was also the fact that they really did share a lot. There was indeed mutual hostility between those more in the line of descent from the agnostic Hume and those more under the sway of the Church of England, but even so:

> As Bentham himself observed, the so-called theological principle was "not in fact a distinct principle", as in practice the will of God always had to be determined by means of the principle of either utility, asceticism or sympathy and antipathy. All told, there are no good historical reasons for playing down the role of theological utilitarians in formulating and popularizing the hedonic standard of morals. Arguably, moreover, its implications were all the more profound for its having occurred in a context in which moral philosophy was still deeply interwoven with theology.[72]

Even Leslie Stephen, who coined the expression "theological utilitarianism," allowed that Bentham was Paley "minus a belief in hell-fire." Paley took moral obligation to be a matter of divine sanctions inducing people to do the right thing, since God willed the greatest happiness; Bentham relied on earthly sanctions.

Bentham was surprisingly reticent about expressing his own deepest views on religion, though he did make it plain enough that most organized religion amounted to a sinister interest breeding superstition, that Christianity had taken a wrong turn with Paul (who was untrue to the message of Jesus), and that human society needed to rely on human sanctions. No belief in revelation or an afterlife, no argument from Design, figured in his vision, in contrast to Paley's. And this certainly gave their arguments a very different feel, even though more orthodox religious figures worried more about the subversive impact of Paley than of Bentham. When Paley addressed the issue of slavery, his cautious, reformist approach was expressed as follows:

> The truth is, the emancipation of slaves should be gradual, and be carried on by provisions of law, and under the protection of civil government. Christianity can only operate as an alterative. By the mild diffusion of its light and influence, the minds of men are insensibly prepared to perceive and correct the enormities, which folly, or wickedness, or accident, have introduced into their public establishments. In this way the Greek and Roman slavery, and since these, the feudal tyranny, has declined before it. And we trust that, as the knowledge and authority of the same religion advance in the world, they will banish what remains of this odious institution.[73]

Like Bentham, Paley opposed slavery and the slave trade and did so without reliance on any notion of basic human rights or a social contract. But, overall, his message was quite different. As D. L. Le Mahieu explains:

> Paley's political thought demonstrated that utilitarianism need not be a radical doctrine. Unlike Bentham, whose invocation of utility constantly revealed the inadequacies and irrationalities of existing practices, Paley employed the notion to justify the *status quo*. In politics and ethics, Paley remained a theorist who, as in his natural theology, judged a practice by how well means were adapted to ends. Unlike his discontented contemporaries, he saw only successes, whether in the British constitution with its unique pattern of checks and balances, or in the legal code with its inconsistent enforcement of the death penalty. Paley sought the rationale of existing practices in the *Principles*, just as … Burke would demonstrate the usefulness of tradition. Both place the burden of proof on those who innovated radically rather than reformed gradually.[74]

Much of Paley's book fits that description; at times, it seems blandly clueless about how subjected Indigenous peoples might regard such things as the "Doctrine of Discovery," which so often served to legitimate the expansions of empire, and in general its gentle, complacently ignorant Enlightenment rationalism veers toward the Panglossian. Of course, there was enough of the Enlightenment, especially the Scottish Enlightenment, in Paley to win him the enmity of Romantics, Evangelicals, and most every less than latitudinarian religious orientation. It is perhaps surprising that it took until the 1840s to undermine his influence at Cambridge, a development that owed much to William

Whewell, the Master of Trinity College, Cambridge and unrelenting opponent of all things utilitarian.

If Paley demonstrated what utilitarianism might look like if one brought more religious complacency to it, another rival of Bentham's demonstrated what it might look like if one was not inclined to have any truck with either Church or State, however reformed. William Godwin, born in 1756, and the radical husband of the radical feminist Mary Wollstonecraft, and father of the author of *Frankenstein*, Mary Shelley, also aimed to do a better job of defending utilitarianism, or what amounted to such. If Bentham's *Principles of Morals and Legislation* is the favored founding text, by academics today, that (misleading) work was initially in the shade of Godwin's colossally successful *An Enquiry Concerning Political Justice* (1793), a more inflammatory defense of the French Revolution coming just after the execution of Louis XVI, the reputation of which would decline as the political reaction to the Terror in France set in. Godwin was less prudent than Bentham, when it came to publishing his more radical views, though both sometimes adopted pen names.

Godwin had published other works, and would go on to publish many more, and this in many genres (he was a philosophical novelist and took a keen, supportive interest in his daughter Mary's work). But his *Enquiry* made his name (and rather tenuous fortune), and in it he set out to build up in a comprehensive systematic way an account of political justice firmly grounded in ethical principles, something that would move public debate beyond pamphleteering and polemical commentary. Although he had a strong religious background – a family of Dissenters, who rejected the Anglican Church – by the time he wrote the *Enquiry* he was a complete atheist. Curiously, his Enlightenment tendencies did not, as with Paley and Bentham, prevent him from winning over many enthusiastic admirers from the Romantic movement, not least his son-in-law, the poet Percy Bysshe Shelley, and he moved in some of the most extraordinary literary circles of all time.

Revealingly, Godwin's philosophy conflicts with both Paley's theological utilitarianism and the (supposedly) defining features of Benthamite utilitarianism – namely, an empiricist naturalism, a qualified and complex hedonistic psychological egoism (again, the assumption that human behavior was largely and by nature narrowly self-interested and pleasure-seeking, or at least to be treated as such for purposes of law, legislation, and policy), and extensive concern with institutional design to insure that utilitarian results came of partial or self-interested human action, such that doing the right thing to promote the general happiness was made easier and properly incentivized in a junction of duty and interest. "Necessity," for Godwin, a metaphysical immaterialist and determinist of a sophisticated type, allowed a dominant role for impartial reason and individual judgment, and his hedonistic account of happiness, like the younger Mill's, made important explicit qualitative distinctions between higher and lower pleasures, denying that, as Bentham purportedly believed (his view was actually more qualified), the pleasure of the children's game of pushpin was as good as pleasure gained from poetry. Godwin believed that humanity was evolving and that the baser pleasures would give way to the higher ones, as mind and reason took ever greater control over the physical world, even eliminating the need for sleep.

In many ways it was Godwin who lent credence to the still pervasive caricature of the utilitarian as a monster of reason, impartially applying the principle of doing the most good as a decision procedure to any and every possible action, at whatever cost to friends, family, and familiar moral rules: "A man is of more worth than a beast; because, being possessed of higher faculties, he is capable of a more refined and genuine happiness. In the same manner the illustrious archbishop of Cambray was of more worth than his valet, and there are few of us that would hesitate to pronounce, if his palace were in flames, and the life of only one of them could be preserved, which of the two ought to be preferred."[75]

In Godwin's example, the famous French Catholic Archbishop Fénelon was to be saved, no matter if the valet happened to be "my brother, my father, or my benefactor" or, for that matter, myself. Reason demands absolute impartiality in the application of the utilitarian standard – "What magic is there in the pronoun 'my,' that should justify us in overturning the decisions of impartial truth?"[76] And reason, Godwin believed, was a matter of individual conscience and impartial, often altruistic, action, leaving the role of the state and commonsense moral rules questionable at best. Although in his earlier work he had been receptive to a reformed state playing an important role in the progress of humanity, as he warmed to the supremacy of guidance by individual conscience, enlightened by Truth with a capital "T," he grew in his anarchism, not that that was the term he adopted for it. Whether the matter was one of keeping a promise or keeping a legal contract, right action was determined by the individual's private judgment of the best consequences, under conditions of political liberty. In fact, promises and contracts were only to be made on the understanding that they would have no force should the felicific calculations run against the keeping of them. On legal/political institutions such as prisons and other components of the carceral state, not to mention marriage, Godwin took what was in effect an anarchist and abolitionist stance that is often echoed today in critiques of the prison-industrial complex and police violence – in, for example, the work of Angela Davis.[77] As Peter Marshall summarizes it:

> Godwin is a thoroughgoing and consistent utilitarian, defining morality as that "system of conduct which is determined by a consideration of the greatest general good". He is an act-utilitarian rather than a rule-utilitarian. While he recognizes that general moral rules are sometimes psychologically and practically necessary, he warns against too rigid an application of them. Since no actions are the same, there can be no clearer maxim than "Every case is a rule to itself." It is therefore the duty of a just man to contemplate all the circumstances of the individual case in the light of the sole criterion of utility. Such reasoning led Godwin to become an anarchist for he rejected all rules and laws except the dictates of the understanding.[78]

Godwin did later soften his position on special obligations and partial attachments always giving way to impartial utilitarian calculations. After the death of his beloved Wollstonecraft (from complications giving birth to Mary), he confessed that "it is impossible we should not feel the strongest interests for those persons whom we know most intimately, and whose welfare and sympathies are united to our own. True wisdom will recommend to use individual attachments; for with them our minds are more thoroughly maintained in activity and life than they can be under the privation of them."[79] Better to avoid such clashes with people's deep loves and attachments, and to be forgiving of, to avoid blaming, those who act on them at some cost to the general good, since they are the very stuff out of which happy people are made. Besides, encouraging people to rashly discount their own future happiness, which does count in the general happiness, for such speculative gains as, say, the beneficent impact of the life of an archbishop, seems like a debatable prescription at best.

At any rate, such maneuvers would prove to be popular with many utilitarians, past and present, who would mostly defend two-level or indirect forms of utilitarianism allowing that often enough it is not utilitarian to have individuals appealing directly to the utilitarian greatest happiness principle in all their daily calculations and decisions. The impartial utilitarian conscience should not always be on duty, only called in at special times, when deep critical reflection is possible and needed, and the stakes are high, and even then applied flexibly, with an eye to avoiding the conflicts. The world could and should be largely arranged to accommodate and facilitate our most meaningful relationships, the loves and friendships that matter even more than economic gain – plausibly, happiness will on balance be better served in the long run and overall by such an approach.

Still, the early Godwin's uncompromising anarchistic utilitarianism led him to take political positions that one can scarcely imagine Paley or Bentham ever entertaining.

> And by what means suppress truth, and keep alive the salutary intoxication, the tranquillizing insanity of mind which some men desire? Such has been too generally the policy of government through every age of the world. Have we slaves? We must assiduously retain them in ignorance. Have we colonies and dependencies? The great effort of our care is to keep them from being too populous and prosperous. Have we subjects? It is "by impotence and misery that we endeavour to render them supple: plenty is fit for nothing but to make them unmanageable, disobedient and mutinous." If this were the true philosophy of social institutions, well might we shrink from it with horror. How tremendous an abortion would the human species be found, if all that tended to make them wise, tended to make them unprincipled and profligate?[80]

The march of truth was global, though Godwin did at times suggest it was proceeding from the advance guard of his literary and philosophical circles.

> How incredible at the present day do the effects of superstition exhibited in the middle ages, the horrors of excommunication and interdict, and the humiliation of the greatest monarchs at the feet of the pope, appear? What can be more contrary to European modes than the dread of disgrace, which induces the Bramin widows of Indostan to destroy themselves upon the funeral pile of their husbands? What more horribly immoral than the mistaken idea which leads multitudes in commercial countries to regard fraud, falsehood and circumvention as the truest policy? But, however powerful these errors may be, the empire of truth, if once established, would be incomparably greater.... No mind can be so far alienated from truth, as not in the midst of its degeneracy to have incessant returns of a better principle.[81]

These may sound like fighting words, but Godwin was just not about violent confrontation: "What I should desire is, not by violence to change its institutions, but by reason to change its ideas. I have no business with factions or intrigues; but simply to promulgate the truth, and to wait the tranquil progress of conviction.... It happens much oftener than we are willing to imagine, that 'the post of honour,' or, which is better, the post of utility, 'is a private station.'"[82] This abiding faith in the role of the intelligentsia, a clerisy given to discussion, would prove disappointing to some of Godwin's more revolutionary admirers, notably his son-in-law.

Bentham may also have been a radical reformer, and one who believed in accommodating and deploying human attachments, but he was worlds away from the Godwinian anarchist. Indeed, he and his followers mistakenly believed that Godwin had been bested in his debates with Thomas Malthus, who had severely criticized Godwin's (largely correct) view that there was a principle in human evolution toward the higher pleasures that would naturally curb excessive population growth, without such harsh Malthusian curbs as famine and disease. Obviously, when it came to prison abolition and suspicion of law enforcement, Bentham was the reformer and Godwin the abolitionist, arguing that such institutions only protected the ruling classes and did more to create violence and criminality than to prevent them.[83]

Was Godwin also a liberal imperialist who, behind a mask of impartial universal truth, countenanced or enabled domination, subjection, and genocide? His anarchism surely weighs against any suggestion that he was part of the "domination of strangers" school of political reform. Not believing in the legitimacy of states at all, whether at home or abroad, he favored freedom now, not the extended tutelage of even a reformed state power, which for Godwin was invariably just a tool of the rich. Freedom was what people needed, not the "quackery" of government.

As Marshall explains, Godwin did not offer an exact blueprint for radical reform in the *Enquiry*, but he did indicate the broad directions of change. Godwin

> looks to a simplified and decentralized form of society based on the principles of justice and equality and which would provide enough security for the free development of all. He found the answer in a loose federation of "parishes", or small face-to-face communities where "the voice of reason would be secure to be heard".... In the first place, there would be no more nation states.

> Colonies and dependencies would be given their independence. Neighbours are best informed of each other's concerns and justice is more likely to be found in a limited circle. But this need not mean insularity, for without nation states the whole of the human species would constitute in a sense one great republic.... Law and government would be gradually abolished ... There would be no need for a permanent national assembly.... there would be an equalization of property.... a form of voluntary communism.[84]

None of this was to come through coercion or intimidation, even of an intellectual variety. Godwin's "whole system is based on the free exercise of private judgment."[85] Dialogue and conversation were to rule. Given Godwin's commitment to non-violence and non-domination, his imperialist tendencies would seem to have been largely confined to a type of atheistic and anarchistic missionary work, spreading the message of No Gods, No Masters, as anarchists put it, and doing this through an extraordinary range of means. His second most well-known work, the novel *Caleb Williams*, was in actuality a serious and informed exposé of the violence and corruption of British law and politics. As Caroline Reitz shows, "Godwin's detective narrative is a product of contemporary social criticism that sought to connect rather than distinguish between the crimes of English law at home and abroad."[86] And this without any suggestion that radical reform at home would come from continuing domination abroad.

Bentham and Godwin, who knew each other slightly,[87] have both been treated as radical monsters, particularly by religious moralists, with Godwin getting the worst of it. His individualism and appeal to the finality of individual, private judgment enjoining universal benevolence, without need of law and government, ironically struck many of the orthodox as a positively evil invitation to egoistic rationalization rather than reason. And this is not to mention his educational views, which were progressive and child-centered to an astonishing degree – about as far from the Dickensian picture painted in *Hard Times* as could possibly be. The strand of educational reform running through all of the classical utilitarians is suggestive of how deep their differences truly were. Their outlooks on what to teach the next generation reveal much.

Consider the following statements on the aims of education:

> to send an uneducated child into the world, is injurious to the rest of mankind; it is little better than to turn out a mad dog or a wild

> beast into the streets … In the inferior classes of the community, this principle condemns the neglect of parents, who do not inure their children betimes to labour and restraint, by providing them with apprenticeships, services, or other regular employment, but who suffer them to waste their youth in idleness and vagrancy, or to betake themselves to some lazy, trifling, and precarious calling: for the consequence of having thus tasted the sweets of natural liberty, at an age when their passion and relish for it are at the highest, is, that they become incapable, for the remainder of their lives, of continued industry, or of persevering attention to any thing; spend their time in a miserable struggle between the importunity of want, and the irksomeness of regular application; and are prepared to embrace every expedient, which presents a hope of supplying their necessities without confining them to the plough, the loom, the shop, or the counting-house.[88]

So far, so Paley. But contrast Godwin:

> It is desirable that a child should partake of both characters, the child and the man. The hilarity of youth is too valuable a benefit, for any reasonable man to wish to see it driven out of the world. Nor is it merely valuable for the immediate pleasure that attends it; it is also highly conducive to health, to the best and most desirable state both of body and mind. Much of it would be cultivated by adults, which is now neglected; and would be even preserved to old age; were it not for false ideas of decorum, a species of hypocrisy, and supersubtle attention to the supposed minutiae of character, that lead us to check our spontaneous efforts, and to draw a veil of gravity over the innocent, as well as the immoderate, luxuriance and wantonness of our thoughts.[89]

Godwin's passion for individual freedom, but not license, extended to his philosophy of education, and it has made him a hero to progressive educators everywhere, the philosophical godfather of Summerhill School, free schools, and many other educational experiments.[90] Godwin himself tried unsuccessfully to start a progressive school – no students turned up – and devoted much of his later life to his Juvenile Library, writing and promoting educational materials for young people that would help to free their minds and immunize them against authoritarianism and domination in their many guises, including those of teachers and schools. His children's books extolled such messages as: "How happy are children, and the inhabitants of certain nations where no people are rich, that they can live without a continual anxiety about jewels and wealth!" He deemed it a "miserable vanity that would sacrifice the wholesome and gradual development of the mind to the desire of exhibiting little monsters of curiosity."[91] Indeed, Godwin seemed to welcome signs of independence and resistance even to his own educational efforts.[92]

Still, there is more shading in Godwin's views than is at first evident. He was not an utter absolutist about the truth of his ethical first principles – the chief of which is that the "true object of moral and political disquisition, is pleasure or happiness" – only convinced of its overwhelming probability. He was not an absolute pacifist – he did after all celebrate the initial phase of the French Revolution and saw that in extreme circumstances resistance was justified – only very, very skeptical about violence as making for real change, rather than begetting more violence. As devoted as he was to freeing minds through education and dialogue, he was all too aware of the failings of human reasoning and did not aim for absolute perfection, only a process of perfectibility steadily making the world a better place. The higher pleasures were qualitatively better, but the lower ones were not to be despised. And if Godwin was at times a committed atheist, in his later years he was more receptive to a comforting, somewhat fuzzy Theistic outlook – a sense of cosmic optimism, or faith that, in the famous phrase from Theodore Parker, the arc of the moral universe was bending toward justice. Even so,

> It is no matter whether the idea of an intelligent Creator, whose essence is love, and who is therefore to be perfect and entirely loved, is the dictate of the purest and the soundest philosophy. The merit of the principle will remain unaltered. Its characteristic is disinterestedness. It stands in direct opposition to the grovelling principle, born in France, and which is the curse of modern times, that all human motives are ultimately resolvable into self-love. It makes virtue to be really virtue, and not a semblance only. It bases the actions of the good man upon a just and irrefragable estimate of the value of things.[93]

Like Bentham, Godwin was influenced by D'Holbach, Helvétius, and other French philosophers, including Rousseau on the fraud of property. But it is more appropriate to think of him as the philosophical heir to Gerrard Winstanley and the Diggers of the seventeenth century. His vision of a voluntary, de-centralized, egalitarian, largely agrarian communism, with no coercive state apparatus and made up of small parishes (in effect, communes) enabling face-to-face human interaction, was in essence the same as that later promoted by Pyotr Kropotkin, the great Russian anarchist thinker who corrected Darwin's account of evolution to capture the importance of cooperation, and in fact acknowledged Godwin as a kindred anarchist spirit. If his anarchism was more that of Kropotkin and Colin Ward than that of Antifa, and his patience with the unfolding of history often too naïve and accommodating of the politics of the time, he still speaks to those who believe that happiness involves non-domination and that the means of radical social change must be consonant with the ends sought, and this for utilitarian reasons. And, of course, to those who recognize, often by being subjected to it, the pervasive, systemic nature of state violence, domestic as well as imperial, marking the neoliberal state in its policing and incarceration policies and practices.[94]

Godwin may have been as dismissive of the fantasies of a social contract and absolute natural rights as Bentham, but the shape of his utilitarianism was very, very different, so much so that his friends and admirers included Coleridge and Wordsworth, and of course Shelley, whose "Prometheus Unbound" is something of a hymn to his father-in-law. And even the core of rights that Godwin championed – basically, the right to private judgment and a "sphere of discretion" not to be interfered with, and the right to receive assistance from one's neighbors when in dire circumstances – were defeasible, not dependent on or constituted by the sanctions of the state, and received whatever force they had from the principle of utility.

To be sure, Godwin appreciated the blessings of maturity as well as those of childhood:

> If you ask men in general, whether they regard life as a blessing, they will perhaps hesitate: but they will recollect some feelings of exultation, some moments in which they felt with internal pride what it was to exist, and many of them will hereby be induced to pronounce in favour of life. But who can suppose himself a child, and look with exultation upon that species of existence? The principal sources of manly pleasure probably are, the feeling that we also are of some importance and account, the conscious power of conforming our actions to the dictates of our own understanding, an approving sense of the rectitude of our own determinations, and an affectionate and heroical sympathy in the welfare of others. To every one of these, young persons are almost uniformly strangers.[95]

But the way there was better facilitated by tasting the sweets of liberty than by being deprived of them. Human nature was quite malleable, but there was a tendency to growth that called for gentle cultivating and persuasion, rather than a pedagogy more akin to the shaping of a bonsai tree. Needless to say, the going methods were more like the latter: "The condition of a negro-slave in the West Indies, is in many respects preferable to that of the youthful son of a free-born European."[96]

That the freedom of the individual happened in community with others and was the hope of happiness might seem to somehow align Godwin with the Mill of both *On Liberty* and *Utilitarianism*, and, of course, the *Chapters on Socialism*. It would be hard to deny that the individualism of private judgment shared much with Millian individualism – finding the magic in the pronoun "I." Even so, the mechanisms of discipline and imperial paternalism found in the Mills are absent in Godwin, who does not figure at all in the works of Lowe, Said, Majeed, Elkins, or the others cited earlier. Understandably so, given Godwin's stance on not only the physical and moral equality of all humanity, but the political implications of that. When it came to "foreign and distant territories":

> The mode in which dependencies are acquired, must be either conquest, cession or colonization. The first of these no true moralist or politician will attempt to defend. The second is to be considered as the same thing in substance as the first, but with less openness and ingenuity. Colonization, which is by much the most specious pretence, is however no more than a pretence.[97]

Godwin is emphatic on "the absolute injustice of coercion" and how it "can only be by the most deplorable perversion of reason, that we can be induced to believe any species of slavery, from the slavery of the school boy to that of the most unfortunate negro in our West India plantations, favourable to virtue."[98]

Thus, Godwin was not one for the "domination of strangers," or domination by or of anyone for that matter. This is a deeply suggestive fact, indicating how many rooms there are in the house of utilitarianism.[99] Certain cautions may be in order, given how even Godwin could compromise his own best insights from an excess of individualistic Enlightenment prejudice.[100] Yet it is still possible to sympathize with Marshall's conclusion that: "As a moral philosopher, he [Godwin] imaginatively challenges the crumbling orthodoxy in contemporary ethics by arguing that facts about human nature are relevant to values and that moral principles can be supported by sound reasoning and truth. In so far as utilitarianism is a living tradition, Godwin provides better arguments than Bentham and anticipates the best of John Stuart Mill."[101]

That is, if "the best of John Stuart Mill" can be decolonized.

2

Utilitarian Virtue?

The New Mill

> Mill characterized Indians as alienated from laws and political structures following from a former "bad" government that had not educated them in the qualities of reason, restraint, and tolerance required for self-government. Although the "rude" people had yet to be adequately instructed to eradicate the ills of "violent passion," "personal pride," and "deplorable states of feeling," so that they might "sympathize" properly with the law, Mill argued that through the education by "good" government, their "mental habits" could be "conquered" to the extent that they would be eventually fit to govern themselves. In situations with an as-yet uneducated populace, he argued, elected government could be easily made an instrument of tyranny. For Mill, India furnished the paradigm of "those unready for liberty," for whom despotism was the only suitable form of government. (Lisa Lowe, *The Intimacies of Four Continents*)[1]

Lisa Lowe is not wrong in her assessment of John Stuart Mill, particularly Mill's 1861 work *Considerations on Representative Government*, which at times reads like "an apology for the East India Company's 'good despotism,' with the final chapter offering an elegy after the Company's recent demise." And in Mill's 1858 "Memorandum of the Improvements in the Administration of India during the Last Thirty Years," his defense of the East India Company's historical record, he "detailed the priorities of colonial governance, from rationalizing revenue collection, public works, and civil society, to the essential use of police and military force to maintain social order." He "measured the efficacy of a colonial state by its suppression of crime and maintenance of social order. He went on to state that owing to the successful suppression of criminal gangs, these policing operations had been extended to address criminal organizations, 'piracy,' 'infanticide,' 'suttee, or the burning of widows,' 'witchcraft,' and 'tragga' or revenge killings."[2] Mill

> explicitly argued that the best colonial government was the corporate colonial state, for which he believed early nineteenth-century British East India Company rule in India to be the ideal. Yet the liberal political reason exemplified by Mill, which combined economic free trade with political liberty, actually furnished the principles and rationale for the apotheosis of British imperialism in the second half of the nineteenth century.[3]

It was much the same template that would be applied in the infamous Opium Wars of 1839–42 and 1856–60, when Britain waged war against China in the name of free trade – free trade in opium, mostly from India, a trade that China had tried to suppress. Britain won both times – the second time in alliance with France – and after the 1842 Treaty of Nanjing took control of Hong Kong. And with the Beijing Convention, at the conclusion of the second war, they took possession of the Kowloon Peninsula bordering Hong Kong. They stayed in control until 1997.[4]

With China, as with India, the term "war" may be euphemistic. As Bernard Porter puts it, "Murder seems an apt word: tens of thousands of Chinese were killed (some killed themselves, out of shame), but the British (and Indian auxiliaries) suffered only minor casualties.... And all in the interests of a bunch of drug-pushers. Hardly any of the British participants felt proud of their victory."[5]

Free trade and the civilizing mission could hardly look worse: "Between the 1770s and the 1830s opium became indispensable to the [East India] Company's financial health. During the first seventeen years of its opium monopoly, the Company made £1,277,000 in profit. By the 1820s it was the company's largest Indian export item and accounted for 15 percent of the Company's Indian revenue."[6] When the Company's charter was up for renewal in 1833, James Mill defended it against its many critics, and it retained its governmental powers, even though losing its monopoly on trade. As Michael St. John Packe concluded long ago, both the Mills

> were convinced that in India, as in primitive communities of the ancient world, despotism was the only possible system for

> the time, and in this sense they believed the Company to be unrivalled. They had faith in its record of systematic expansion, of slow and steady enlightenment, and in its long tradition of loyal service. Dangerous radicals as they were as far as Europe was concerned, for India they were more tory than the Tories.[7]

And as John Stuart Mill remarked in another context, the Tory party, by the "law of its constitution," was "the stupidest party."

The previous chapter sketched or rehearsed a number of key themes: the variability of utilitarianism even in its familiar Eurocentric and Anglo-American contexts; some of the ways in which, or enabling factors by which, certain classical utilitarians – Bentham in some ways, but especially his followers – embedded (and compromised) their reformism in the colonialism, settler colonialism, and imperialism of the British Empire, buying into and rationalizing the ideology of "civilizing" supposedly uncivilized subjects lower on the utilitarian "scale of civilization" and unfitted for self-government; and some of the pretensions, erasures, delusions, and hypocrisies involved in such complicity, which historical research has increasingly exposed for what they were. It cannot be stressed strongly enough that, outside of the relatively narrow purviews of certain internal academic philosophical debates over utilitarianism, it is often taken as uncontroversial that, in Caroline Elkins's words, James Mill, by "portraying Indian society as morally degraded," was actually "formulating a different justification for British rule. Replacing Oriental despotism with good governance, or instituting political and legal reform, would transform so-called natives, ridding them of their superstitions and stupid character." And, as Elkins demonstrates at length, even if "Britain's civilizing mission was reformist in its claims, it was brutal nonetheless. Violence was not just the British Empire's midwife, it was endemic to the structures and systems of British rule."[8]

In fact, in recent decades, the reception of the younger Mill has shifted so much in the direction of this view of his father's accomplishments that it is now, in many academic quarters, considered reckless to mount a defense of Millian liberalism, such as that of Inder S. Marwah's *Liberalism, Diversity and Domination: Kant, Mill and the Government of Difference*.[9] But Marwah's example is instructive – he stresses that his defense of Millian liberalism is not an attempt

> to defend Mill's views, or liberalism more generally, root and branch. Mill's political philosophy justified imperialism, and his professional life was dedicated to its extension.... Many

> other liberals shared in his views, and many other liberalisms bear the marks of their presumptions. He (and they) readily advanced a wide range of Eurocentric confabulations that shaped the modern world and continue to resonate in contemporary global relations. As postcolonial scholars have demonstrated, a wide swath of western thinkers – liberals, Marxists and others – adopted historicist frameworks and civilizational hierarchies upholding injustices ranging from the dispossession and extermination of Indigenous peoples, to slavery, to imperial and colonial domination. Still further, critics of neo-colonialism have drawn out their ongoing impacts, as the imperial era's structural foundations – legal, political and economic – endure, cementing the subjugation of subaltern peoples through uneven global institutions and associations.[10]

Indeed, Marwah does a superb job of spelling out many of the problems that Mill's anti-colonial and postcolonial critics have emphasized – "it is in no way set against the spirit and ambitions of postcolonial theorists, critics of liberal imperialism or scholars of neo-colonialism" – while also straightening out various misunderstandings of Mill's views on the stages of historical progress and scale of civilization, where he drew from Comte and others, but added considerable nuance. His ultimate aim, however, is to provide a contextually sensitive reading of the roots of liberalism that serves an admittedly presentist purpose, valorizing the Millian legacy over the Kantian one:

> the Kantian orientation leaves little conceptual space to acknowledge the internal value of diversity: non-European cultures are legible only as immature, irrational and aberrant, and non-European races, as instruments of a purposive natural history anchored by humanity's moralization. Kant's frequent invocations of morally salient racial characteristics (Negroes' cognitive ceiling, Amerindians' developmental stuntedness, etc.) are certainly troubling, but the teleological framework shaping his response to pluralism more broadly is the real problem, suffocating any possibility of envisioning human diversity in terms that might register its worth. If we take Kant's full theorization of our moral nature, as he laid it out – incorporating both our transcendental freedom as rational beings and our lifelong moral evolution as phenomenal ones – it appears difficult to uncouple his moral system's egalitarian pretensions from its limitations.... If we remove Mill's parochial assessments of

> given cultural groups – Indians, Basques, the Chinese and so on – from his account of human development, its philosophical coherence remains and its structure is unaffected. If we do the same for Kant, his theorization of our moral nature and moral progress lapses into unintelligibility. The movement from nature to freedom is, for Kant, precisely humanity's evolution from unenlightened, "raw," non-European social forms to the cultured civilizations cradling the dominion of reason. That movement is our moral and political vocation, and is incoherent outside of its racial and culturalist presumptions.[11]

So far, so good, as least as concerns Kant. Whether Mill can be so reconstructed is another question, and one that is perhaps not quite as relevant to decolonizing utilitarianism as it might at first seem, since Marwah hives Mill's liberalism off from his utilitarianism and treats it (or tries to treat it) largely independently. He stresses how Mill's utilitarianism shifted over time, which is true, but claims that with the mature Mill, "the true utilitarian spirit," as Isaiah Berlin put it, "has fled": "This Mill self-consciously avoided ideological stringency in general, and all the more so in matters of social and political life that he saw as especially poorly served by it. This Mill is no more a strict utilitarian than the libertarian he's sometimes miscast as; he is sensitive to the cultivation of social virtue, but not quite a virtue ethicist; he is as much an eighteenth-century rationalist as a nineteenth-century romantic."[12]

Whether this is still Mill, as opposed to John Gray, is a good question, but at any rate, Marwah, like Berlin, seems to be working with a very narrow, simplistic view of utilitarianism and, oddly enough, does not, any more than the Kantian apologists, develop his critique with an adequate account of race and racism. Like other defenders of Mill, he seems to think that it would be anachronistic to charge Mill with racism, even while allowing that it is useful overall to charge him with ethnocentrism and to charge Kant with racism.[13]

But, clearly, the violence of the Empire was racialized, with the scale of civilization regularly placing white populations as closer to self-governance than populations of color, even if it would only be later in the nineteenth century that Rudyard Kipling's infamous declaration of the "White Man's Burden" would become part of the popular imperial imagination, and a virulent, so-called "scientific" racism would be added to the legitimating ideologies of empire. As the century wore on, liberal imperialism both matured and gave way to a not very liberal imperialism, as fears of democratization and rebellious subjects intensified. The peculiar irony of the classical utilitarian canon is that the trajectory of philosophical progress and insight – as celebrated by Rawls, Parfit, and so many others – is taken as steadily improving from Bentham through Mill to Sidgwick, with Sidgwick being lauded as the philosophical pinnacle of classical utilitarianism. Viewed through the lens of the effort to decolonize utilitarianism, however, the ideological subservience to the Empire grows steadily worse – and more authoritarian – as the move from Bentham to Sidgwick unfolds, with the latter buying into defenses of colonialism, settler colonialism, and imperialism that were more compromised – and more racist – than anything in Bentham and the Mills. The younger Mill was perhaps the liberal peak of this complex trajectory of liberal imperialism, a trajectory that can only make one wonder about what exactly was being prized by Rawls and company.[14] But he was also, along with his father, a bridge to these later developments, to the expansion of academic philosophical professionalization that was mostly in harmony with, not opposition to, the expansion of England, to invoke the title of Seeley's famous apologia.

This trajectory is not a simple one; there were serious differences between Bentham and his followers. As Pitts argues: "Even if James and John Stuart Mill questioned whether possession of colonies profited the European colonizers, both insisted that colonial rule benefited its backward subjects. Bentham never adopted such ardor for despotic colonial rule, though his views about whether Indians and others – including citizens of the United States – could benefit from British rule remain somewhat enigmatic and indeed contradictory."[15] But even so, Bentham's somewhat ironic saving graces – being enigmatic and contradictory – do not exactly remove him from the company of early liberal imperialists, as even his warmest defenders in the end admit. He was no Godwin, and however much he allowed for this special circumstance or that, his disagreements with the two Mills stayed within certain parameters. Rightly or wrongly, the name of Godwin scarcely gets invoked in such contexts. Anarchist utilitarianism did not fit with any of the contending sides – Tory, Whig, Liberal, or Philosophical Radical. It is very pleasant to think of what might have happened to the East India Company had Godwin been a force in running the organization.

It should also be acknowledged that other disciples were far more troubling, including some in the US. Crimmins and Spencer, in their magisterial *Utilitarians and Their Critics in America, 1789–1914*, do justice to such Benthamites as the English-born South Carolinian Thomas Cooper (1759–1839), a lawyer, reformer, and sometimes chemistry teacher who enthusiastically promoted Benthamism – even Bentham's critique of Adam Smith's restrictions on usury – but turned the view into a defense of slavery. As noted on the Farleigh Dickenson College webpage on "Dickenson and Slavery," in his 1826 work "Two Essays" "Cooper claims that 'emancipation of the Slaves, would surely convert them into idle and useless vagabonds, and thieves; as every Southern man conversant with negro habits and propensities well knows.'"[16]

As Crimmins and Spencer note of Cooper, "that he could also use this formula [the greatest happiness] to justify slavery leaves a question mark against the consistency of his utilitarian thinking. On the other hand, this could be cited as evidence of the pliability of utilitarian theory in different hands."[17] Bentham himself had been impressed enough by Cooper's avowed utilitarianism to ask John Quincy Adams to forward to him some of his – Bentham's – works.

Educating the Educator

So, what, then, is "the best of John Stuart Mill"? And where does this leave the "utilitarian self"? And education for the utilitarian outlook?[18]

There is little agreement about these topics, even among the most canonical of the classical utilitarian patriarchs. All agreed that happiness, conceived as some form of pleasure over pain, was the great end, and that consequences, outcomes, mattered most. But when it came to the nature of the creatures pursuing that end, and the appropriate means and methods, including the role of the state and of England in particular, there was so much serious disagreement that, practically speaking, they lived in different worlds – though not, for the most part, the world of Thomas Cooper.

Still, given the fundamental importance accorded to education by the classical utilitarians, whatever their differences, the topic seems inescapable. So, how did they go about teaching a utilitarian outlook, in the more conventional sense of teaching?

The answer is: not very well, even by their own standards, and even in the case of the Mills. As everyone who knows the name John Stuart Mill knows, the education crafted by his father and Bentham to make of him a perfect utilitarian ended up landing him in a personal crisis. By the time Mill junior was 20, his life looked, from the inside, like an existential crisis. He credited his father with having deprived him of the pleasures of childhood, indeed, of any childhood whatsoever, having stunted him in a way that was all too "Benthamite," in the familiar pejorative sense. The "hilarity of youth" was not part of the curriculum. John DiIulio provides a neatly condensed biographical snapshot:

> Those familiar with Mill will probably already know the beats to the story: a rigorous, experimental education under the tutelage of James Mill, his imperious father; raised to carry the torch for the Utilitarian reform projects of his father and godfather, Jeremy Bentham, the leading light of England's Philosophical Radicals; a nervous, near suicidal, breakdown at age twenty; recovery via Romantic poetry, which filled the sentimental and aesthetic void left in his soul by his exhausting, emotionally barren upbringing; meeting Harriet Taylor, the then-married love of his life, and carrying on a scandalous courtship with her; making deep and abiding friendships with many of his Conservative rivals; working at the East India Trading Company; his marriage to and intellectual partnership with Taylor; serving a storied spell in Parliament; and all the while pondering and scribbling away as he produced some of the most momentous and famous philosophical treatises of all time.[19]

But it was one thing for Bentham to be tortured as a child by an ambitious, social-climbing father who was forever pushing him to push himself onward and upward, or for James Mill to have been forced into a childhood of constant study by devout Scottish parents, particularly a mother set on her son rising up in the world (she even changed the family name from Milne to Mill because it was more English). Why would a similarly oppressive educational regimen be imposed on a child by enlightened utilitarian educators determined to produce a perfect utilitarian self, happy and productive of happiness in others?

The younger Mill complained in his celebrated *Autobiography* that his education in effect suffered from some of the same flaws as Benthamism in general. His secular godfather Bentham, he argued, was "one-eyed," seeing only the unpoetic, mechanical, business side of life, remained "a boy to the last," was incapable of "deriving light from other minds," missed the significance of "national character" (and character in general), and did not appreciate how human acts needed to be assessed not just by their morality, but by their prudence, beauty, and lovableness.[20] There was much more to the "Art of Life," as Mill called the comprehensive sphere of normative reasoning about how to live.[21] Bentham was the heir to the empiricism and naturalism of the eighteenth century, but something more was called for with the new generations, who witnessed the Romantic, Coleridgean, and Wordsworthian reaction against dry rationality in the name of creativity, spirit, feeling, intuition, mysticism, imagination, the sublime, and everything else that Romanticism would promote. Mill sought to appropriate these oppositional forces for a more capacious, more historically aware and sensitive, liberal utilitarian vision.[22] This is the Mill who became Victorian England's leading public moralist, the Mill whom many celebrate for having broken with the Philosophical Radicals, reinventing or even abandoning utilitarianism even while clinging to the term – not that Mill saw it that way.

But for all his complaints, John Mill was as much a product of, as a rebellion against, the educational regimen devised by his father and Bentham. The story is familiar, but there are aspects of it that the familiar accounts miss, especially concerning, once again, the differences between Bentham and Mill. These differences had a lot to do with Plato, the classics, and classical languages. And character. And virtue.

Bear in mind that John Mill arguably became the most highly educated man in England, despite being home-schooled and for most of his life despising Oxford and Cambridge as bastions of idleness and religious bigotry. That he came to expect a lot from education is evident from his 1867 "Inaugural Address" as the Rector of the University of St. Andrews, with its vision of liberal education as including the classics and Greek and Latin, along with mathematics and natural philosophy and a vast range of other subjects. As Alan Ryan notes, in comparing Mill's view of education to the literary education championed by Matthew Arnold,

> a concern for the classics was to feed a concern for a lively democratic politics, and for a kind of political and intellectual ambition that Mill thought Victorian Englishmen lacked ... when Mill asked the question whether we should seek an education for citizenship or an education in the classical tradition, he inevitably answered Both, and when he asked whether such an education ought to be a scientific or a literary education he unhesitatingly answered Both once more.[23]

Along with intellectual education and moral education, there is "a third division, which ... is barely inferior to them, and not less needful to the completeness of the human being; I mean the aesthetic branch; the culture which comes through poetry and art, and may be described as the education of the feelings, and the cultivation of the beautiful." Art, "the endeavour after perfection in execution," is a vital educational component for cultivating the love of virtue and making people feel

> not only actual wrong or actual meanness, but the absence of noble aims and endeavours, as not merely blamable but also degrading: to have a feeling of the miserable smallness of mere self in the face of this great universe, of the collective mass of our fellow creatures, in the face of past history and of the indefinite future – the poorness and insignificance of human life if it is to be all spent in making things comfortable for ourselves and our kin, and raising ourselves and them a step or two on the social ladder. Thus feeling, we learn to respect ourselves only so far as we feel capable of nobler objects.[24]

Just how the younger Mill came to such high-minded views is a story suggestive of the deep differences between James Mill and Bentham, as well as father and son.

John's home schooling was, like that of his father and Bentham, essentially a lifelong intensive track, and profoundly if unsurprisingly Eurocentric. He had begun studying Greek when he was three, and Greek and arithmetic, along with reading and writing, took up most of his early years, until he began on Latin at about age eight. By the time he was a teenager, he had "read Plato's dialogues called Gorgias and Protagoras, and his Republic," and, as he explained in the draft of his *Autobiography*:

> There is no author to whom my father thought himself more indebted for his own mental culture, than Plato, and I can say the same of mine. The Socratic method, of which the Platonic dialogues are the chief example, is unsurpassed as a discipline for abstract thought on the most difficult subjects. Nothing in modern life and education, in the smallest degree supplies its place. The close, searching *elenchus* by which the man of vague generalities is absolutely compelled either to express his meaning to himself in definite terms, or to confess that he does not know what he is talking about – the perpetual testing of all general statements by particular instances – the siege in form which is laid to the meaning of large abstract terms, by laying hold of some much larger class-name which includes that and more, and *dividing down* to the thing sought, marking out its limits and definition by a series of accurately drawn distinctions between it and each of the cognate objects which are successively

> severed from it – all this even at that age took such hold on me that it became part of my own mind; and I have ever felt myself, beyond any modern that I know of except my father and perhaps beyond even him, a pupil of Plato, and cast in the mould of his dialectics.[25]

This stress on Greek and Greek literature clearly did not owe much to Bentham. Although James Mill enthusiastically endorsed Bentham's *Chrestomathia*, there is scarcely any mention of Plato in that work, or of the value of Greek and Latin. Indeed, Bentham was almost invariably as snarky in his references to Plato as he was in his references to Blackstone. As Crimmins records, the "Lockean fictions of natural law and contract theory upon which Blackstone based his account of the English constitution led Bentham to a ceaseless campaign against the abstractions of law, philosophy, and politics. If the works of Plato were 'the grand original mint of moral unintelligibles', radicals like Thomas Paine were the purveyors of political fictions, and Blackstone was pre-eminent among the 'dealers of fiction' in the field of law."[26] James Mill never disrespected Plato in that way.

And Mill senior did pay close attention to his son's education, though in the earlier and more candid draft of the *Autobiography* John confessed that his father "reproached me when I read a sentence ill, and *told* me how I ought to have read it," but "never *shewed* me … how it ought to be read." And this "was a defect running through his modes of instruction as it did through his modes of thinking" – namely, that "he trusted too much to the intelligibleness of the abstract when not embodied in the concrete."[27]

But the final version of the *Autobiography* largely stressed how he owed to his father his many-sidedness, love of learning and Plato, grounding in political economy, much of his utilitarianism, and more. He defensively claimed that, although his father had not been directly involved in starting the *Westminster Review*, he was more truly the voice of the Philosophical Radicals than Bentham. James Mill's associationist psychology, appreciation of Malthus, and other factors made it so, and John attributed to his father "an almost unbounded confidence in the efficacy of two things: representative government, and complete freedom of discussion. So complete was my father's reliance on the influence of reason over the minds of mankind, whenever it is allowed to reach them, that he felt as if all would be gained if the whole population were taught to read, if all sorts of opinions were allowed to be addressed to them by word and in writing, and if by means of the suffrage they could nominate a legislature to give effect to the opinions they adopted."[28] Bentham is dismissed as more of an eccentric voice behind the scenes, one whose judgment was called into question by both father and son for his designation of James Bowring as a favorite, a favorite to some degree displacing Mill senior as Bentham's confidant. Bowring became not only Bentham's literary executor but also the first editor of the *Westminster Review*, after James Mill declined Bentham's offer, but the younger Mill simply scorned him.[29]

What was James Mill's side of the story? What did he think that he was doing, with his familial educational experiment? His son's account of the paternal pedagogy at times obscures the philosophical relationship between father and son. Mill senior was formidable, the author of not only *The History of British India*, but also such works as the *Elements of Political Economy* (1821), the *Essays on Government, Jurisprudence, Liberty of the Press, Education, and Prisons and Prison Discipline* (1823), and the two-volume *Analysis of the Phenomena of the Human Mind* (1829). If he was an ally of Bentham, he was also an ally of Ricardo and others who had their reservations about Bentham. His "Essay on Government," composed for the "Supplement" to the fifth edition of the *Encyclopædia Britannica*, sparked a witty critique of the Philosophical Radicals from the Whig Macaulay, who objected that the "style which the Utilitarians admire, suits only those subjects on which it is possible to reason *a priori*."[30] Macaulay skewered a priori or deductive economistic reformism, though he did allow that Bentham had taught people "*how*, in some most important points, to promote their own happiness; and if his school had emulated him as successfully in this respect, as in the trick of passing off truisms for discoveries, the name of Benthamite would have been no word for the scoffer."[31]

But Mill's views were more complex than Macaulay's account allowed, and he certainly considered himself a philosopher of education. "Education," an article written in 1815 for the *Encyclopædia Britannica*, praised the monitorial system famously implemented by Bell and Lancaster,[32] which had excited Bentham to no end with its vision of non-punitive, but efficient, tutoring of younger students by older students in a spirit of friendly competition. And it defended utilitarianism: "the end of Education is to render the individual, as much as possible, an instrument of happiness, first to himself, and next to other beings." But part of this rendering would come through the inculcation of certain virtues, since "intelligence and temperance have a reference not less direct to the happiness of others than to that of the possessor; and Benevolence cannot be considered as less essential to his happiness than intelligence and temperance … the happiness of the individual is bound up with that of his species, that which affects the happiness of the one, must also, in general, affect that of the other."[33]

Happiness depends partly on the condition of the body, partly on the condition of the mind, and the latter is the distinctive concern of the educator. Naturally, the overriding significance of political education, via law and government, is emphatically reiterated: how legal and political systems with all their sanctions are the lead socializers. The study of human nature in general is just a branch of education. But the cultivation of virtuous character nonetheless plays a key role.

Unfortunately, Mill senior's practical applications of this educational philosophy were severe. As John admitted, "Temperance" was one of the ancient Greek virtues that his father endorsed in the Platonic extreme. Achieving maximal pleasure for either the individual or humanity demanded something akin to a Platonic ordering of the soul, but through cognitive behavioral conditioning rather than intuitive insight: "A perfect command, then, over a man's appetites and desires; the power of restraining them whenever they lead in a hurtful direction; that possession of himself which insures his judgement against the illusions of the passions, and enables him to pursue constantly what he deliberately approves, is indispensably requisite to enable him to produce the greatest possible quantity of happiness."[34] Happiness is of course "the end; and we have circumscribed the inquiry, by naming Intelligence, Temperance, and Benevolence, of which the last two parts are Generosity and Justice, as the grand qualities of mind, through which this end is to be attained." The issue is "how can those early sequences be made to take the place on which the habits, conducive to intelligence, temperance, and benevolence, are founded; and how can those sequences, on which are founded the vices opposite to those virtues, be prevented?[35]

This is indeed a training in virtue, a very strenuous virtue:

> A man can affect the happiness of others, either by abstaining from doing them harm, or by doing them positive good. To abstain from doing them harm receives the name of Justice; to do positive good receives that of Generosity. Justice and generosity, then, are the two qualities by which man is fitted to promote the happiness of his fellow-creatures. And it thus appears, that the four cardinal virtues of the ancients do pretty completely include all the qualities, to the possession of which it is desirable that the human mind should be trained.[36]

The "sequences" in question are "those sequences among our sensations which have been so frequently experienced as to create a habit of passing from the idea of the one to that of the other" – that is, the sequences of mental associations that Mill took to be the building blocks of the mind, described at great length in his *Analysis of the Phenomena of the Human Mind.* The emphasis on conditioning was to such a degree that the father was always warning his eldest son that there was absolutely nothing special about him, and that with the right education, any child could rival his accomplishments. For James Mill, it was clear that just as "we strive for an equal degree of justice, an equal degree of temperance, an equal degree of veracity, in the poor as in the rich, so ought we to strive for an equal degree of intelligence, if there were not a preventing cause." And it would help matters if the young were not

> bound close to labour before they are fifteen or sixteen years of age ... if those years are skilfully employed in the acquisition of knowledge, in rendering all those trains habitual on which intelligence depends, it may be easily shown that a very high degree of intellectual acquirements may be gained, that a firm foundation may be laid for a life of mental action, a life of wisdom, and reflection, and ingenuity, even in those by whom the most ordinary labour will fall to be performed.[37]

Mechanical education, he owned, would chiefly have to do with intelligence.

Curiously, when it came to the exact nature of happiness, Mill outlined two distinct approaches: one ultimately rooted in simple sensations and their combinations, as with Bentham; the other, a more Platonic one that moves beyond such humble origins and "affirms that there is something in human happiness, and in the human intellect, which soars high above this corporeal level; that there are intellectual as well as moral forms, the resplendent objects of human desire, which can by no means be resolved into the grosser elements of sense." Oddly, he leaves the matter at that, exhorting philosophers "to perfect this inquiry."[38] Such open-mindedness was not one of his signature traits, alas.

As a model of education, this Millian approach missed much, in theory and practice. Even setting aside the complexities of the reasons-versus-causes literature and interpretive social science, there is an obvious difference between what is in effect a simple mental conditioning model and a purposive or rational actor (or Platonic actor) model, and Mill did not show how the two models could be reconciled, something that his son would come to realize in an all too painful way, as he sought a better reconciliation of freedom and necessity.[39] Indeed, getting to the utilitarian self from one's individual happiness would demand a different approach to the virtues of happiness.

The Crash

When it came to the utilitarian experiment that was his son, James Mill no doubt aimed high, trying to demonstrate what the best education might achieve. As Terence Ball shows, in a nice synthesis of Mill's writings:

> James Mill thought that "of all the circumstances which affect the happiness, the beauty, and order, and well-being of society, by far the most important" is individual character (Mill 1813a, 97). The shaping of character was no simple matter.... To adapt a famous Stoic idea, as we move from the inner to the outer concentric circles of affection and concern for one's self and for others, it becomes increasingly difficult (impossible even without conducive physical and moral circumstances), to abstain from doing harm or do positive good to others... without strong associations, the knowing subject's mind hardly takes cognizance of the interests or even the existence of others outside the narrow circle of one's self, family, friends and associates.... Good education strengthens virtuous motives so that they do not "give way, habitually, whenever they are opposed by any other motive even of moderate strength" (Mill 1829a, II.241).... Only when one cares enough to sacrifice that "part of the self which the good of our species requires" (Mill 1818, V.527) can individual exertion be directed towards the pursuit of social happiness.[40]

John was apparently meant to be an example of education's "most perfect work," but the product proved defective. His polishing in France, which in part took place while staying with Samuel Bentham, did help round him out, giving him among other things his enduring love of mountains, rural or natural scenery, botany, and France, and a model of a strong, independently minded woman, Lady Bentham. And he did become, after his strategically timed teenage reading of Bentham, the great utilitarian hope – something his education was designed to achieve – and, through his discussion and debating societies and such friends and allies as Charles and John Austin, George Grote,

John Roebuck, and others, he championed the cause with considerable enthusiasm. Despite his dislike of Bowring, he contributed to the *Westminster Review* and other publications, and defended utilitarianism – a term he mistakenly believed had originated in Galt's "Annals of the Parish" – against an array of opponents, from Tories and Whigs to Owenites and anyone who dared to criticize Ricardo's economics or its Malthusian premises. Thus, as Richard Reeves has put it, by "his late teens … Mill had a creed, comrades and a career."[41]

But in 1826, when he was 20, this carefully constructed self collapsed in a dejected heap:

> It was in the autumn of 1826. I was in a dull state of nerves, such as everybody is occasionally liable to; unsusceptible to enjoyment or pleasurable excitement; one of those moods when what is pleasant at other times, becomes insipid or indifferent … In this frame of mind it occurred to me to put the question directly to myself, "Suppose that all your objects in life were realized; that all the changes in institutions and opinions which you are looking forward to, could be completely effected at this very instant: would this be a great joy and happiness to you?" And an irrepressible self-consciousness distinctly answered, "No!" At this my heart sank within me: the whole foundation on which my life was constructed fell down. All my happiness was to have been found in the continual pursuit of this end. The end had ceased to charm, and how could there ever again be any interest in the means? I seemed to have nothing left to live for.[42]

The "cloud of dejection" did not pass over – "A night's sleep, the sovereign remedy for the smaller vexations of life, had no effect on it." He awoke to "a renewed consciousness of the woeful fact" and indeed for "some months the cloud seemed to grow thicker and thicker." Nothing helped.

He kept all this from his father. "My education, which was wholly his work, had been conducted without any regard to the possibility of its ending in this result; and I saw no use in giving him the pain of thinking that his plans had failed, when the failure was probably irremediable, and at all events, beyond the power of *his* remedies." After all, his father's model of mind was the problem:

> I had always heard it maintained by my father, and was myself convinced, that the object of education should be to form the strongest possible associations of the salutary class: associations

> of pleasure with all things beneficial to the great whole, and of pain with all things hurtful to it. This doctrine appeared inexpugnable; but it now seemed to me on retrospect, that my teachers had occupied themselves but superficially with the means of forming and keeping up these salutary associations. They seemed to have trusted altogether to the old familiar instruments, praise and blame, reward and punishment. Now I did not doubt that by these means, begun early and applied unremittingly, intense associations of pain and pleasure, especially of pain, might be created, and might produce desires and aversions capable of lasting undiminished to the end of life. But there must always be something artificial and casual in associations thus produced. The pains and pleasures thus forcibly associated with things, are not connected with them by any natural ties; and it is therefore, I thought, essential to the durability of these associations, that they should have become so intense and inveterate as to be practically indissoluble, before the habitual exercise of the power of analysis had commenced. For I now saw, or thought I saw, what I had always before received with incredulity – that the habit of analysis has a tendency to wear away the feelings: as indeed it has when no other mental habit is cultivated, and the analysing spirit remains without its natural complements and correctives. The very excellence of analysis (I argued) is that it tends to weaken and undermine whatever is the result of prejudice; that it enables us mentally to separate ideas which have only casually clung together: and no associations whatever could ultimately resist this dissolving force, were it not that we owed to analysis our clearest knowledge of the permanent sequences in nature; the real connexions between Things."[43]

Indeed, teaching the Socratic elenchus or the greatest happiness principle was a task that called for a more humanistic method than that used to condition a rat to run a maze, which can hardly be called a dialogical relationship. Coming to see the arbitrariness of one's social conditioning can surely be disheartening, especially if one is championing one's outlook as the salvation of humanity. Such debunking can be carried even further, as in evolutionary arguments exposing various moral beliefs as explainable in terms of their survival value rather than their truth.[44] But for John, finding meaning in his life via the utilitarian principle required making it his own in both reasoned and emotional terms, rather than regarding it as an arbitrary piece of his psychology, the result of mechanical processes of socialization. To recognize this was to recognize the value of autonomy, of uncoerced and authentic self-direction, of character. His father had theorized character, with the virtues of the ancients, but he had not understood how to inculcate it.

Mill carried on through "the melancholy winter of 1826–7" in his usual ways, but mechanically, from "mere force of habit." He frequently asked himself if he "was bound to go on living when life must be passed in this manner," something he could not envision doing for more than a year. But then darkness broke in a very suggestive way:

> When, however, not more than half that duration of time had elapsed, a small ray of light broke in upon my gloom. I was reading, accidentally, Marmontel's *Memoirs*, and came to the passage which relates his father's death, the distressed position of the family, and the sudden inspiration by which he, then a mere boy, felt and made them feel that he would be everything to them – would supply the place of all that they had lost. A vivid conception of the scene and its feelings came over me, and I was moved to tears. From this moment my burthen grew lighter. The oppression of the thought that all feeling was dead within me, was gone. I was no longer hopeless: I was not a stock or a stone. I had still, it seemed, some of the material out of which all worth of character, and all capacity for happiness, are made. Relieved from my ever present sense of irremediable wretchedness, I gradually found that the ordinary incident of life could again give me some pleasure; that I could again find enjoyment, not intense, but sufficient for cheerfulness, in sunshine and sky, in books, in conversation, in public affairs; and that there was, once more, excitement, though of a moderate kind, in exerting myself for my opinions, and for the public good.[45]

That a scenario of fatherly death should prove so therapeutic is not surprising, given the son's emotional suffocation.

What credibility can the utilitarian educator possess, as a personality that fails to exemplify or impart the very thing that forms the end of the educational enterprise?[46] As Lowe suggested, the younger Mill saw his crisis as a case of the microcosm within the macrocosm, as a tale of progress, achieving freedom after a kind of slavery:

> though my dejection, honestly looked at, could not be called other than egotistical, produced by the ruin, as I thought, of my fabric of happiness, yet the destiny of mankind in general was ever in

> my thoughts, and could not be separated from my own. I felt that the flaw in my life, must be a flaw in life itself; that the question was, whether, if the reformers of society and government could succeed in their objects, and every person in the community were free and in a state of physical comfort, the pleasures of life, being no longer kept up by struggle and privation, would cease to be pleasures.

That is, if he could see some "better hope than this for human happiness in general," then he might be able to "look on the world with pleasure; content as far as I was myself concerned, with any fair share of the general lot."[47] This intimate entangling of egoism and utilitarianism, such that the former takes on the aspect of one's "fair share" of the general happiness, and the views converge in subtle ways, is a leading theme of classical utilitarianism, and one that would undergo further development with Sidgwick, Mill's philosophical successor.[48] The ultimate aim promised the convergence of personal and general happiness.

Given the texture of Mill's crisis, it is unsurprising that the cure came in the shape of Romanticism, of Wordsworth and the cultivation of the feelings:

> What made Wordsworth's poems a medicine for my state of mind, was that they expressed, not mere outward beauty, but states of feeling, and of thought coloured by feeling, under the excitement of beauty. They seemed to be the very culture of the feelings, which I was in quest of.... From them I seemed to learn what would be the perennial sources of happiness, when all the greater evils of life shall have been removed. And I felt myself at once better and happier as I came under their influence.[49]

As Mill grew more distanced from his early Philosophical Radical friends, he "fell more and more into friendly intercourse with our Coleridgeian adversaries in the Society, Frederick Maurice and John Sterling." Maurice, Mill observed, "was the thinker, Sterling the orator," and it was the passionate Sterling who was destined to become Mill's closest friend, next to Harriet Taylor.[50]

But when it came to what Mill deemed the lasting effects of his crisis, the impact of Maurice and other representatives of the Coleridgean alternative is plain:

> I, for the first time, gave its proper place, among the prime necessities of human well-being, to the internal culture of the

> individual. I ceased to attach almost exclusive importance to the ordering of outward circumstances, and the training of the human being for speculation and for action. I had now learnt by experience that the passive susceptibilities needed to be cultivated as well as the active capacities, and required to be nourished and enriched as well as guided.... The maintenance of a due balance among the faculties, now seemed to me of primary importance. The cultivation of the feelings became one of the cardinal points in my ethical and philosophical creed.[51]

The impact was evident, too, in Mill's recognition that although "happiness is the test of all rules of conduct, and the end of life," it was an end that "was only to be attained by not making it the direct end. Those only are happy (I thought) who have their minds fixed on some objects other than their own happiness; on the happiness of others, on the improvement of mankind, even on some art or pursuit, followed not as a means, but as an ideal end. Aiming thus at something else, they find happiness by the way." If one does, "and if otherwise fortunately circumstanced you will inhale happiness with the air you breathe, without dwelling on it or thinking about it, without either forestalling it in imagination, or putting it to flight by fatal questioning. This theory now became the basis of my philosophy of life."[52]

Thus, the enduring effect of this period was to highlight the importance of character, virtue, and "aesthetic education," which was what would, Mill hoped, carry humanity forward and improve the content and aid the reform of common morality, which was the sphere of rules enforceable by blame and/or punishment. According to Wendy Donner, "the unifying theme of the entire period is that in the realm of aesthetic education and experience, the philosopher-poet is the prime model and exemplar, the source of the uplifting and ennobling experiences and inspiration."[53] The aesthetic was the driving force, in Mill's "Art of Life" – what made the utilitarian clerisy a clerisy. All this still resonated with his father's vision of a perfect education, but as a better way to inculcate the character virtues bringing together one's own happiness and the happiness of all, reducing the reliance on purely external sanctions.

John Mill took these developments so far as to frame a new science. As Janice Carlisle has persuasively suggested: "in conceiving of ethology as a new field of inquiry that he would establish single-handedly, Mill was resorting to one of the most effective ways in which nineteenth-century writers characteristically defended themselves against the marginality inherent in their careers: by setting as their goal works of epic ambition, they defined the writer as hero."[54] Announced in his *Logic*, ethology was to be the science of character formation, which Mill confusingly described in both individual terms and as extended to considerations of "national character." It was a side of psychology he thought his father had missed, and it probably did not sit at all well with such associationism as Mill clung to, but it defined his approach to politics both at home and abroad as more sensitive to the peculiarities of time and place, to difference. As Carlisle explains, in connection with the discussion of ethology in the *Logic*:

> The clearest statement about what ethology might achieve appears ... when Mill discusses the generally recognized differences in the characters exhibited by the French and English or by men and women. He suggests that such differences – "peculiarities," he calls them – may result from "diversities" in institutions, climate, customs, education, and such physical factors as "bodily strength and nervous susceptibility." If, Mill argues, one can link general and empirical laws, the results of reasoning by observation and by deduction, "we need be under no difficulty in judging how far [such differences] may be expected to be permanent, or by what circumstances they would be modified or destroyed".... Mill affirms that it is possible to know which characteristics of a group are inherent – "permanent" and "congenital predispositions" ... as he calls them elsewhere – and which characteristics are transitory, the result of circumstances that can be changed and that, being changed, will change character ... ethology can create a hierarchy of the "effects" that it is "desirable to produce or to prevent" and, therefore, become the basis for the "corresponding Art" of "practical education."[55]

The ambition of Mill's envisioned science of ethology took him beyond both his father and Bentham, though Mill senior was the midwife to it. As Stephen Engelmann claims, John Mill's "most fundamental objection to Bentham was the latter's lack of concern with character. This, argued Mill, was a scientific, moral and aesthetic and political mistake."[56] But his fundamental objection to his father was deeper. James Mill was hardly unconcerned with character, though he badly misconceived it.

Plausibly or not, Mill always insisted that these innovations were still consistent with hedonism – after all, happiness was a complex, with parts, analogous to health, as Aristotle had famously held. One desired the parts for their own sake, just as one valued friends for their own sake. But what made them desirable was, ultimately, the pleasure afforded by them. To subtract that would be to subtract such goodness as they have, as parts of happiness or means to it.[57] As he memorably put it in *Utilitarianism*,

> the ultimate end, with reference to and for the sake of which all other things are desirable (whether we are considering our own good or that of other people), is an existence exempt as far as possible from pain, and as rich as possible in enjoyments, both in point of quantity and quality.... This, being ... the end of human action, is necessarily also the standard of morality; which may accordingly be defined, the rules and precepts for human conduct, by the observance of which an existence such as has been described might be, to the greatest extent possible, secured to all mankind; and not to them only, but, so far as the nature of things admits, to the whole sentient creation.[58]

True, in advancing happiness, the philosopher-poet has reasons running rather ahead of concern about what calls for moral censure; there is more to the Art of Life than moral censure. Moreover, as DiIulio neatly puts it, "while Mill's conception of happiness affirms the importance of simply enjoying a multiplicity of higher pleasures, it also has a deeper developmental layer. Mill distinguishes between *experiencing* happiness and *being* happy."[59] That is,

> According to Mill, the mind's eye fixes not only on *doing* but also on *being* – on cultivating the virtues or excellences by which we become increasingly *like* the higher pleasures. What strikes the mind's eye as pleasant is not just the ideals that people pursue, but, more deeply, the characters of those who embody these ideals. Thus, in *On Liberty*, Mill defines happiness in the words of Wilhelm von Humboldt: "the end of man" is "the highest and most harmonious development of his powers to a complete and consistent whole."[60]

Thus, the lessons Mill learned from his crisis still called for the cultivation of character, but in ways freeing the self from a morbid self-consciousness and an excess of – capital-T –Temperance.[61]

Fairly or not, Mill's construction of the causes and cures of his breakdown reflects, is in fact embedded in, his construction of the views of Bentham and his father. His critical assessments of Bentham – from his Obituary of him in 1832, to his "Remarks on Bentham's

Philosophy" in 1833, to his somewhat more moderated "Bentham" of 1838 – amount to so many reflections on what went wrong with his education and life, and what was needed to repair the damage. His father was to an astonishing degree exculpated, credited with having given him that interest in learning from others and seeing all sides of a question that, on his reckoning, were conspicuously absent in Bentham. But the affirmations and forgettings in Mill's autobiography are telling: the father may have bequeathed to the son more about the value of character and virtue than the latter realized, and, relatedly, more of the culture of imperialism. And even if Mill junior sought more light from other minds and theorized that quest, his mature educational self-experiment also ended in failure.

The Outcomes of Mill's Utilitarian Education

For all his times of turmoil, John Mill produced works that became the standard fare of a liberal arts education – notably *On Liberty*, *Utilitarianism*, and *The Subjection of Women*, and he dominated the mid-Victorian intellectual world like no one else. Although not an academic, he was a powerful influence on the academic institutions he criticized, particularly through his more textbook-style *A System of Logic*, *Considerations on Representative Government*, and *Principles of Political Economy*. His more metaphysical and logical writings, for example his 1865 *Examination of Sir William Hamilton's Philosophy*, have not proved as popular, in the Western canon, as his comprehensive liberalism foregrounding freedom of speech, press, and conscience – and "experiments in living" – a vision frequently cited today in defense of political and academic freedom, and one that even some anti- and post-colonial critics seek to redeem. Mill sought a political world that could accommodate and advance that individual autonomy or self-direction which was a key component of the complex, multifaceted form of happiness that the utilitarian should promote, the better to advance the long-term progress of civilization. The State should be strongly anti-paternalistic and could only justifiably constrain individual liberty to prevent harm to others; otherwise, people should be left free to live their lives as they themselves saw fit. At least, those people who did not require despotic government.

Obviously, he also favored a highly educative state – educative in part through political participation – and a high-minded, deliberative, but elitist form of democracy weighted in favor of the educated. Like his father and Bentham, he never lost sight of the importance of political socialization, and the many ways in which it happened. In his later years, especially, he strongly endorsed socialistic or cooperative forms of economic organization of a non-Statist, non-bureaucratic variety, as in Robert Owen's utopian social experiments. His feminism was grounded in his liberalism, and neither was deemed by him to be in tension with his utilitarianism. In explaining the benefits of full equality for women, he stressed "the most direct benefit of all, the unspeakable gain in private happiness to the liberated half of the species; the difference to them between a life of subjection to the will of others, and a life of rational freedom. After the primary necessities of food and raiment, freedom is the first and strongest want of human nature."[62]

But the attractions of internal culture, the development of virtuous character capable of acting against various of one's desires, were also vividly elaborated by Mill, along with a vision of the progressive, educational development of civilization in bringing this rich individualism forth out of times of transition, though his vision surely strained the limits of psychological associationism, determinism, hedonism, and empiricist naturalism in general, not to mention the interpretation of the top end of the "scale of civilization."[63] The doctrine of the higher pleasures – those qualitatively different pleasures judged worthier by individuals with adequate knowledge of the alternative possibilities – has generated an extensive critical literature devoted to the question of whether Mill was inconsistently introducing another, non-hedonistic criterion for the good, which he denied.[64] But the further question of how it was meshed to his work with his father at the East India Company has not received quite the same attention.

In his sensitive reading of Mill's actual liberalism, rather than the better liberalism that might be salvaged from it, Marwah rightly stresses how Mill's political philosophy often mirrored the lessons of his home schooling. He is concerned to explain how Mill's view of good government involved both "pedagogic and machinery criteria," such that government ought "equally to develop a population's capabilities and manage its existing resources."[65] And echoing Mill junior on Mill senior, he highlights the affective as well as the cognitive components of political life:

> Mill's attention to the aims, ends and conditions of government bespeaks a subtler view of politics than the catch-all liberalism he is often made to ventriloquize. If governments are to shape themselves to a people's character and foster its capacities, if they are to command and maintain social solidarity, and if they are to balance order and progress, they're bound to account for

> that people's cultural, sociological and historical circumstances. They're bound to lean on the psychological and institutional networks that sustain unique and idiosyncratic forms of collective life. Government, Mill saw, is neither neutral, minimal nor a bare guard for liberty. It is, rather, embedded in the affective, dispositional and habituated fabric of social and political life.[66]

For Mill, Marwah argues, "democracy is a character-dependent good: more than other forms of government, it relies on citizens' public-mindedness, civic trust and public engagement, and not just on their rational capacities." Consequently, Mill is less apt to sound like his father when it comes to the scale of civilization, since there is less a set pattern of developmental stages and more historical variation. The crucial factors, cognitive and affective, that form the glue holding a democratic society together under the rule of law in a shared public life amount to a pedagogy for humanity "writ large": "institutions such as jury trials, public service, accessible education, and 'industrial and philanthropic enterprises by voluntary association' comprise invaluable schools of public spirit, drawing us past our parochial spirit. Service to juries and parish offices are modern equivalents of the Athenian dicastery and ecclesia, developing public-mindedness, while newspapers and railroads serve as Britain's agora."[67] The real problems with those Mill deems unfit for democracy are basically twofold: "First, while they might accept representative government, they're incapable of fulfilling its conditions of action and self-restraint. Second, representative institutions not only fail to improve the uncivilized, but actually exacerbate their pathological character, detracting from government's ultimate end." The "rude" peoples are incapable of Millian Temperance, and given too much representative democratic freedom too early on, they only become "Incapable of dispassionate debate, violent, intemperate, envious and vindictive."[68]

Mill's strictures might sound like a fair description of the present results of the American experiment in representative democracy, or the UK's, but of course he was for most of his life not skeptical enough about the English-speaking world, and all the erudition and public spirit in the world did not, as Marwah acknowledges, prevent him from carrying on the familial commitment to the British Empire. And this despite how the utilitarian foundations of his liberalism, which Marwah does not do justice to, were scarcely unproblematic even by his own admission.

Indeed, on the ethical front, Mill's views can be thrown into sharp relief by considering his exchanges with one of his most cogent critics

– William Whewell, the Master of Trinity College, Cambridge and a supreme polymath with an extensive knowledge of modern science and its history (he coined the term "scientist"). Whewell was one of the "Cambridge Moralists" influenced by Coleridge and Romanticism, but far more rigorous philosophically in his defense of a deontological system flatly at odds with utilitarianism and grounded on a type of rationalism that is often referred to as "dogmatic intuitionism" – a system of what were deemed to be self-evident truths. History, for this camp, was indeed progressive – it revealed a progressive understanding of the necessary ideals or laws unifying both the physical and moral worlds, which had their own distinct spheres of truth, accessed by the same reason. The familiar moral duties – charity, truth-telling, promise-keeping, justice, and so forth – together form a deontological Supreme Rule: the "Rule of Human Action is expressed by saying Be benevolent, be just, be true, be pure, be orderly. To be this in our actions, is to act rightly."[69] These duties are not derived in axiomatic fashion, but represent the moral knowledge that humanity already possesses, albeit often only in implicit, crude, or confused form that requires refinement by the moral philosopher, whose job is to extract a rationally satisfactory system out of commonsense morality, a system that can resolve casuistical questions, comprehensively guide action in all spheres of life, and demonstrate how the different spheres and principles do not conflict.[70] For Whewell, the long, unfolding historical process of inductive and moral science steadily illuminated a Platonic universe: how "there were in the Divine Mind, before or during the work of creation, certain archetypal Ideas, certain exemplars or patterns of the world and its parts, according to which the work was performed: so that these Ideas or Exemplars existed in the objects around us, being in many cases discernible by man, and being the proper objects of human reason."[71]

Thus, for Whewell, utilitarianism in any form, whether it was from Bentham or Paley, was just wrong-headed from the start. The "Dependent Morality" of utilitarianism, invoking the external object of happiness, started in the wrong place, with actions and their consequences. "Independent Morality" was the true scheme: "We maintain, with Plato, that Reason has natural and rightful authority over Desire and Affection; with Butler, that there is a difference of kind in our principles of action; with the general voice of mankind, that we must do what is right at whatever cost of pain and loss."[72] "Conscience" – the voice of reason including the grasp of self-evident moral truth – rules, and rightly so.

Mill responded to Whewell's challenges with a vituperation worthy of Bentham. In remarks venting the at times characteristic utilitarian disdain for reliance on intuitions, whether cognitive or non-cognitive, Mill described Whewell as someone who regarded "all moral propositions familiar to him from his early years as self-evident truths."[73] For Mill, "intuition" was invariably just a dogmatic argument-stopper, and the intuitional moralists were hypocrites who had to resort to the principle of utility to resolve ethical conflicts anyway.[74] The so-called Laws of the Divine Mind failed to reflect the inductive, empiricist nature of both science and logic.

Mill held that it would be a disaster if, as seemed to be happening, "the doctrine of a priori or self-evident morality, an end in itself, independent of all consequences, became the orthodox theory."[75] But Mill at his most metaethically basic was not Mill at his best. Whewell had argued that the intuitional morality did not deny the importance of progress or of promoting happiness, properly understood – only that that duty was but one among others and in various ways tied to and constrained by the understanding of morality as a system incorporating other principles. True happiness is already moralized, relying on moral principles as part of its content. Also, utilitarians had no right to help themselves to secondary rules, commonsense norms, or intermediate principles, and Bentham's animal liberation arguments, shared but downplayed by Mill, were a *reductio ad absurdum*, as if human suffering, the suffering of free rational beings, could be justified if it "produced great happiness in, say, pigs and geese." To be sure, cruelty to any sentient being was wrong, but there was a fundamental difference in moral standing between human beings and non-human animals, marked by the use of language, a criterion that also demonstrated the immorality of slavery, though Whewell allowed the legitimacy of states with legalized slavery.

Mill's response to such ethical and metaethical challenges was surprisingly weak, in response to Whewell and in general. Whewell and other critics could plausibly claim that, with Mill's epistemology, both ethics and science would collapse into skepticism or mere question-begging assertion, taking his political philosophy with it. Mill's so-called proof of the principle of utility – that happiness is desirable because desired, and the general happiness desirable because each individual's happiness is – has struck many as less compelling than his plea that in "an improving state of the human mind, the influences are constantly on the increase, which tend to generate in each individual a feeling of unity with all the rest; which feeling, if perfect, would make him never think of, or desire, any beneficial condition for himself, in the benefits of which they are not included."[76]

Here it is worth recalling that Bentham and the two Mills explicitly denied that ultimate ends or first principles were susceptible of proof in the most rigorous sense. At best, there were "considerations capable of determining the intellect," such as the laborious critical process of pointing up the failings of the alternatives so that an impartial concern for promoting the greatest happiness was the last, most fundamental, most inescapable alternative, after a process of elimination. Admittedly, it could seem like an alternative that was too often more or less unconscious in the popular mind, and the metaethics of the bedrock reached after digging through so many commonsense confusions often seemed too unstable, shifting between the descriptive and the prescriptive. Exactly how and when did justification come to an end?[77]

For Mill, there are both external and internal moral sanctions, the first coming from the approbation or disapprobation of others, the second from internalized norms: conscience. Both can importantly support utilitarian morality, and likely will increasingly do so as society progresses because "there is a natural sentiment in human beings which encourages social life. Each person desires to be in harmony with others, and … this has the result that human beings will find their own individual greatest happiness in living in accordance with utilitarianism" – a higher pleasure, and, on this reading, one not unlike Bentham's.[78]

To this, Whewell, and Mill's successor Sidgwick, would reply that any such naturalistic account of the mechanisms of human ethical development is probably descriptively erroneous and, at any rate, being merely descriptive, not a normative justification.[79] More is needed. Much more.

One might conclude that there is a sense in which Bentham and Mill senior succeeded – Mill junior did become a world-class champion of utilitarianism, or at least an expanded version of utilitarianism able to some degree to assimilate much from the perspectives of the critics. More historical and less mechanically analytical, more inductive and comparative, more admiring of Tocqueville and Macaulay, more cognizant of difference and national character than his father – perhaps, though the Platonic bond was still strong.

But what difference did all this really make, when it came to the ideological uses of the "scale of civilization" and attempted legitimations of the work of the East India Company and the British Empire in general? Were all the Millian refinements turned to the purpose of adding rungs to the utilitarian ladder of civilization and anxious warnings about the dangers of premature democracy and the need for better education at home and abroad? Although Mill himself insisted on some very big differences between his views and those of his mentors, especially when it came to character, national character, and the new science of ethology, how real were these and how did they actually play out in the age of imperialism?

Tipping the Scale of Civilization

Framing Mill's educational experiences and perspectives within a broader political and psychological account of utilitarian education is revealing. Consider how Blake, in her determined effort to locate the liberal in liberal imperialism, casts the issues at stake in the infamous controversies over what educational policy in India should involve. While allowing that on "education East India Company policy looks perhaps its least liberal," given that it opted for a policy of educational "diffusion" such that "England presumed to teach India in English, apparently taking no lessons home to itself," she nonetheless advances some of her characteristic counterpoints.

> The teaching of English and English literature to Indians is the least vigorously backed element in J. S. Mill's account of education. The famous – or infamous – proposal for English studies is Macaulay's 1835 "Minute on Indian Education", calling for Westernization and Anglicization. Macaulay says he has found nobody "who could deny that a single shelf of a good European library was worth the whole literature of India and Arabia". He proposes to form educated natives to be interpreters to the millions, "a class of persons, Indian in blood and colour, but English in taste, in opinion, in morals, and in intellect" … The proposition was co-masterminded by Charles Trevelyan, who wanted natives to "become more English than Hindus."[80]

This policy represented a shift "away from preserving classical Oriental learning and providing training in Muslim and Hindu law important for the courts," and both the Mills took a very different line. A draft dispatch of the younger Mill's "Memorandum" on the subject, ultimately overridden, "shows him deeming it chimerical to expect the mental cultivation of the people to take place in a foreign language." Although valuing modernization,

> He considers the greatest need to be for Sanskrit and Arabic scholars able to create new terms for science and philosophy,

> which can then feed into the various vernaculars. He does not want these scholars to be alienated by disrespect for their learning and lost to good service as translators and teachers to the people. Mill questions the benefit of producing students who aim only at getting government jobs through knowing English without more meaningful wider influence ("Previous Communication 1828").[81]

Of course, both the Mills favored, in stock Enlightenment fashion, the spread of knowledge, though compared to James, John "speaks with greater respect for the traditional learned class and its role in expanding education." The younger Mill made it clear that other matters were also important in these policies: "greater inclusiveness, such as counteracting prejudices against female education, stimulus to education through open civil-service exams, extension of vernacular education, direct central-government backing, with funding, guidelines, and inspection, and support of secular instruction."[82] This was the utilitarian agenda that would in due course find greater favor in England. But the way was paved in India, which was well in advance of England when it came to English as a school subject, civil service reforms, and a state-supported secular educational system. For Blake, "there is a lot to call liberal in this."

Yet, once again, it is difficult to see just why achieving the liberal "through" liberal imperialism should be considered a triumph, particularly when the costs of the imperialism, the violence, brutality, and exploitation, are given as little attention as they are in Blake's book. No doubt history is full of perverse paradoxes, and benefits can come in strange ways. That may not be much of a consolation for those whose suffering is not counted in the felicific calculus, and whose education was compulsory, not Godwinian. How liberal is such a liberal education, if the purpose is still to make subject populations "English," in the sense of embodying the virtues enabling "self-government," which was as much Mill's aim as Macaulay's. Mill had little doubt that bringing an Indian elite around to an appreciation of political economy and Plato would make for progress. In that, he scarcely differed from the Idealists sent forth from Benjamin Jowett's Oxford.[83] For his part, Bentham might well have regarded Sanskrit as yet another dead language with a stranglehold on the present, but he was probably even more open-minded than either of the Mills in acknowledging the unavoidable realities of other cultures and how they needed to be accommodated in reform programs. John Mill might have taken a more historically sensitive approach than his father, embracing a more hermeneutical, interpretive approach to understanding the meaning of other cultures, but this was still with an eye to where they fell on some type of progressive scale of civilization, even if a modified one, looking to the potential for democratic character.

Indeed, however much the younger Mill may have felt that he had evolved into a better version of himself, if not a different self, his erudite self-fashioning did not fundamentally alter his faith in the legitimacy and practices of the East India Company or Britain's Government Houses, at least for most of his life, and late in life this set him up for another melancholy turn. As Pitts explains in *A Turn to Empire*, a candid letter of Mill's from 1866 was unusual in confronting some of the uncomfortable realities that he had studiously avoided for most of his career, both pre- and post-crisis:

> My eyes were first opened to the moral condition of the English nations (I except in these matters the working classes) by the atrocities perpetrated in the Indian Mutiny & the feelings which supported them at home. Then came the sympathy with the lawless rebellion of the Southern Americans in defence of an institution which is the sum of all lawlessness, as Wesley said it was of all villainy – & finally came this Jamaica business the authors of which from the first day I know of it I determined that I would do all in my power to bring to justice if there was not another man in Parlt to stand by me. You rightly judge that there is no danger of my sacrificing such a purpose to any personal advancement.[84]

As Pitts notes, this letter marks "an uncommon moment of reflection about the connections among British atrocities in a variety of colonial settings" and it "is in fact rare in its willingness to confront the problem."[85] All the Plato and Wordsworth in the world had not kept Mill from remaining oblivious to the realities of the British Empire; the civilizing mission had stayed with him, and it was only late in life that he suffered a growing anxiety about being part of a club that was rather worse than just exclusionary.[86]

The rest of this section will shift the focus back to issues of settler colonialism, colonialism, and imperialism, and the ways in which the younger Mill did or did not share the views of his father and Bentham.[87] But the focus will extend to other parts of the world, addressing Mill's views on the Maori, Native Americans, and especially the Blacks of Jamaica, the better to illustrate other dimensions of his imperialism, and how his imperialism was entangled with racism.

As Katherine Smits has argued,

> In the 1830s and 40s Mill was an enthusiastic advocate of colonization schemes for South Australia and New Zealand. He wrote in support of them, contributed money and bought land in New Zealand. Like Wakefield and other Radicals, he saw settler colonies as arenas to both absorb surplus labour and capital and to allow for capital and market growth. His early support of colonial settlements in the Pacific developed into advocacy of the rights of these new colonies to self-government. But in light of the reports of colonial brutality against Australian and New Zealand indigenous peoples, Mill expressed increasing concern about race relations in the colonies. As evidence of settler violence and genocide mounted from the middle of the century, his enthusiasm for both the civilizing potential of the imperial project, and the unmitigated good of settler self-rule, gradually cooled. His correspondence during the 1860s suggests that Mill feared that settler violence compromised the progressive promise of imperialism, and challenged the utilitarian benefits of self-rule.[88]

Mill's enthusiasm for Edward Gibbons Wakefield's work on colonization – a bubble that achieved fame by bursting – was shared by many of the Philosophical Radicals, and reflected the assumption that such settler colonies were different from cases like India, a dependency with a subordinated population. The "key difference here was the assumption propounded by Wakefield, that the lands in the Australasian colonies were *terra nullius* – unowned in any sense recognizable to the British."[89] Bentham had also supported Wakefield's scheme, and even drew up a charter for South Australia – "a colony designed, as he put it, with the utilitarian purpose of transferring 'persons of indigence' to 'persons of affluence.'"[90] Consequently, it is not surprising that Mill did not think, for most of this period, that there was a civilizing mission at issue in this colonization effort, since he did not realize that there were Indigenous peoples there to be "civilized." When in the 1860s he finally did grow increasingly aware of the displacement and settler colonial violence being inflicted on them, his faith in the ethical state of the settlers as candidates for self-rule was shaken, and the alternatives to it were left unclear, though he never indicated that perhaps the Indigenous peoples did not need the civilizing mission:

> In the case of India, Mill had been able to convince himself that at least the supposedly impartial and professional servants of the

> East India Company were dedicated to ruling in the best interests of local peoples. In Australia and New Zealand, the very peoples on whose behalf he had argued the right to self-government were by their own actions proving themselves incapable of good government over others. By the end of his life, Mill was forced to acknowledge, however briefly, that the realities of power, so passionately documented in gender relations in *The Subjection of Women*, equally subverted any hopes for progress in the paternalistic government of other peoples.[91]

It should have been enough to shake his faith in the progress of Western civilization, but apparently almost nothing really could.

Indeed, it is quite evident that, for much of his life, Mill, and his ethology, were preposterously and culpably naïve, as when he claimed that the "conduct of the United States towards the Indian tribes has been throughout not only just, but noble."[92] The truth was so obviously otherwise even in Mill's time that such lines leave one dumbfounded.[93]

In this context, the many attempts to position Mill as something else, as a multicultural feminist hero, do not strike the right chord. Martha Nussbaum has long urged that Mill's critique of male power is strengthened by a conception of happiness that makes it "a richer resource" for "contemporary feminist and, more generally, anti-hierarchical thinking."[94] And the Mill celebrated by Nussbaum – obviously quite different from the one celebrated by Marwah – has also been appropriated for purposes of cosmopolitan critiques of patriotism. Georgios Varouxakis, in *Mill on Nationality*, argues that "Mill's conception of the relationship between obligations to country and obligations to mankind was close to that of Nussbaum." For both, patriotism is commendable only when it conduces "to the interests of the whole of humanity."[95] Such accounts of patriotism and particular loyalties and attachments are clearly at a far remove from old-fashioned communitarian love of country, right or wrong.

Although these appropriations of Mill do take their point of departure from very real aspects of Mill's views, particularly his *The Subjection of Women*, they cannot be said to address those critics of Mill, from Lowe to Pitts, Mamdani, Marwah, et al., who regard him as an unlikely hero for anti-hierarchical thinking, given the way his elitist higher pleasures doctrine and notions of national character entailed so many colonialist entanglements, refining the "scale of civilization" but hardly junking it. Mill also figures in Appiah's *The Ethics of Identity*, a subtle book that addresses the charge, common to Uday Mehta, Bhikhu Parikh, and John Gray, that "Mill was an autonomist, and that autonomism is an ethnocentric preference, ruled out by pluralism." Appiah counters that, in fact,

> Mill is truly ethnocentric precisely where he suspends the requirement of autonomy.... The Mill who says that even the despotism of an Akbar or a Charlemagne can be beneficial for backward societies cannot be accused of foisting an ethic of autonomy upon cultures for whom autonomy is not a value. It is not the smallest of ironies that these critics of Mill accept his arguments at their weakest – and reject them at their strongest.[96]

But, of course, Mill was all too willing to help impose despotism en route to autonomism, and nothing Appiah says licenses one to ignore how the younger Mill was grotesquely Eurocentric, complacently and arrogantly imperialistic, and "politely" or "functionally" racist, using such claims to justify imperial domination. And as Lynn Zastoupil's collection *John Stuart Mill and India* repeatedly demonstrates, England's Indian subjects were often described in the most offensive terms, as "niggers," etc. "Progress" was racialized in ways that were as systemic as they were obvious.[97] Mill was not above it all.

The issue of Mill's racism remains one that even many of his critics are reluctant to confront. Lowe, Pitts, Marwah, and many others back off when the R word comes up. But that is a bad mistake, often betraying a failure to recognize how, as Olivette Otele notes (in discussing Goldberg's approach), "in the case of 'racial historicists', nineteenth- and twentieth-century racial paternalism was characterized by the belief that Africans and Asians, deemed inferior, could improve their intellect and behaviour through education."[98] The "could" was of course consistent with the various ideologies of empire justifying ongoing domination, even as the historical trajectories of racializing and racism from the formation of modern Europe to today witnessed, in Goldberg's words, the "extended culturizing of the racial, its repetitive expression through cultural distinction. Whites, stereotypically, have taken themselves throughout modernity to be hard-working, blacks to be criminally lazy, Muslims to be violent, Asians to be inscrutable."[99]

To be sure, some of Mill's critics have followed Mehta, whose *Liberalism and Empire* argued that: "In India ... especially following the mutiny of 1857, there was in fact an unmistakable tilt toward the hardening of authoritarian policies ... that they justified in their theoretical writings. For example, in *Considerations on Representative Government*, Mill had made clear that in colonies that were not of

Britain's 'blood and lineage' any move toward greater representation was not to be countenanced."[100] For Mehta, the younger Mill "invests race with far greater seriousness than most of his liberal contemporaries, who generally view it as a catchall term that loosely designates what might be called cultural difference. Instead Mill elaborates the term through the biological notion of 'blood.' Hence for example in the *Considerations on Representative Government* … he draws what he takes to be the crucial distinction in terms of readiness for representative institutions by reference to 'those of our blood' and those not of our blood."[101]

But Goldberg, in his seminal essay "Liberalism's Limits: Carlyle and Mill on 'The Negro Question,'" builds his cogent critique of Mill as follows:

> Mill's argument for benevolent despotism failed to appreciate that neither colonialism nor despotism is ever benevolent. Benevolence here is the commitment to seek the happiness of others. But the mission of colonialism is exploitation and domination of the colonized generally, and Europeanization at least of those among the colonized whose class position makes it possible economically and educationally. And the mandate of despotism, its conceptual logic, is to assume absolute power to achieve the ruler's self-interested ends. Thus colonial despotism could achieve the happiness of colonized Others only by imposing the measure of Europeanized marks of happiness upon the other, which is to say, to force the other to be less so. Mill's argument necessarily assumed superiority of the despotic, benevolent or not; it presupposed that the mark of progress is (to be) defined by those taking themselves to be superior; and it presumes that the ruled will want to be like the rulers even as the former lack the cultural capital (ever?) quite to rise to the task. Mill's ambivalence over the inherent inferiority of "native Negroes", even as he marked the transformation in the terms of racial definition historically from the inescapable determinism of blood and brain size to the marginally escapable reach of cultural determination, has resonated to this day in liberal ambivalence regarding racial matters.[102]

Goldberg is of course referring to Mill's 1850 response to Thomas Carlyle's virulently racist "Occasional Discourse on the Negro Question," which was republished in pamphlet form (after Mill's response) with the contemptuous title "Occasional Discourse on the

Nigger Question."[103] Carlyle endorsed nearly every vicious prejudice against Blacks known to humanity, depicting a stereotype of "Quashee," a lazy, laughing, watermelon- (or "pumpkin-") eating inferior fit only for paternalistic control and direction by "the beneficent whip" of whites, who are superior by birth. Indeed, Carlyle calls for – or at least strongly suggests the desirability of – the reinstitution of slavery, condemning, in his usual way, the cruelties of laissez-faire. The entire disgusting show is cast in humorous vein, satirizing a "Universal Abolition of Pain Association."

Goldberg admits that Carlyle's essay provoked a scathing critical rejoinder from Mill, who remarked of the slave trade: "I have yet to learn that anything more detestable than this has been done by human beings towards human beings in any part of the earth." Mill charged Carlyle with:

> the vulgar error of imputing every difference which he finds among human beings to an original difference of nature. As well might it be said, that of two trees, sprung from the same stock, one cannot be taller than another but from greater vigour in the original seeding. Is nothing to be attributed to soil, nothing to climate, nothing to difference of exposure – has no storm swept over the one and not the other, no lightning scathed it, no beast browsed on it, no insects preyed on it, no passing stranger stript off its leaves or its bark? If the trees grew near together, may not the one which, by whatever accident, grew up first, have retarded the other's development by its shade?[104]

Moreover, the "great ethical doctrine" of Carlyle's "Discourse," "than which a doctrine more damnable, I should think, never was propounded by a professed moral reformer, is, that one kind of human beings are born servants to another kind." Mill identified himself with the "thinking persons" who "either doubt or positively deny" the innate inferiority of Blacks. And he derides Carlyle's insane views about work being the be-all and end-all of existence, even while making it clear enough that more capital-T Temperance was needed with the Jamaicans as with other "backwards" or "stationary" subject populations to bring them up to the appropriate level of affluence and democratic character.

Mill's replies, however, do not in the least undercut Goldberg's argument. After all, it "was Carlyle's call to reinstitute slavery to which Mill principally objected ... [His] critical concern with Carlyle's racist sentiment was only secondary and much more understated.

Moreover, not only did Mill not object to colonial domination, he insisted on it, albeit in 'benevolent' form."[105] And Mill only doubted that Blacks were biologically inferior – he did not effectively deny Carlyle's claim that Blacks were somehow inferior, so much as recast the inferiority as a historically contingent matter. As Joseph Miller has also observed, "Mill agrees with Carlyle that blacks generally are less capable than Europeans, comparing blacks to trees that grew in poor soil or poor climate or that might have suffered from exposure, storms or disease."[106] And in this case, for Goldberg, Mill's defense of laissez-faire, rather than limitation of it, was suspect on racial grounds:

> In objecting to Carlyle's racist hierarchical naturalism … Mill inscribed in its place, and in the name of laissez faire and equal opportunity, an imputation of the historical inferiority of blacks. Mill implied that this assumption of inferiority, because historically produced and contingent, was not always the case (Egyptians influenced Greeks) and might one day be overcome. Yet Mill's superficial bow to what has become an Afro-centric cornerstone barely hid beneath the surface the polite racism of his Euro-centric history. Contingent racism is still a form of racism – not so usual, not so bald, not so vituperative, and polite perhaps, but condescending nevertheless even as it is committed to equal opportunity. Equal opportunity among those with the unfair, historically produced inequities of the colonial condition will simply reproduce those inequities, if not expand them.[107]

Thus, if Carlyle's racism was "bald and vicious," Mill's was merely "polite and effete." Still, "polite and effete" racism remains racism:

> Mill's erasure in the name of nonracialism rubs out at once the history of racist invisibility, domination, and exploitation, replacing the memory of an infantilized past with the denial of responsibility for radically unequal and only superficially deracialized presents … savages become the permanently unemployable, the uncivilized become crack heads, the lumpen-proletariat the underclass. Distressed Needlewomen become sweated labor, poor Irish peasants turn into distressed defaulting family farmers and, well, "Niggers" become "Negroes," or blacks scarcely disguised beneath the seemingly benign nomenclature. For every Mill of yesteryear there is today a William Bennett or a Gary Becker.[108]

Or a Donald Trump, to update the story, though Trump seems rather closer to Carlyle.[109] As Goldberg's searing book on *The War on Critical Race Theory* pointedly demonstrates, racism in the guise of nonracialism – colorblindness, a focus on individual racist expression – has become a favored tactic of those working assiduously to restore the racial hierarchies of previous times, though these recent white supremacists are often doing so with book bans and legislative interferences that make Mill look good by comparison. Even if one agrees with Goldberg that ultimately "it is better, on balance, to say of an expression or action rather than an individual that it is racist, unless especially and unapologetically so, or an extension of a pattern by the person in question," and to treat individual racist expressions as "learning opportunities" to educate people on the realities of enduring structural racism, the case against Mill remains vitally important, given his emblematic role as a leading player in the history of utilitarianism.[110]

A closely related line of critique has also been advanced by Anthony Bogues, in "John Stuart Mill and 'The Negro Question': Race, Colonialism, and the Ladder of Civilization":

> So what we have here in the debate between Mill and Carlyle are the following. In one current of English political thought, difference was innate, created by nature, and as a consequence there was no chance of political and social equality for those who were nonwhite subjects of the empire. Another current admitted that the black and colonial subjects were indeed inferior but argued that this inferiority was not ordained by nature and therefore could be overcome by contact with civilization and a process of tutelage. Both currents were united in their belief about black inferiority but disagreed on its root causes and naturalness. For those who thought that this so-called inferiority could be overcome, we should note that the goal was envisioned in terms of white normativity. To become fully human and a citizen, the colonial and black subject had to master the protocols of Western civilization, to become in the words of the nineteenth-century English writer Anthony Trollope, a "Creole Negro."[111]

These critiques combine to depict Mill as a racist and nascent neo-conservative elitist – like one of those racists, so common in the US and Europe, who talk the talk of compassion and colorblindness to support policies that serve to ratify or restore structural racism. On these readings, Mill is suspect on the count of racism both when urging the spread of "representative" government and laissez-faire, and when qualifying their applicability, both when recognizing difference and when being "blood blind." Goldberg is justifiably incensed both by Mill allowing the English to play Charlemagne in India and by his supposed call for laissez-faire in Jamaica.

The case made by Goldberg and Bogue is grounded on both a realistic account of the harsh realities of colonialism, settler colonialism, and imperialism, and a sophisticated account of how racisms come in different forms, not all of them invoking biological essentialism or supposedly noncontingent factors making for inherent inferiority. Unfortunately, too much of the literature on Mill is lacking on one count or the other (or both), even when taking a critical perspective.

Consider Pitts's conclusion, in *A Turn to Empire*, that:

> Mill, for all his radicalism with regard to domestic politics, placed considerable faith in colonial government as a well-intentioned and legitimate despotism designed for the improvement of its subjects. Both his writings on India and his role in the Eyre affair suggest that he hesitated before a full-scale inquiry into the structure of colonial rule and the repeated abuses that structure invited. He avoided such an inquiry even though he came to acknowledge, late in life, a mistrust of British political judgment on colonial matters.[112]

Pitts is analyzing Mill's theoretical and practical work on both India and Jamaica. In the latter case as well as the former, Mill was practically and politically involved. He became the moving force on the Jamaica Committee investigating – or, rather, condemning – Governor Eyre's atrocities in response to the Morant Bay Rebellion of 1865, when Eyre brutally repressed the (justifiable) uprising and judicially murdered such rebel leaders as Paul Bogle and George William Gordon, the latter being a well-to-do mulatto landowner and member of the Assembly who had long been critical of Eyre but was not directly involved in the rebellion.[113] Eyre's ferocity recalled the British response to the Sepoy Rebellion, and Mill's response to it was – as Goldberg, Bogues and Pitts agree – singularly revealing, suggestive of what he did and did not dissent from in Carlyle, who was a vociferous leader of those defending Eyre, Carlyle's ideal of a hero.

Mill wanted Eyre brought to justice, but that was apparently all he wanted, beyond his usual hopes, now tinged with greater doubt and melancholy, for improving the quality of imperial rule. Mill's

> belief in the incapacity of non-European subjects for self-rule meant that he failed to argue for – perhaps even to imagine – conditions of accountability to colonial subjects. Until backward peoples were deemed, presumably by European administrators, capable of participating in their own governance, Mill seemed content to rely on colonial administrators themselves for appropriate restraints on the exercise of power. Other than his expressions of mistrust of the local legislature, Mill said little about how progress toward collective self-government in Jamaica might take place. He resorted, as in India, to the tidier and less political solution of administration checked by criminal courts. Mill, that is, tended to regard colonial subjects as objects of administration rather than participants in a political process.[114]

Like Mehta, Pitts allows that Burke was more attuned than Mill to the abuses of colonial rule. But, like Goldberg and Bogues, she recognizes how Mill's context was more virulently racist: "liberal colonial reform itself, and liberal cosmopolitanism, had changed by the mid-nineteenth century. British superiority and the justice of British colonial rule were nearly taken for granted by the bulk of the population by the mid-nineteenth century."[115] Thus, in this context, "Mill's continued opposition to racist argument and his commitment to benevolent and improving colonial government was perhaps the most ambitious posture liberalism could muster. The Eyre trial gives some indication of the constraints on humanitarian discourse more generally in the nineteenth century."[116]

But if Pitts refrains from describing Mill as a "polite and effete" racist, she does come quite close: "both Mill and Tocqueville insisted that claims about biological differences or inequalities were unprovable and morally and politically pernicious. And yet their willingness to see the moral and political standards that governed relations within Europe suspended in dealings with other peoples bore the mark of a discourse increasingly founded on the assumptions about the inequality of different peoples."[117] And, in fact, fierce as Mill's response to Carlyle was, he did not actually deny that there might be inherent biological racial differences; he only claimed that scientific, ethological knowledge was insufficiently advanced to demonstrate these, that factors like climate also mattered, etc. Even the late John Robson concluded, in his essay "Civilization and Culture," that if Mill was sketchy on "race" – the term "national character" being his more common idiom – which he considered an "accident of birth" like sex, he did, like others of his time, tend "to apply it to groups that were indeed genetically loosely interrelated, but distinguished from one another by behaviour and belief." His position was made clear in a letter to Charles Dupont-White, in which Mill emphatically denied that his condemnation of the "vulgar error" of attributing everything to race meant that he attributed no influence to race – "he did not deny, but in fact admits 'pleinement,' 'l'influence des races.'"[118]

In a spirited defense of Mill against Goldberg, Varouxakis has argued that the difference between Carlyle and Mill should be counted as a difference between racist and non-racist: "I think that the two things are separate and that the term 'racism' is not appropriate to describe Mill's attitude; 'Euro-centric' would do."[119] But even so, "Mill's thought was indeed Euro-centric, and, despite his efforts to be open-minded, he did show himself deplorably ignorant and prejudiced about non-European cultures, not least those of the Indian Peninsula. And his belief that a benevolent despotism was a legitimate mode of governing those he called 'barbarians' ... was paternalistic and based on assumptions that we cannot accept today."[120] Varouxakis claims, against Mehta, that what "Mill actually means when he talks of colonists 'of our blood' is their cultural traits, coming from the mother country, the metropolis. He does not use 'blood' literally."[121]

Such defenses of Mill may help clarify just how Mill used such key terms as "race," "blood," "national character," etc., but they concede so much – and reek of such rearguard desperation – that those who describe Mill as racist really ought to (and largely do) feel vindicated. And this is not to mention Mill's avowed receptiveness to the possibility that science might in the future make out some significant (biological) racial differences.

The crucial point, however, is that such terminological maneuvers to dodge the "R word" are premised on inadequate notions of race and racism. "Race blindness" or "colorblindness" are in fact ways in which white domination can be perpetuated, can erase the very concepts needed to be anti-racist. Mill's views on, say, the Jamaicans justified a Victorian equivalent of racial profiling, a presumption that these were people in need of imperial discipline and control, and supported institutions that were structurally, enduringly racist in their functioning.[122] Given the conceptual confusions that invariably swirl around the notion of "race," such that one can find biological essentialists about race cast as anti-racists and anti-biological essentialists cast as racist, one might easily conclude that on the count of racism, there is no serious exoneration of Mill to be found in the responses to Goldberg.[123] The systemic implications of Mill's position would still leave the Jamaican Blacks in that "waiting room of history" – a holding cell really – waiting for more research on educational aptitude and ethology to determine their fate.

Moreover, it is perfectly obvious that there was an anti-racist, Black subjectivity for Mill to ignore in this context. He plainly did so when he was confronted with the Jamaicans Paul Bogle and George William Gordon. As one history of Jamaica puts it,

> Bogle and Gordon, in their last years, defined the central themes of justice and concern for the "many," which widened into a struggle against the monopoly of political power that was taken up by Robert Lowe, Sandy Cox and Bain Alves with their trade unions, Marcus Garvey, Norman Manley in his campaign for universal adult suffrage and Alexander Bustamante in his formation of the labour movement, and led to political independence in 1962.[124]

In short, they were freedom fighters. To understand this, one need only consult the histories portrayed in C. L. R. James, *The Black Jacobins: Toussaint L'Ouverture and the San Domingo Revolution*, or in Kris Manjapra's *Black Ghost of Empire: The Long Death of Slavery and the Failure of Emancipation*, or any number of other works.[125] As Bogues notes, during the Morant Bay Rebellion, the rebellious crowds at points confronted those police officers who were Black with cries of "Cleave to the black."

Of course, the historical situation in the Caribbean and Latin America was very complex; as Holt observes, of the treatment of mulattos and mixed-blood peoples, "they came to occupy a social status not unlike the Jewish and Muslim converts. They were not classified with blacks but as a separate caste, and they filled the interstitial jobs – and some of high status – that American frontier societies with small white settler populations required. In the British West Indies there were legal procedures – if one could pay for them – for having oneself actually declared white by an act of the legislature. In Jamaica in the 1830s the white planters hoped that the brown population could be assimilated to the white side of the racial divide so that they would form a protective bulwark against the soon-to-be-emancipated black slave majority."[126]

Still, it is safe to say that, even when confronted with a compelling Black resistance movement and a possible extension of (genuine) political equality to Jamaican Blacks in response, Mill, as Pitts admits, "sought a solution in the imposition of reforms through the colonial authority."[127] It would seem, then, that to say that he was good for his cultural context is to define his cultural context by (a problematic construction of) English "whiteness," when he himself was actively engaging with the Jamaican situation and an avowedly Black liberation movement in a way that can only be described as a racist failure to appreciate the meaning of his historical moment, a failure in his own effort – and in his own terms – to see all sides of a question.[128] He was in fact helping to set the stage for the horrors of "scientific racism" that would, in the decades following his death, give the logic of empire another turn.

Why try to salvage Mill's philosophical reputation by arguing that he was not working with a biological racial essentialism, only "Eurocentrism"? The racialism involved in racism is never coherent or consistent, and although the term "racism" may have gained greater currency in the early twentieth century and have many contested meanings, there is no reason to resist applying it to earlier periods, when such terms as "blood," etc., seemed to carry a mix of biological and cultural features, just as they often do in more recent times. Indeed, although his account of racism misses some of the considerations Goldberg highlights, this point is made by George Fredrickson in his book *Racism: A Short History*: "Deterministic cultural particularism can do the work of biological racism quite effectively."[129] As he observes, with reference to the case of South African apartheid, "the extent to which Afrikaner nationalism was inspired by nineteenth-century European cultural nationalism also contributed to this avoidance of a pseudoscientific rationale. No better example can be found of how a 'cultural Essentialism' based on nationality can do the work of a racism based squarely on skin color or other physical characteristics."[130]

It is scarcely anachronistic or judgmental to worry about racism in this context; it is more anachronistic and judgmental to insist in advance on accepting the "limits" of the "cultural context," "times," etc. For Fredrickson, although we must take care not to invariably make "racism the ideological essence of imperialism," we must, nonetheless, recognize how the "view of colonial rule as a lengthy and problematic apprenticeship for civilized modernity can be viewed as functionally racist to the degree that it justified denying civil and political rights to indigenous populations for the foreseeable future."[131]

As Mill said, of the treatment of Gordon: "The great majority of people, especially people in power, are ready to believe almost anything against their political enemies, especially those who have said or published things tending to excite disapprobation of their conduct."[132] But he did not pursue such thoughts to their uncomfortable conclusion.

Complain as he did about "the overbearing and insolent disregard of the rights and feelings of inferiors which is the common characteristic of John Bull when he thinks he cannot be resisted," he did not seriously rethink his view of the "inferiors."

As suggested, about the best "anti-hierarchical" thought one can find in Mill comes in that 1866 letter to David Urquhart: "But my eyes were first opened to the moral condition of the English nation …"[133] But Mill prefaces this late-in-life explanation with the admission: "You approve of my speech because you see that I am not on this occasion standing up for the negroes, or for liberty, deeply as both are interested in the subject – but for the first necessity of human society, law." Again, his overwhelming concern, throughout the Eyre business, was with the rule of law. As Kinzer, Robson, and Robson observe, "The moral legitimacy of such imperial rule turned on the intent and capacity of the dominant country to provide the subject people with a government better – in the sense of promoting 'the permanent interests of man as a progressive being' – than they could provide for themselves," but the "men representing the British crown in Jamaica in the autumn of 1865 had disgraced the British Empire and desecrated the principles for which it ought to stand."[134]

Of course, although he was recalled and his career effectively ended, Eyre never was brought to justice; rather, Mill lost his seat in Parliament in part thanks to his efforts against the former governor, the Jamaican Assembly was dissolved (by itself, out of fear of Black participation) and Crown rule imposed.[135] Such outcomes, along with the death threats he received, should have provided Mill with rather more food for thought than they apparently did. If, in his case, the life is obviously extremely helpful in understanding the work, neither serves to exonerate him on questions of racism and empire. His refashioned utilitarian self-development also failed him – he remained too limited in his quest to seek light from other minds. Quite unlike Godwin, he proved himself to be mostly incapable of truly fathoming the violence and brutality of law and government. Where is the virtue in that?

And things would only get worse.

3

The Worst of the Best

> I propose in these lectures to examine historically the tendency to expansion which England has so long displayed. We shall learn to think of it more seriously if we discover it to be profound, persistent, necessary to the national life, and more hopefully if we can satisfy ourselves that the secession of our first colonies was not a mere normal result of expansion, like the bursting of a bubble, but the result of temporary conditions, removable and which have been removed. (Sir John Robert Seeley, *The Expansion of England*)

> Seeley's *Expansion of England* was published in 1883, and Froude's *Oceana* in 1885. Two things are interesting to the readers of these books … The Colonies are no longer fruits that drop off when they are ripe. Both writers consciously alter the metaphor, preferring that of leaves and branches that nourish while they spread the influence of the tree; or, better still, of the banana tree, whose branches root themselves in the ground and add support to the parent stem. In the second place the argument from America is turned. America is no longer an argument for separation, but for retention. (J. H. Muirhead, "What Imperialism Means")

The chapters so far have told a story – an admittedly and deliberately Anglocentric and patriarchal story – about various cross-currents flowing through the work of the best-known classical utilitarian patriarchs, who clearly were not of one utilitarian mind about a host of fundamental matters, including even the legitimacy of the British Empire. What is supposed to be a simple narrative, and is often presented as such in established histories of philosophy, turns out to be a difficult, contested terrain mapped out only by the general idea that promoting the happiness of all (an "all" that was in reality often highly exclusive) is somehow what ultimately matters most and somehow to be sought, directly or indirectly, individually or collectively, via empire or the abolition of empire, and so on. Many of these figures were hampered by a commitment to a simplistic associationist model of mind that was at best speculative, and at any rate simply got in the way of what they really wanted to say about human happiness and education. Not all of them were, and even those that were struggled in different ways with the challenges of being able to theorize what they were really about, as might be suggested by the failures of their educational experiments. Bentham and John Stuart Mill both believed in the vital importance of cultivating a healthy self-respect, but their ego ideals looked very different, and even Mill's fondest admirers allow that there is a type of elitism in his view that was foreign to Bentham, who was less disdainful of the "lower" pleasures of the board, the bed, and the beasts. But neither Bentham nor the Mills are good guides when it comes to the question of how to teach utilitarianism, then or now.

One could go further. In *Completely Free*, John DiIulio casts history's most famous utilitarian as something of a unicorn in this canonical history:

> To Bentham, "the greatest happiness of all those whose interest is in question" is "the only right and proper and universally desirable *end* of human action: of human action in every situation"; to Sidgwick, "the conduct which, under any circumstances, is objectively right, is that which will produce the greatest amount of happiness on the whole"; and to Moore, our duty "can only be defined as that action" which "will cause more good to exist in the Universe than any possible alternative." To act morally is to do that which best advances the happiness of all persons within our sphere of influence.
>
> Given my analysis thus far, it should be immediately apparent that Mill does not (*cannot*) ascribe to this Benthamite ethic. According to Mill, morality is only one sphere of life, and it encircles only those (in)actions that have an evident, intrinsic association with the general happiness, such that they naturally engage our moral sentiments.[1]

DiIulio ultimately wants to deny that Mill adopts a maximizing ethic, but he allows that there are complications. He acknowledges that Mill insists that utility is "the ultimate principle of Teleology" and that "all rules of practice" must be assessed by their "conduciveness to the happiness of mankind." Thus, one might plausibly reconstruct Mill as claiming "that the general happiness would be best served by establishing, first, a moral sphere, filled with rights and duties, and, second, a nonmoral sphere, filled with liberties, discretion, and free play. Thus, indubitably, we can soundly argue that the moral and nonmoral spheres alike are justified insofar as they maximize the general happiness."[2] DiIulio wants to resist this reconstruction, which casts Mill in too ideal, Platonic terms, missing his real-world emphasis on people and politics as they are. It is, however, a plausible reading.

Thus, even something as fundamental as John Stuart Mill being a maximizing utilitarian can be intelligently debated in this way. And in light of the debates over Mill's qualified hedonism and possible perfectionism, it could even be said that it is up for grabs whether the best known of the classical utilitarians was committed not only to maximization, but even to a hedonistic account of the happiness that was to be, or not to be, maximized. There is more foggy ambiguity hovering over Mill's views than over Godwin's.

In this chapter, the fog will not lift, and it may even take a more toxic form. Henry Sidgwick, who carries little of Mill's name recognition, is the figure often singled out as, philosophically, the greatest of the classical utilitarians, the one who saw the argumentative cracks in Bentham and the Mills and repaired them, and this with all the keen analytical rigor of a true professional academic philosopher – not someone taking time off from their day job of ruling India, though he was a very well-connected reformer.[3] He was, beyond any reasonable doubt, a superlative academic philosopher, and in that respect his work is as alive today as it was in the nineteenth century. But he was also the classical utilitarian who did the most to speed through the turn to empire, and he did so in racist terms that were less "polite" when it came to theorizing the civilizing mission of Greater Britain and legitimating the international system that carries the stamp of empire down to the present day, though he appears not at all in the works of Lowe, Pitts, Elkins, Mehta, Mamdani, Stokes, Said, and so on. In the era of "scientific racism," Sidgwick struggled just to cling to a type of racial historicism, against the essentialist accounts of supposed biological racial inferiority that seemed to be taking over his life-world.

Perhaps unsurprisingly, given all the paradoxes of classical utilitarianism, it is also debatable whether or in what way Sidgwick himself was a utilitarian, and whether, even if he was, he could defend his position by his own standards. He would take the psychological underpinnings of utilitarianism in new, often better, directions, being influenced by William James and others who had a better grasp of how mind actually mattered. But, as with Mill, his psychology, in theory and practice, produced a crisis of self-legitimation. Indeed, his life and work perfectly exemplify Judith Butler's gloss on Adorno: "If the human is anything, it seems to be a double movement, one in which we assert moral norms at the same time as we question the authority by which we make that assertion."[4] Sidgwick, it seems, was all too human, much to his dismay.

This chapter will start with Sidgwick, but at the end transition into more recent times and the task of moving from the decolonization of utilitarianism to the sources for a critical utilitarian alternative.

The Sidgwickian Academy

Both Mill's priorities and Whewell's strong points would be appropriated by Sidgwick, who shared Whewell's admiration for Joseph Butler and helped utilitarianism shake off the problems and ambiguities of a reductive empiricism and psychological egoism. Like Godwin, he allowed instead that humans were capable of genuinely disinterested and benevolent action – that is, genuine, conscience-dictated self-sacrifice of their own good for the greater good. However, Sidgwick worried endlessly about the rational justification for such self-sacrifice – more particularly, the justification when religion was failing, morality was confused and imperiled, and social institutions very imperfect. Sidgwick loathed Whewell, but agreed with him that the metaethical justifications for utilitarianism offered up by Bentham and Mill were inadequate and question-begging, conflating descriptive and normative considerations; and that utilitarianism, like any ethical theory, needed a rational grounding. It could only find that if it rested on fundamental cognitive intuitions, self-evident truths akin to mathematical truths. As he put it, in a short intellectual autobiography: "Thus, in spite of my early aversion to Intuitional Ethics, derived from the study of Whewell, and in spite of my discipleship to Mill, I was forced to recognise the need of a fundamental ethical intuition."[5] Consequently, despite his seeming utilitarian sympathies, he was often critical (often unfairly so) of Bentham and Mill, even while going further than Mill in co-opting the opposition and seeking to do justice to commonsense moral norms and principles. Perhaps paradoxically, he brought more cogent skepticism to bear on utilitarianism and its rivals than any of the other figures treated here, and the philosophical critics of classical utilitarianism have long been living off the food Sidgwick supplied.

Sidgwick never dominated the Victorian philosophical landscape the way Mill did, but he has, after some periods of neglect, enjoyed a legacy that has been perhaps even more important in the realms of academic ethical philosophy, especially English-language ethical philosophy.[6] Others who overshadowed him, such as Herbert Spencer, the anti-imperialist who came to be regarded as one of the philosophical architects of Social Darwinism (though his early work predated Darwin), may have their defenders, but they are not celebrated for their work making, in Parfit's words, more "true and important claims" than any other work on ethics ever. Spencer himself described Sidgwick as the "foremost representative" of and heir to the utilitarianism of Bentham and Mill.[7]

Yet Sidgwick was in many ways from another planet, philosophically speaking. He was an academic – and Academic Liberal reformer – from beginning to end.[8] His larger family connections reflected considerable wealth coming from cotton spinning mills, though his father had not gone into that business – he was the Revd. William Sidgwick, the headmaster at the Free Grammar School of Skipton – and died when Sidgwick was a young child. A talented student (like his siblings), Sidgwick excelled academically and opted for an academic life, staying at Cambridge University from the beginning of his college career until nearly the end of his life, when he resigned because of illness. He was influenced in his life plan by the elite, selective discussion group the Cambridge Apostles, who were committed to free and fearless conversations in pursuit of truth, which inspired Sidgwick and brought him around to utilitarianism. Despite some drama early on, when, after much religious soul searching, he in 1869 resigned his Trinity fellowship because he could no longer sincerely assent to the Thirty-Nine Articles of the Church of England – a requirement that Bentham had very reluctantly gone along with – he was able to carry on in his academic work, eventually being elected Knightbridge Professor of Moral Philosophy in 1883. He was initially passed over for that position in favor of the less controversial T. R. Birks, whose criticisms of utilitarianism echoed Whewell's: "Utilitarianism … has one main defect … It dwells on the third aspect of moral action, the results to which it leads, to the exclusion of two others, equally essential, and more fundamental, the fountain from which it must proceed, and the channel through which it must flow. There is a standard of Divine perfection and essential right, which must go before."[9]

Through family connections, especially his marriage to Eleanor Mildred Balfour of the powerful Balfour family – his brother-in-law and former student was Arthur Balfour, the future prime minister and earl – Sidgwick would play a role in politics in general, though his emphasis, when not obsessing about the role of religion in the moral order of progressive society, was mostly on academic reform. He was devoted to the professionalization and modernization of academic institutions in general, and philosophy in particular, generously helping to finance the needed innovations, which included everything from funding new academic positions, to getting the fledgling academic journal *Mind* up and running, to setting the stage for the launch of the British Academy. The Sidgwicks are recognized as founders of Newnham College, one of the first women's colleges in England, and they played a crucial role in building up and legitimizing the British Society for Psychical Research, which proved to be a vehicle for psychological research on Sidgwick's part, cementing his friendship with William James. Unlike Bentham, who was morbidly afraid of ghosts, Sidgwick pursued them tirelessly (and weirdly), hoping that proof of an afterlife might support a reformed, Theistic religion. His break with the Anglican Church had been painful, not least because another brother-in-law, and beloved early mentor, was Edward White Benson, who became Archbishop of Canterbury.

As with Mill, Sidgwick's interests were wide-ranging, and his works spanned ethics, political economy, political and legal theory, metaphysics and epistemology, education, parapsychology, and literature, usually with an acute and erudite historical perspective on the subject. The three major treatises he published during his lifetime were *The Methods of Ethics* (1874), *The Principles of Political Economy* (1883), and *The Elements of Politics* (1891), but there was much else besides, and some of his important writing only appeared posthumously. Sidgwick's aim in much of his work was thoroughly academic and hardly meant for popular audiences. His best-known and most highly praised work has always been *The Methods of Ethics*, which went through five editions within his lifetime. But, as he explained, his purpose in that book was not to edify or exhort, but only "to expound as clearly and as fully as my limits will allow the different methods of Ethics that I find implicit in our common moral reasoning; to point out their mutual relations; and where they seem to conflict, to define the issue as much as possible."[10] He even conceived of this project as more or less in the spirit of Aristotle's approach in the *Nicomachean Ethics*, an effort to determine what "we," the many and the wise, really think on reflection.

For such reasons, labeling Sidgwick a "utilitarian" is hazardous. He treated ethics in broad terms as a concern with how to live, with what one has most reason to do and desire. Methods of ethics are, as he puts it, ways of "obtaining reasoned convictions as to what ought to be done." In *The Methods*, he singled out for extensive analysis three prime, but seemingly incompatible, candidate methods, casting two of them in terms of a hedonistic account of the good. Thus, there was, first, egoistic hedonism (or rational egoism, holding that one ought to promote one's own greatest good), followed by two more recognizably ethical perspectives: second, universal hedonism (or utilitarianism – that one ought to promote the greatest good of all); and, lastly, commonsense or "dogmatic" intuitional morality, construed as either commonsense moral duties or the revised versions of these set out in the systems of absolute duties of Whewell, Birks, Henry Calderwood, or other such moral theorists. Although the book as a whole seems to lean toward the utilitarian method, and critics have always charged Sidgwick with stacking the deck in its favor and/or ignoring other important methods,[11] it is more in line with his explicit disclaimers to say only that Bk. IV of the work (supplemented with other sections) contains the best, clearest, and most consistent statement of the classical utilitarian ethical theory, duly purified, but the book overall does not claim success in justifying that view, despite its upgraded, cognitivist metaethics and moral psychology. Remarkably, Sidgwick concluded his great work, especially the first edition, with a confession of failure – there was a "dualism" of practical reason that had universal hedonism in a stand-off with egoistic hedonism, leaving practical reason in chaos. Thus, although Sidgwick personally often indicated his utilitarian inclinations, he was candid about their shaky foundations, and his overall practical outlook was more complicated and controversial.[12]

Sidgwick's outlook is not as familiar as John Stuart Mill's, and it deserves more fleshing out. Not unlike Whewell, but with less Platonic baggage, Sidgwick argued that ethical theories demanded a non-tautological, non-reductive, and non-naturalistic rational foundation. The "science" of ethics had its own irreducible subject matter – its sphere was not the same as or reducible to those of empirical psychology, physiology, or biology, though all were susceptible to rational inquiry. Sidgwick believed that whatever its psychological, physiological, or biological sources, in any given situation there is something that one ought to do, and that the most basic normative notion of 'ought' or 'right' is irreducible to any natural or descriptive properties. Moral approbation is "inseparably bound up with the conviction, implicit or explicit, that the conduct approved … cannot, without error, be disapproved by any other mind."[13] Such judgments about what one truly ought to do or desire could, as Godwin held, also be motivating to at least some degree – if not always decisively so – simply on their own, as objective reasons.

In *Principia Ethica*, Sidgwick's later Cambridge student G. E. Moore (1873–1958) conceded that, unlike Bentham or Mill, Sidgwick did not commit the so-called "naturalistic fallacy." It is far from clear that anyone ever actually did, but the standard point is that it is question-begging to define such notions as "right" or "good" in terms of, or equate or reduce them to, natural, merely descriptive properties, provoking the "open question" of whether, say, pleasure really is good.[14] But here it must be admitted that Sidgwick's efforts to defend a non-tautological, non-question-begging account of the good as pleasure, rather than (to his mind) such vague and conflictual alternatives as virtue, excellence, or perfection, may not be his most lucid efforts. He was clear that the philosopher had to show that pleasure – or, better, conscious feeling apprehended as desirable when experienced – really is the sole ultimate good, what one ought to desire and promote, how Bentham and Mill had failed at this, and how Mill had also muddied the waters with his seemingly separate classification and weighting of pleasures in terms of quality, in addition to quantity. But the exact wording of his case is not always consistent, and the cognitive intuition at stake seems less certain, perhaps best put as the claim that pleasure can and should be "defined as feelings apprehended to be desirable," since it "is not a tautology to say feelings apprehended to be desirable are in fact desirable."[15]

For all that, Sidgwick did conclude that the hedonistic view of the good was the most rationally defensible option, a view that, despite much criticism in the twentieth century, has undergone something of a revival in more recent decades, despite Nozick's famous "Experience Machine" objection that, on such a view, a simulated world is as good as the real one.[16]

For Sidgwick, however, the notion of "ought" or "right" was the more fundamental one, and it reflected a more distinctly modern, imperative understanding of the normative, which he thought Cumberland had adumbrated in his modern natural law variant of utilitarianism. It was more determinate, more lawlike or "deontological" (to use the term introduced by C. D. Broad), with respect to action than the "attractive" notion of "good," which figured more prominently in the ancient ethicists. It is the difference between thinking one must "do this" (or "not do this") and finding oneself drawn toward some end such as happiness. Interestingly, one point on which Sidgwick was not in line with either Mill or Kant was in his rejection of the idea of free will, against or for, as of crucial relevance in ethics. On his view, people could act on reasons, either "agent relative" egoistic ones or "agent neutral" impartialist ones, but the deliberative mindset involved might not be importantly altered by thinking of oneself or others as either determined or free, except on the important topic of punishment and responsibility. Here too, his tendency to minimize metaphysical entanglements may be less than persuasive.[17]

At any rate, Sidgwick held that, on pain of endless regress, justifications for normative 'ought' claims had to come to a halt somewhere, and that bedrock was in propositions that had some serious claim to being self-evident truths, cognitive intuitions (not mere considered convictions, or gut feelings) the truth of which rested on their own content when properly apprehended. Rather confusingly, intuitionism figured both as a method of ethics, and, in a more abstract philosophical (non-dogmatic) form, in the assessment of all the methods of ethics, though some details of that more sophisticated level are kept in the background until the end of Book III and the detailed interrogations of rational egoism and commonsense or dogmatic intuitionism. In comparing, contrasting, and trying to reconcile the different methods insofar as possible, Sidgwick ended up effectively demonstrating to the dogmatic intuitional moralists how commonsense morality, even theoretically upgraded commonsense morality, demanded additional principles – how such supposedly intuitively self-evident principles as veracity, promise-keeping, justice, purity, etc., were only apparently self-evident and not truly fundamental, even when strung together as a Supreme Rule. They were at best only vague and crude (but still useful) general rules allowing various exceptions and qualification (not to mention conflicts with other duties), as Mill had insisted. They required further principles for systematizing and subordinating them, and for rendering their prescriptions consistent, coherent, and clear. A duty like telling the truth might be presented as absolute and clear, but when it came to lying to spare an invalid a terrible, possibly fatal shock, few decent people would follow the absolutist line but would instead appeal to more or less utilitarian considerations, also needed to determine just how much shock might be allowable, when and where exceptions were needed, and so on.

After a long, disenchanting tour through such failings in commonsense or dogmatic intuitional morality in Book III of *The Methods of Ethics*, Sidgwick concluded that there were better candidate intuitions than commonsense or Whewellian ones, but these were less concrete and more general and abstract, less mired in the confusions and inconsistencies of commonsense morality. As it happened, these intuitions included principles, or axioms, supporting the utilitarian position, the better option for cleaning up and straightening out the confusions of commonsense or dogmatic intuitional morality, while still according it an important practical role. The better axiomatic principles were: (1) that the good of one is no more important than the good of another; (2) that, other things equal, future good is as important as present good; (3) that what is right for one must be right for anyone similarly circumstanced; and (4) that it is right to promote the good generally. These appear in different wordings in different places in Sidgwick's writings, and there is a small scholarly industry devoted to sorting them out.[18]

It is noteworthy that, in sharp contrast to Bentham and Mill, Sidgwick had an extensive knowledge of the works of Kant and Hegel (not to mention Plato and Aristotle), but like Mill, or later utilitarians such as R. M. Hare, he held that the best of Kant's insights, concerning universalizability, could be assimilated by utilitarianism, which also added content to the formal test of universalizability, which by itself and contra Kant, could justify rational egoism or other views. One can consistently will the utilitarian maxim of maximizing the good of all to be a universal law, but one can also consistently will that each individual should maximize his or her own good. Still, Kant's universalizability principle (interpreted as in 3 above), along with his readings from Clarke and More, had helped Sidgwick realize that cognitive intuitions could take a more compelling form than in Whewell's work – not that Kant thought of his grounding principles in any such rationalist or intuitionist terms.

Sidgwick's reconciliation of intuitional morality and utilitarianism was extensive and subtle, and, again, it relied on what he called "philosophical intuitionism," a sophisticated fallibilistic approach applying four criteria: clarity, careful reflection, consistency, and consensus of experts. Like Whewell, he certainly allowed that there had been historical progress in the discovery, or at least clarification and refinement, of intuitive truths, even if he did try his best to make good on Mill's claim that the principles supporting utilitarianism were the truly foundational ones. And again, neither Whewell nor Sidgwick believed in some mysterious special faculty or sense for grasping self-evident truth, only reason, which included the capacity to apprehend non-naturalistic self-evident a priori truth. But getting to the point where one even had serious candidates for genuinely self-evident principles or axioms took a lot of effort, including the extensive dialogical and dialectical work involved in applying all the criteria, and Sidgwick sometimes suggested that the best that could be done was to reduce the likelihood of error.[19] He always seemed to leave it open that principles or axioms presenting themselves as self-evident truths were actually only apparently so, as one could come to see upon more informed reflection and an effort to derive light from other minds as likely to be correct as one's own.[20]

And in fact, in the end, Sidgwick himself doubted that he had succeeded in fully rationalizing and upgrading commonsense morality and in the process vindicating the principles undergirding utilitarianism, which, he agreed, held that "It is the Good Universal, interpreted and defined as 'happiness' or 'pleasure,' at which a Utilitarian considers it his duty to aim: and it seems arbitrary and unreasonable to exclude from the end, as so conceived, any pleasure of any sentient being."[21] With a painful personal sense of failure, he concluded that there remained a "dualism of the practical reason" because rational egoism, unlike intuitional morality, could not be reconciled with utilitarian principles; moreover, it was equally self-evident that one was rationally justified in aiming at one's own greatest happiness. In the world as it seemed to be, this led to serious conflicts between one's own good and the good of others – rational, hedonistic egoism was both at odds with utilitarianism and more limited in its capacity for systematizing commonsense morality. Without a different epistemology, or something akin to Paley's God, there was a "fundamental contradiction in our apparent intuitions of what is Reasonable in conduct," such that "the 'Cosmos' of Duty is thus really reduced to a Chaos, and the prolonged effort of the human intellect to frame a perfect ideal of rational conduct is seen to have been foredoomed to inevitable failure."[22] Hence his dogged, ghost-chasing efforts to somehow, perhaps Theistically, harmonize these two methods, though those also fell before his discerning and relentless critical scrutiny. In one of his most candid academic statements of his position, which comes in the course of his lectures on Spencer, Sidgwick addresses Spencer's claims about the necessity "with a view to the general happiness" of a compromise "between Egoism and Altruism" and expresses some degree of agreement with Spencer, but with important caveats:

> It may be said to me: How do *you* deal with it? My answer is, that unless we assume or prove the moral order of the world, there is a conflict between rational convictions. – Do I assume it? Yes, practically, as a man; provisionally, and with due recognition of the need of proof, as a philosopher. The assumption is normal to reflective man, and a postulate of Common Sense.[23]

Thus, to judge from both his life and his writings, Sidgwick, like Mill, was not actually the purest distillation of impartial utilitarianism as it is canonized today, exemplary as his description of that view may have been, though it also seems plausible that, despite some key differences in metaethics and metaphysics with his philosophical predecessors, he shared a good deal of the actual Benthamite/Millian outlook when it came to seeking to harmonize and reconcile the conflicting sides of the human psyche – "I have recognized clearly, though without either the emphasis of Bentham or the eloquence of Mill, the practical claims of egoism."[24] He was always driven, albeit in a fashion more receptive to theological possibilities, to try to harmonize the interests of self and the interests of others so that best for all was also best for oneself. Even if the justificatory reasons, impartial benevolence versus rational egoism, were fundamentally different, both had force and it was better to minimize the need for uncompensated self-sacrifice and try to effect that Millian unity in an ambitious way redolent of a more religious perspective on the moral order of the universe. The very idea of a perverse, conflictual, or rationally abusive universe in which such harmonization could not be achieved (or achieved in the right way) profoundly disturbed Sidgwick, figuring in his biggest existential crises. He was horrified at the thought that the "wages of virtue" might be "dust," in the words of Tennyson, one of his favorite poets (along with Arthur Hugh Clough). What kind of ultimate cosmic victory was there in demonstrating that one was indeed rationally required to sacrifice oneself whenever impartial benevolence demanded it (which might be for marginal but numerous and widespread gains to others), with no reward in this life or the next? As Phillips aptly notes, with respect to de Lazari-Radek and Singer's ingenious effort to overcome the dualism in favor of impartial utilitarianism through an evolutionary debunking argument against the alternatives, their argument might give Sidgwick "one thing he would certainly have liked – an argument for the truth of utilitarianism – at the cost of losing another thing he also very much wanted, an argument for the existence of God."[25] If not God, at least a "friendly universe" in which the moral order of reason took a less hard-hearted and demanding form.

Sidgwick never did claim success in his search for the moral order of the universe, and at times, in the 1880s and 1890s, he was close to utter despair, feeling that all methods, including his ghosthunting, had failed him. But his approach remained flexible and dynamic, always adapting to address new philosophical developments in the quest for progress in ethics. By the 1880s, intuitionism had receded and another famous rebellion against the utilitarian legacy was in the ascendant with the work of the British Idealists, especially T. H. Green, F. H. Bradley, and Bernard Bosanquet, which development would also shape the later pragmatist movement. This revolution began with attacks on utilitarianism, such as Bradley's "Mr. Sidgwick's Hedonism." Idealism was not a mere continuation of intuitionism, being more thoroughly metaphysical and holistic, though Green was influenced by Maurice's Christian Socialism and the movement rather obviously reflected many of the same religious concerns.

The best Idealist criticism essentially tried to demonstrate, sometimes successfully, how utilitarianism, psychological egoism, naturalism, and empiricism all had the seeds of self-destruction built into them, for more or less analogous reasons – namely, an overly reductive, atomizing view of human experience that could only yield Humean skepticism about human knowledge, whatever the domain. The utilitarian philosopher best able to withstand such criticism was Sidgwick, but this was because he had already abandoned the empiricist naturalism of his predecessors, even while being cautious and rather minimalist in his metaphysical and ontological entanglements. His detailed writings engaging with Idealism point up how Sidgwick's approach was an evolving work in progress.[26]

Two more points about Sidgwick's *Methods* must be introduced here. First, Sidgwick recognized, apparently for the first time in ethical philosophy, that there was a crucial difference between calculating total and calculating average utility when the population in question could vary in size, such that a smaller but deliriously happy population would by the felicific calculus be deemed inferior to a much larger population with much lower average happiness, but more happiness in total because of the additional numbers.[27] This issue has generated a vast critical literature on obligations to future generations and the question of whether the utilitarian duty to make people happy also demands making additional happy people, a policy that could, as Parfit famously argued, lead to a repugnant, vastly populated world of creatures with lives only just barely worth living.[28] Yet, if it is wrong to bring people apt to suffer terribly into existence, why is it not right to bring people apt to be very happy into existence?

Parfit's *Reasons and Persons* pursued such questions in a truly Sidgwickian way, while heaping even more intractable philosophical difficulties onto the original one, with such issues as the Non-identity problem – that is, to give but one facet of it, the challenge of assessing the damage of, say, injustices, if the people suffering from them would not have existed had it not been for them. Avoiding the injustices would not have made those same people better off, but instead led to a different set of existing people, as with an impersonal utilitarian consideration of which population of future people would produce the most happiness. This raises the question of whether it is possible to somehow do wrong, but without actually wronging any existing present or future people.[29] It also, among other things, raises difficult issues about such matters as reparations for slavery, given that the people to be compensated would for the most part not have existed at all had the injustices of slavery not existed.

Second, it was Sidgwick who most clearly articulated the potentially extreme self-effacingness of utilitarianism, how it could be so indirect as to take an esoteric form:

> on Utilitarian principles, it may be right to do and privately recommend, under certain circumstance, what it would not be right to advocate openly; it may be right to teach openly to one set of persons what it would be wrong to teach to others; it may be conceivably right to do, if it can be done with comparative secrecy, what it would be wrong to do in the face of the world.[30]

This, Sidgwick admits, is paradoxical given the general aversion to such a view, but that only means that such implications should themselves be kept secret in a more comprehensive esotericism. In the world as it is, which then as now was hardly to be counted as one of perfectly enlightened utilitarians, such esotericism on the part of utilitarians could well be justified to Sidgwick's mind, and it would not be wholly self-defeating. For example, it might be more productive of general happiness to have the comforts of religious morality linger on for a time, undisturbed by the troubling theological doubts of the Sidgwicks of the world. Sidgwick himself held and practiced such a view. He largely refrained from openly attacking religion or various aspects of commonsense morality, including those concerning prohibitions on the same-sex "Greek Love" that was preached and practiced in his more intimate friendship circles.[31] And he at times confessed that it would probably be better if young people believed in Green's Idealism rather than anything that he might teach them.

Bernard Williams famously cracked that this might well be called "Government House" utilitarianism, a view fitted to colonialist administration, and went further in arguing that, if it is not a matter of different sets of people, a utilitarian elite and the uncomprehending others, then it creates a problematic disjunction in individuals between theory and practice, given that the ordinary dispositions of common-sense morality are now being used to implement utilitarianism rather point up the problems with commonsense morality.[32] Can one adopt, in Sidgwick's phrase, the impartial benevolence of the utilitarian "Point of View of the Universe" – of an impartial spectator or godlike superperson incorporating the perspectives of all – with respect to one's own dispositions to act morally, without altering those very dispositions, psychologically recasting them as instrumental rather than really right, and this in ways inimical to one's integrity? Perhaps the cool hour of critical reflection is parasitic on the practices and commitments of life when lived, in one's projects and relationships. But defenders of Sidgwick from Parfit to Singer have counterargued that, just as in certain contexts it is important, as Williams claims, not to have "one thought too many," in other contexts it is important not to have "one thought too few," recognizing the truth that one is only one pebble on the beach, so to speak. This lively and very long-standing debate, which calls to mind the evolution in Godwin's stance on burning palaces, continues in ever more sophisticated versions.[33]

It is indeed intriguing – revealing, perhaps – that Williams could make this point without seriously considering whether Sidgwick was a Government House utilitarian. Like so many who have written on Sidgwick, he focused almost exclusively on *The Methods of Ethics*. It is an ironic fate for the person so often praised as the best of the classical utilitarians to have his economic, political theoretical, and historical work studiously ignored, even by political philosophers, while his ethical work gets all the scholarly attention. But this carefully curated reception of Sidgwick is illustrative of the problem of systemic racism in academic philosophy.

Government House Utilitarianism

Much could be said here about Sidgwick's important contributions to the Cambridge School of economics, his relationship to such figures as Alfred Marshall, W. S. Jevons, and F. Y. Edgeworth, and how his works opened the way for A. C. Pigou's *The Economics of Welfare*. But the focus here will be on those aspects of his economic, political, and historical work bearing directly on matters of settler colonialism, colonialism, imperialism, and racism – that is, the aspects of Sidgwick that parallel the growth of a utilitarian ideological subservience to the aims of empire described in earlier chapters.[34] The challenge, of course, comes in no small part from Sidgwick's calculated evasions and affirmations, which can obscure his agenda in ways uncharacteristic of his predecessors.

In his more academic way, Sidgwick was as embedded in imperialism as the Mills were with the East India Company. His academic environment was a hotbed of liberal imperialism, and of not so liberal imperialism for that matter – James Fitzjames Stephen, a fellow Apostle, defended violent suppression of democratic resistance everywhere, as did his colleague Henry Sumner Maine, whose anti-democratic claims Sidgwick deemed impressive.[35] He was close to, indeed edited the posthumous work of, Sir John Seeley, widely regarded as the historical and intellectual spokesperson for the imperialism of the late-Victorian era, given his book *The Expansion of England*, which famously suggested that "We seem, as it were, to have conquered and peopled half the world in a fit of absence of mind."[36] Like Seeley, and perhaps reflecting the influence of Comte, Sidgwick believed that the advance of scientific authority (the consensus of experts) would and should serve as an effective countervailing power to the spreading democratic enthusiasms of the era.[37] He devoted considerable attention to the Indian Civil Service (ICS) – he was even invited to teach at Haileybury, though he declined – and had very close friends associated with that, including George Otto Trevelyan (the author of *Cawnpore*, who hated India) and Oscar Browning.[38] And, of course, his relations with his former pupil and brother-in-law Arthur Balfour were close, and their influence on each other was mutual. Even before the conservative Balfour became Irish Secretary, and earned the nickname "Bloody Balfour," Sidgwick would opine "the only tolerable alternative for Home Rule *now* is Coercion, and vigorous coercion; any intermediate scheme has become irrelevant, even to stupidity."[39] Like Mill, Sidgwick harbored doubts about the Irish, and like his friend Seeley, he defended Liberal Unionism (indeed, he parted company with many other Liberals in opposing Home Rule). And he had an admirer in the Princeton professor, and later US president, Woodrow Wilson, an ardent imperialist who shared Balfour's commitment to a strong Anglo-American alliance to establish international order of the right kind. Wilson had high praise not only for Sidgwick's *Elements*, but also for the early film *The Birth of a Nation*, a profoundly racist production that had white actors in blackface attacking white women, with the Ku Klux Klan riding to the rescue. The list goes on.

To be sure, the transition from the mid-Victorian to the late-Victorian era was momentous, with many dramatic changes in the culture of imperialism. Again, Caroline Elkins gives a clear summary of a very complex history:

> The fear of too much too soon also ascended in liberal imperial thought. For mid- and late Victorians, convulsions in the empire were the result of British reform efforts rather than the injustices of British rule. Traditional societies had dissolved in the face of a too-rapid civilizing mission and created massive disorder. Going forward, as Karuna Mantena elaborates in *Alibis of Empire*, indigenous political and social forms would be rehabilitated, and often invented, to stabilize indigenous populations. Britain would rule indirectly through local systems and their pashas, princes, and chiefs whose power was directly contingent on British support and the execution of imperial policies on the ground. Alongside Britain's evolving policy of indirect rule was a paternalistic ethos. Imperial actors, such as frontline administrators and missionaries, implemented reform measures with the anticipation that it would now take generations, if not more, for these measures to yield results. At the same time, a parallel legal system evolved that Britain did not entrust to local rulers. Comprised of penal codes, restrictive regulations, and the ability to declare martial law or a state of emergency (statutory martial law), this system suppressed challenges to British rule.[40]

Indirect rule, with such theoreticians as Maine behind it, was an important twist on the domination of strangers, but the steel frame of legal codification persisted and at points hardened.

It should be admitted here that Sidgwick found himself, as the century wore on, quite distressed by the jingoist, John Bull militaristic political rhetoric of the 1890s, especially evident at the time of the second Boer War. He feared the growth of a militaristic and Machiavellian form of self-interested power politics, whether domestically or globally. Against the ruder and cruder forms of self- or national interest – aggravated by a practical reason in chaos – he sought a continued moral and political evolution, led by the European powers, toward a greater federalism and cosmopolitanism that would generate the institutional mechanisms and political morality needed to avoid war and avert other forms of strife – that is to say, the very world order that continues the imperialist project down to today, though with Sidgwick this had a more up-front Eurocentric and Anglo-Saxon cast. Ethical socialism, the fostering of humanity's sympathetic and cooperative tendencies, was the road he favored in all regions, and education, in a broad sense, remained the vehicle of reform and moral order to which he would ever return, though he allowed that genuine cosmopolitanism was an ideal for the further future. This was at best the "liberal" in liberal imperialism – Sidgwick did not even think militarism an indicator of a lower degree of civilization.

Sidgwick's political writings did not achieve anything approximating the inspiring tone of John Mill, and for all of his indebtedness to *On Liberty*, *Considerations on Representative Government*, etc., he tended to highlight rather different concerns – concerns that often reflected his anxieties over the dualism of practical reason.[41] And strangely, but quite deliberately, he made it difficult for readers of his major works to discern his views on such hot topics as India by writing in a bland, colorless, and abstract way about the supposed principles involved, rarely making it clear which particular historical or contemporary cases he had in mind. In a weird way, he took the outlook of James Mill a step further, in the belief that writing in this distanced manner would achieve greater objectivity and impartiality of judgment, even as he "developed a cautious internationalism grounded in structural-liberal claims," as Bell puts it.[42]

Thus, in his *Elements*, as in the *Principles*, where one would expect to find an extensive, explicit treatment of India, he rarely makes any serious direct mention of it at all, though his sympathies with the work of Maine (rather than James Mill) on land tenure in India are evident: "competent judges hold that it might have prevented serious mistakes in our government of India, if the governing statesmen had had before their minds the historical development of land-tenure, as we now conceive it to have taken place in European countries."[43] There is more express referencing of India and other parts of the Empire in Sidgwick's correspondence. Consider his somewhat obsequious January 6, 1889 letter to Lord Lytton:

> My dear Lord Lytton
>
> I am exceedingly obliged to you for your very full and interesting letter; and much gratified to find that you do not take more objections to my formulation of international duty, and that your disagreements are only on minor points. I was probably led to exaggerate our difference from the fact that, as you say, we approached the matter from opposite [*sic*] – your object being to show that the ordinary moralist had got considerably out of his proper place and function in his dealings with international questions, and <u>my</u> object being rather to put him if possible in his proper place and keep him there!
>
> I thought all you said in your address about the feminine personalities of nations and the [*sic*] their misleading effects

opportune as well as entertaining. I quite feel that popular talk on this subject is rife with absurdities which are liable to become worse than ridiculous in their practical effect. I have sometimes thought that the uncertainty whether national identity depends on physical continuity of *race* or identity of *land* inhabited was perhaps the most striking cause of muddled sentiment on the subject. Do you remember how in Tennyson's "Boädicea" the queen is consoled by loosely robed prophetesses depicting power and glory awaiting the "isle" in the future? – when it would be inhabited by Angles who had managed to [extirpate?] Boädicea's kinsfolk, except from "Little Wales"! All the same I suppose you would agree that as the notion of national identity is indispensable if we are to have any international morality, all this muddled sentiment does more good than harm *on the whole*, – though it is an excellent thing that it should from time to time be sharply criticized.

I am much interested in what you say of the perplexities of Federal States in international relations. I suppose however that they would only come in so far as matters of "*international comity*" are concerned, as distinct from matters of *strict duty* according to the received law of nations. I mean, at least, that U.S.A. took this view of the treatment of British niggers by South Carolina in 1849–51, for the Federal Government is constitutionally bound to punish "offences against the law of nations."

I should myself be inclined to say that this distinction between Offices of "Comity" and duties of strict obligation was required in applying my principle that "internal Constitution" cannot be an excuse for neglecting international duty. I am particularly pleased with your approval of what I have said about this; as it seems to me one of the points – they are perhaps few! – in which a theoretical, systematic treatment of international duty may really do practical good. For I can hardly conceive any one approaching the subject from a theoretical point of view, and considering the question in relation to the received principle that no nation's internal Constitution is to be interfered with by other nations – I can hardly conceive him not coming to my conclusion. And yet the opposite view has often been loudly maintained by Englishmen, at the time of the Conspiracy Bill to which you refer and at other times. I think it partly belongs to a conviction that the moral superiority of a free country, quâ free, justifies it in taking liberties that cannot be allowed to despots!

Still on this point, as I said, I should distinguish between points of strict duty and points of mere friendliness or courtesy.

It seems to me that as regards the latter "internal Constitution" may fairly be considered. To adapt your metaphor, a man with a wife whom he cannot control must not be therefore excused from paying his just debts, but he may be excused for not asking his friends to stay with him.

Now a word or two as regards minor points of disagreement. I am afraid I have no effective answer to what you say about my discussion of the moral validity of compacts imposed by "unjust victors." I am afraid it must seem all rather "in the air," to practical statesmen. All I would urge is that the international moralist is bound to have some view on the morality of breaking treaties, and he cannot quite bring himself to say that a defeated State may legitimately tear up an irksome treaty whenever it has a favourable opportunity or feels strong enough. And though the moralist may have but little influence on the decision of such a question, do you not think that he may have some – always supposing that a tolerably complete consensus of moralists could be attained? At least if ^the Statesmen of^ such a State were balanced between the pros and cons on the question of tearing up a treaty, would not the probable verdict of X impartial moral opinion have some weight? And might I not even quote the case of Russia and the Black Sea on my side? Do you think Russia would have dared to do what she did (say) ten years earlier, and with no excuse of breaches on the other side?

As to arbitration, – I am impressed with what you say of the objections to it as a means of solving the minor disputes to which alone we agree in thinking it possible to apply it effectively. Do you think that your objection would be at all removed or diminished by adopting Maine's suggestion (in his last posthumous book) of a permanent Court of Arbitration appointed by the Concert of Europe to deal with all questions that might be referred to them by any State? This seems to me partly to get over the danger of conscious and interested partisanship of the arbitrator.

I am really most grateful to you for giving so much attention to my proofs. I fear very few will read my chapters carefully even once, when published – except unhappy wights preparing for examination – but one must at least imagine readers, so in writing the rest I shall imagine you. I am yours aff^{ly}
H Sidgwick[44]

Lord Lytton was Edward Robert Bulwer Lytton (1831–91), the first Earl Lytton, who had served as Viceroy in India from 1876 to 1880; he had given Sidgwick comments on the proofs of *The Elements of Politics*, first published in 1891, and it is rather telling that Sidgwick considered him something of an ideal reader of his last major tome. But the rest of their correspondence is devoted to parapsychology, with Sidgwick working to recruit Lytton to the Society for Psychical Research, not draw him out on his experiences in India.

Still, *The Elements* did include an important chapter on "Principles of External Policy" that discusses, in a typically nuanced Sidgwickian way, the advantages and disadvantages of colonization, and in the course of his analysis he explains, in connection with the case where "the conquered, though not uncivilized, are markedly inferior in civilization to the conquerors," that the advantage of "increased strength for war" may "easily be outweighed by increased difficulty of defense if the conquest is distant or otherwise inconveniently situated, – e.g. England is rather weakened than strengthened for formidable conflicts by her possession of India."[45] He carefully, if abstractly, considers the advantages and disadvantages for the colonized as well as the colonizers, concluding with respect to the former that the benefits of civilization outweigh the disadvantages, given the potential for "completer internal peace and order, improved industry, enlarged opportunities for learning a better religion and a truer science."[46] Of course, given the skeptical results of so much of Sidgwick's work, it is not obvious what "a better religion and a truer science" amounted to. Green's Idealism and parapsychology?

These points come just prior to his account of the "sentimental satisfactions" involved in the civilizational mission of "spiritual expansion." Indeed, in this work, Sidgwick carries on in glowing terms about how, even if colonies are an economic or military liability, there

> are sentimental satisfactions, derived from justifiable conquests, which must be taken into account … Such are the justifiable pride which the cultivated members of a civilized community feel in the beneficent exercise of dominion, and in the performance by their nation of the noble task of spreading the highest kind of civilization, and a more intense though less elevated satisfaction – inseparable from patriotic sentiment – in the spread of the special type of civilization distinctive of their own nation, communicated through its language and literature, and through the tendency to imitate its manners and customs which its prolonged rule, especially if on the whole beneficent, is likely to cause in a continually increasing degree.[47]

This is the process of "spiritual expansion," a form of cultural imperialism that can occur even in the absence of political and economic imperialism.

Moreover, in chapter XXVI, on "Federal and Other Composite States," Sidgwick does roll around to a general analysis of dependencies that seems relevant to the particulars of the East India Company:

> If we ask the best mode of governing dependent part-states, the answer must vary with the varying conditions under which the relation is suitable. Where the dependence is compulsory or semi-compulsory, – due to what we may assume to be legitimate conquest, – there is an obvious reason for not allowing the unwilling members any influence on the government of the whole: which is also a sufficient reason for keeping the organized force of the dependency entirely in the hands of an executive organ appointed and controlled by the dominant government, and for making the assent either of this organ or of the dominant government practically as well as formally necessary to any special legislation required for the dependency. It is a more difficult question how far such legislation should be ordinarily allowed to be framed by a representative assembly, freely elected by the citizens of the dependent community – supposing them to be adequately homogeneous and civilized, and otherwise fitted for representative institutions. On the one hand, such an assembly is likely to become the mouthpiece of disaffection, and to render combination easier for the purpose of hampering and resisting the dominant government: on the other hand, so far as it works effectively within the sphere assigned to it, its operation is likely to diminish discontent and improve legislation; since it will be generally difficult to devise a satisfactory substitute for such a body, as a means of ascertaining the real needs of the population of the dependency. The decision in any particular case must depend largely on the extent and intensity of disaffection in the dependency; since, so long as this is extensive and violent, the risk of facilitating dangerous organized agitation, through the election and operations of a representative legislature, would generally outweigh any probable gain in the way of pacification or useful legislative work. Similar considerations must also largely determine the answer to another important question, – viz. how far the subordinate posts of the executive and the judiciary in the dependent country should be filled from the inhabitants of the dominant country.[48]

There is no explicit account of the East India Company, only some distant echoes of Mill's defense of it. Indeed, like Mill in his later years, Sidgwick harbored many suspicions about the wisdom of democracy, especially what he deemed premature democracy, at times out of an understandable fear that in settler colonies the settlers would treat native populations atrociously. As with Mill, his fears arose from the domestic scene as well, and he championed the need for a cultural "clerisy" or elite vanguard of educated opinion pretty much everywhere, often sounding a note not unlike that of Walter Lippmann in the twentieth century, stressing how an educated elite should benevolently shape public opinion and guide policy. Again, he greatly admired the work of his friend James Bryce, author of *The American Commonwealth*, which pointed up both the vitality and the dangers of the US political system. But he shared Mill's concerns about a seriously uneducated electorate and was quite content to exclude such people and many others from the franchise – criminals, paupers receiving public funds, young people, and even those "guilty of disgraceful conduct not amounting to crime," such as "keeping a brothel." Also, "policemen and soldiers on service," the better to keep them "impartial in political conflicts."[49] He devoted comparatively little effort to proclaiming the benefits of freedom of conscience and speech, was quite critical of Mill's schemes for proportional representation, and worried at length about how "to correct the erroneous and short-sighted views of self-interest, representing it as divergent from duty, which certainly appear to be widely prevalent in the most advanced societies, at least among irreligious persons." In fact, for the government to supply teachers of this view might even be "indirectly individualistic in its aim, since to diffuse the conviction that it is every one's interest to do what is right would obviously be a valuable protection against mutual wrong," though it would probably detract from the credibility of such teachers if they were salaried employees of the state.[50]

Thus, Sidgwick's political writings do in their way effectively underscore the crucial role of education, broadly conceived, which seems a clear parallel to and continuation of the projects of Mill and the earlier utilitarians. The more sinister aspects of his anxieties about the supposed educational deficiencies of what he termed the "lower classes" and the "lower races" may make one suspect that the enabling conditions of academic philosophical excellence shared much with other imperial institutions. If his more academic research indicated, as a practical political point, the need for expanding and improving educational offerings and opportunities, the backdrop to this was surely his larger anxieties about the direction of civilization, including premature democracy. However, in a turn the sheer strangeness of which rivals Bentham's Auto-Icon, those anxieties were woven into a profound dissatisfaction with a reductive, materialistic scientistic worldview, and a profound longing for something more meaningful – a longing that was manifested more in Sidgwick's psychical research than in his academic writing. That is, even if he did not succeed in finding proof of an afterlife, he did conclude that telepathy was real and that the conscious self was, as James believed, not the whole story. Sidgwick remained undecided about the very constitution of the self in ways unparalleled by his utilitarian predecessors. Although he ended up debunking it, he was initially enthusiastic about Theosophy and hoped it might turn out to be true.[51] Esotericism spoke to him.

This is not to deny his more worldly accomplishments, his devotion to advancing higher education for women and many attempts to improve the curriculum of Cambridge University (by including Bentham, modern literature, physiology, and other new subjects) and expand its audience and felicific social impact.[52] Beyond formal educational institutions, Sidgwick was indefatigable in promoting and participating in discussion societies, ever aiming at the elusive "consensus of experts" that his epistemology called for. If, toward the end of his life, his participation in such vehicles as the "Ethical Societies" reflected some despair over the possibility of achieving such a consensus, this was scarcely his characteristic attitude, at least when it came to his personal commitment to exploring the deepest questions of human life.[53]

Overall, then, it is very difficult to deny that, with Sidgwick, the economic arguments about the value of colonies, dependencies, etc., counted for far less than the concerns about ethical and political duty (and comity), and the now rather more anxious civilizational mission to educate and discipline the world, such that, in Seeley's words with respect to India, "the experiment must go forward … we cannot leave it unfinished if we would."[54] Unlike Seeley, however, Sidgwick at times anticipated the sentiments of the liberal imperialist J. H. Muirhead, who, in the immediate aftermath of the second Boer War, worried, albeit rather complacently, that the Empire had historically made a huge mistake, the mistake that "in setting about the education of these people we have taken no trouble to understand the people we are educating. We have not yet taken to heart and applied abroad what we have known for the last half-century at home, that there can be no true education where the ideas we aim at imparting stand in no organic connection with the ideas already there."[55] Added to that, for Sidgwick, was the gnawing doubt that his civilization had any truly justifiable ethical and political positions to teach – after all, the educators teaching the harmony of interest and duty could hardly resort to Sidgwick's *Methods* to support their case.

It is impossible to do justice here to all dimensions of Sidgwick's life and work, his various entanglements in the complexities, both theoretical and practical, of the British Empire and the other empires that he studied (including the Belgian Colonial Empire under King Leopold, which was arguably worse than the British Royal African Company in the nineteenth-century "scramble for Africa"). At most, as in previous chapters, only a few more illustrative, revelatory episodes can be considered, the better to draw out or decode Sidgwick's positioning with respect to the racism, colonization, and imperialism addressed earlier. Sidgwick's nervous agnosticism regarding hereditary racial differences, which was a descendant of Mill's but more anxious, clearly had an even more problematic side.[56] Unlike Mill, Sidgwick in his correspondence (for example, with Lord Lytton) sometimes used the "N word" – "nigger" – and this in an offhand, derogatory way suggestive of the type of casual racism characterizing his general company.[57] Indeed, despite ample opportunity to blast "bald and vicious" forms of racism of the Carlylean type, as in the work of E. A. Freeman, Sidgwick never did so, preferring instead to decorously sidestep such issues.

Although Sidgwick did not actually comment on Mill versus Carlyle, his line was extremely close to Mill's – while conceding in stock fashion that, historically, things are not so simple and that the Egyptians and other non-whites played important roles in cultural advance, he nonetheless allowed that future science might demonstrate significant racial differences; that "savages" were "inferior," even if this might be a contingent inferiority and race only one possible determining factor; and that "civilized" Europeans, to whom we owed constitutional government, were for the foreseeable future to be the judges and schoolmasters of the world. In familiar Millian fashion, he recognized how the rights of subjected peoples had to be protected from the abuses of colonial governments – on that count, he was rather better than Mill, even the later, melancholy Mill – bringing to his work a much keener sense of the ferocious cruelty and bigotry that marked the history of settler colonialism. Mill's late-in-life mistrust of British political judgment on such matters was in fact developed and systematized by Sidgwick, who dealt with the subject in the *Elements*. He was every bit as cosmopolitan as Mill, looking to a future in which duty to humanity would increasingly trump love of country. But he was perhaps rather soberer than Mill, unless it be the Mill of the late 1850s, when it came to recognizing the obstacles to this cosmopolitanism, which he thought would need to be led by the "Concert of Europe" (a very white Europe). But neither the late Victorian Sidgwick nor the mid-Victorian Mill ever came close to the anti-colonialist and anti-imperialist elements in Godwin.

There are in fact passages in the *Elements* that sound more like the defenders of Eyre than like a good Millian. In the section on "Principles of External Policy," Sidgwick discusses "special restrictions on freedom of contract" in a singularly revealing way:

> [I]f such contracts are left unrestricted, there is some risk that the inferior race may be brought too completely into the power of private employers. This point is of course peculiarly important in the case of colonies in which the superior race cannot or will not undertake the main part of the manual work required: in this case the demand of the capitalist employer for a steady supply of reliable labour led modern civilization in its earlier stage back to the institution of slavery in an extreme form: and prompts even now to longing aspirations after some system of compulsory labour, which shall have the economic advantages of slavery without its evils. But I know no ground for thinking that such a system can be devised: and should accordingly deprecate any attempt to approximate to it. I do not therefore infer – as some have inferred – that contracts of long duration ought to be prohibited altogether; but only that they ought to be carefully supervised and closely watched. The need for this vigilance arises equally – it may be even greater – when the labourers in question are not natives, but aliens belonging to a lower grade of civilization; at the same time there are strong economic reasons for introducing labour from abroad in colonies of this class, where the natives are either not sufficiently numerous or wanting in industrial capacity.[58]

The plausible suspicion that Sidgwick was referring to the Jamaican case, as construed by Mill, is strengthened by a footnote a couple of pages earlier: "in our own empire, the South African colonies form, from this point of view, a series of links intermediate between Australia and New Zealand which are clearly colonies of settlement, and the West Indian islands which are clearly not." "Colonies of settlement" are those in which "the manual labour can be and will be supplied by the civilized race"; the other colonies, only loosely so called, being those "in which it can only supply capital and superior kinds of labour." Moreover, Sidgwick emphasizes that:

> the protection of the lives and property of the settlers will require effective prosecution and exemplary punishment of crimes against them: at the same time, it will be the imperative duty of Government to keep such punishment within the limits of strict justice. The difficult task of fulfilling this double obligation is likely to be better performed if those charged with it are not hampered by pedantic adhesion to the forms of civilized judicial procedure: what is important is that substantial justice should be done in such a manner as to impress the intellect of the aborigines with the relation between offence and punishment.[59]

These passages lend themselves to a far from Millian reading. The Morant Bay Rebellion was set off precisely in reaction to reassurances in "the Queen's Letter" that "The prosperity of the labouring classes, as well as of all other classes, depends, in Jamaica, and in other countries, upon their working for wages, not uncertainly, or capriciously, but steadily and continuously, at the times when their labour is wanted, and for so long as it is wanted."[60] This only served to evoke memories of slavery and fears of an attempt to reinstitute it by other means. And, of course, the defenders of Eyre were the very ones who complained about how unfair it was to insist on "pedantic adhesion to the forms of civilized judicial procedure" in the case of a rebellion by those whose labor was needed but not forthcoming, these rebels being equally identifiable by race.

Such openness to the case for Eyre appears to have been a longstanding Sidgwickian posture. At the very time when Mill was working for the Jamaica Committee, and Sidgwick was supposedly a younger and more radically Millian figure, Sidgwick confided to his mother that, although all of his friends were joining the Committee, he could not make up his mind on the matter.[61] There is no record of his having departed from that stance. Rather, he was apt to complain, at that time, about Mill's influence waning because of the public displays of his radicalism. And in his own defense, he might well have invoked Mill's own (earlier) words:

> To civilize a savage, he must be inspired with new wants and desires, even if not of a very elevated kind, provided that their gratification can be a motive to steady and regular bodily and mental exertion. If the negroes of Jamaica and Demerara, after their emancipation had contented themselves, as it was predicted they would do, with the necessaries of life, and abandoned all labour beyond the little which in a tropical climate, with a thin

> population and abundance of the richest land, is sufficient to support existence, they would have sunk into a condition more barbarous, though less unhappy, than their previous state of slavery. The motive which was most relied on for inducing them to work was their love of fine clothes and personal ornaments. No one will stand up for this taste as worthy of being cultivated, and in most societies its indulgence tends to impoverish rather than to enrich; but in the state of mind of the negroes it might have been the only incentive that could make them voluntarily undergo systematic labour, and so acquire or maintain habits of voluntary industry which may be converted to more valuable ends. In England, it is not the desire of wealth that needs to be taught, but the use of wealth, and appreciation of the objects of desire which wealth cannot purchase, or for attaining which it is not required. Every real improvement in the character of the English, whether it consist in giving them higher aspirations, or only a juster estimate of the value of their present objects of desire, must necessarily moderate the ardour of their devotion to the pursuit of wealth.[62]

Here again the somewhat paradoxical point – that the Jamaicans supposedly needed a more stringent materialistic work ethic (greater Temperance) to bring them to the civilizational level of the English, who needed to get over their materialistic work ethic – indicates the ambivalence of the utilitarian economic analysis of colonialism and how Mill's uses of the notions of civilization and barbarism really were at work throughout. Sidgwick would have had a case for claiming that the older Mill's criticisms of Carlyle obscured their potential points of agreement – after all, Mill and Sidgwick were as convinced as Carlyle that, in Hall's words, "colonization could provide a key to a better world," however much they differed from him in the grounds for such convictions.[63]

As usual, some might argue that both Mill and Sidgwick appreciated the accomplishments of other historical civilizations and were primarily concerned to stress European superiority in science and self-government. Even if true, which is debatable, this does not mitigate the forms of racism (not terribly polite, at times historicist and contingent, but enduring) in their works, which often did blend biological and ethnic notions in conceptions of race featuring such things as capacity for self-government. As Fredrickson put it:

> Nativists seeking to restrict immigration from eastern and southern Europe stressed an association between a capacity for

> self-government and Anglo-Saxon, Anglo-American, or Nordic (not simply white or European) ancestry. Hence the United States was not immune from its own variety of ethnic nationalism. But what the right kind of people inherited from their ancestors was the capacity to be liberal or democratic in the manner prescribed by the Enlightenment and the founding fathers. In Germany, *völkisch* nationalism was explicitly promoted as antithetical to liberalism and the heritage of the Enlightenment, and it had relatively weak opposition from those who sought to make the national project a prototype for humanity as a whole or even a large segment of it.[64]

In short, an emphasis on certain European civilizational contributions to self-government is not, in this context, at all reassuring, since such constructions have often served the purposes of white supremacism, the "dreamworlds of race" – or, in Sidgwick's case, the nightmarish threats of declining white civilizational control.

If Sidgwick's notions of race and civilization seem incoherent, it should be recalled that the Millian notion of "blood" was also incoherent, and in both cases, their agnosticism about the determinants of "nature" got washed out at the practical political level, where the "character" of the "savages" – the stunted trees, whose growth had been "retarded" – was immutable enough for purposes of maintaining colonial rule and de facto racial segregation and domination.[65] More theorizing went into the problem of who was fit for manual labor than of how to grant self-rule. Such racisms were perfectly consistent with support for abolitionism, the cause of the North in the American Civil War, etc., though Sidgwick even waffled on that.

Thus, Mill and Sidgwick shared much on matters of race and imperialism, and the leaders of the resistance in Jamaica and other countries would and could have effectively labeled them as racist, in the equivalent terminology of the day, with Sidgwick perhaps being the more offensive of the two.[66] But it is illustrative of how the times were changing that one cannot quite find in Mill the type of perspective that one finds in the work of Sidgwick's friend Charles Henry Pearson. Born in 1830, Pearson, who had studied at King's College London, under F. D. Maurice, and at Oriel College, Oxford, would become education minister in Victoria, Australia, and a stalwart of the Liberal Party in general. He was brought to Cambridge by Sidgwick at the point when the changes in the curriculum meant that Sidgwick would no longer have to teach history as part of the Moral Sciences. They would work together closely for two years and correspond for many years afterward, and Sidgwick even came to hope, in the mid-1870s, that Pearson would receive a professorship in history. He thought very highly of Pearson, and in a telling review, which appeared in the *National Review* in 1894, he praised Pearson's book *National Life and Character*:

> prophecies are not always put forward, even by the most highly educated prophets, as based on a scientific grasp of the laws of social evolution. Indeed, in the most impressive book of a prophetic nature which has appeared in England for many years – I mean Pearson's *National Life and Character* – the prophecies are not announced with any such pretensions; they always rest on a simply empirical basis, and only distinguish themselves from the common run of such forecasts by the remarkably wide and full knowledge of relevant historical facts which the writer shows, and the masterly skill with which the facts are selected and grouped. His predictions are almost always interesting and sometimes, I think, reach a degree of probability sufficient to give them a real practical value.[67]

The distressing thing about this glowing review is that Pearson's book was concerned to make such arguments as the following, in which Mill's worries about the loss of cultural vitality get transmuted into a Nietzschean mode:

> Summing up, then, we seem to find that we are slowly but demonstrably approaching what we may regard as the age of reason or of a sublimated humanity; and that this will give us a great deal that we are expecting from it – well-ordered polities, security to labour, education, freedom from gross superstitions, improved health and longer life, the destruction of privilege in society and of caprice in family life, better guarantees for the peace of the world, and enhanced regard for life and property when war unfortunately breaks out. It is possible to conceive the administration of the most advanced states so equitable and efficient that no one will even desire seriously to disturb it. On the other hand, it seems reasonable to assume that religion will gradually pass into a recognition of ethical precepts and a graceful habit of morality; that the mind will occupy itself less and less with works of genius, and more and more with trivial results and ephemeral discussions; that husband and wife, parents and children, will come to mean less to one another;

> that romantic feeling will die out in consequence; that the old will increase upon the young; that two great incentives to effort, the desire to use power for noble ends, and the desire to be highly esteemed, will come to promise less to capable men as the field of human energy is crowded; and generally that the world will be left without deep convictions or enthusiasm, without the regenerating influence of the ardour for political reform and the fervour of pious faith which have quickened men for centuries past as nothing else has quickened them, with a passion purifying the soul. It would clearly be unreasonable to murmur at changes that express the realisation by the world of its highest thought, whether the issue be good or bad. The etiolated religion which it seems likely we shall subside upon; the complicated but on the whole satisfactory State mechanism, that will prescribe education, limit industry, and direct enjoyment, will become, when they are once arrived at, natural and satisfactory. The decline of the higher classes as an influence in society, the organisation of the inferior races … throughout the Tropical Zone, are the natural result of principles that we cannot disown if we would. It would be impossible for a conservatively-minded monarch to reconstruct the nobility of the eighteenth century in the twentieth; and even now no practical statesman could dream of arresting Chinese power or Hindoo or negro expansion by wholesale massacres. The world is becoming too fibreless, too weak, too good to contemplate or to carry out great changes which imply lamentable suffering. It trusts more and more to experience; less and less to insight and will.[68]

The tone here is reminiscent of Carlyle on heroism and great men, with Pearson sweating over the fate of a society of sheepish men, a society that "has no purpose beyond supplying the day's needs, and amusing the day's vacuity." What has such a society "to do with the terrible burden of personality"? But there "seems no reason why men of this kind should not perpetuate the race, increasing and multiplying till every rood of earth maintains its man, and the savour of vacant lives will go up to God from every home."

There are Millian thoughts in such lines, about a stationary state of society, character development, and ethology, but they have been twisted to a more expressly racist purpose. For Pearson, the human predicament has everything to do with race, construed in the typically incoherent but politically charged way:

> Even during historical times, so-called, the world has mostly been peopled by races, either like the negro very little raised above the level of brutes, or at best, like the lower-caste Hindoo and the Chinaman, of such secondary intelligence as to have added nothing permanent to our stock of ideas. At this moment, though the civilised and progressive races have till quite recently been increasing upon the inferior types, and though the lowest forms of all are being exterminated, there seems, as we have seen, good warrant for assuming that the advantage has already passed to the lower forms of humanity, and indeed it appears to be a well-ascertained law that the races which care little for comfort and decency are bound to tide over bad times better than their superiors, and that the classes which reach the highest standard are proportionally short-lived.[69]

Pearson consoles his readers with invocations of the Norse "twilight of the gods" as the possible future, when, although there may be a "temporary eclipse of the higher powers," even the losing struggle is a kind of vindication. As the Nietzschean thought continues:

> We are so accustomed to the fierce rapture of struggle and victory, to that rough training of necessity by which the weak are destroyed, to revolutions of the political order, transferences of power and wealth, and discoveries in science, that we can hardly conceive a quiet old age of humanity, in which it may care only for sunshine and food and quiet, and expect nothing great from the toil of hand or thought.... It is now more than probable that our science, our civilisation, our great and real advance in the practice of government are only bringing us nearer to the day when the lower races will predominate in the world, when the higher races will lose their noblest elements, when we shall ask nothing from the day but to live, nor from the future but that we may not deteriorate. Even so, there will still remain to us ourselves. Simply to do our work in life, and to abide the issue, if we stand erect before the eternal calm as cheerfully as our fathers faced the eternal unrest, may be nobler training for our souls than the faith in progress.[70]

Pearson's melancholy racism can make Sidgwick's concern with colonization and manual labor look singularly suspicious, as though his doubts about progress and faith in federation and the "Concert of Europe" might have reflected an all-too-conservative faith in a saving remnant of civilization holding out against the peril of the "lower races." After all, his views on the difficulty of determining what made for scientific and cultural change and development certainly left a very wide field for alternative explanations, such as Pearson's. And it is clear what Pearson has in mind, given his account of the attitudes that he deems overly complacent:

> No one, of course, assumes that the Aryan race – to use a convenient term – can stamp out or starve out all their rivals on the face of the earth. It is self-evident that the Chinese, the Japanese, the Hindoos, if we may apply this general term to the various natives of India, and the African negro, are too numerous and sturdy to be extirpated. It is against the fashion of modern humanity to wish that they should suffer decrease or oppression. What is assumed is that the first three of these races will remain stationary within their present limits, while the negro will contribute an industrial population to the states which England and Germany will build up along the Congo or the Zambesi. The white man in these parts of the world is to be the planter, the mine-owner, the manufacturer, the merchant, and the leading employee under all these, contributing energy and capital to the new countries, while the negro is to be the field-hand, the common miner, and the factory operative. Here and there, in exceptional districts, the white man will predominate in numbers, but everywhere he will govern and direct in virtue of a higher intelligence and more resolute will.[71]

Pearson is insistent that the "character of a race determines its vitality more than climate," and he strikes a more pessimistic, alarmist note than the assumption concerning stationary racial divides, arguing that the day will come when the globe is

> girdled with a continuous zone of the black and yellow races, no longer too weak for aggression or under tutelage, but independent, or practically so.... The citizens of these countries will then be taken up into the social relations of the white races, will throng the English turf, or the salons of Paris, and will be admitted to intermarriage. It is idle to say, that if all this should come to pass our pride of place will not be humiliated.

As he elaborates on this vision – in something of a Sidgwickian anxiety attack – those who had been struggling "for supremacy in a world which we thought of as destined to belong to the Aryan races and to the Christian faith" will wake up to find themselves "elbowed and hustled, and perhaps even thrust aside by peoples whom we looked down upon as servile, and thought of as bound always to minister to our needs." Against the "solitary consolation" that the changes were "inevitable," he confesses that "in some of us the feeling of caste is so strong that we are not sorry to think we shall have passed away before that day arrives."[72]

No surprise that in Australia Pearson fanned fears of "the Yellow Peril," the Chinese workers who could swamp the white laborers of the country, or that he cited with approval the racist American laws restricting Chinese immigration. As Sidgwick put it, Pearson seemed to envision, and fear, how "the human world would gradually become mainly yellow, with a black band round the tropics, and perhaps an aristocratic film of white on the surface!"[73]

In his contribution to *Charles Henry Pearson: Memorials by Himself, His Wife, and His Friends*, Sidgwick made it all too clear not only that he knew Pearson very well and thought very highly of him, but also that he had long known of his views:

> though I had much interesting talk with him on these subjects, the impression derived there from has become, in the main blended with or obliterated by the impression derived … from his remarkable book on "National Life and Character" … many of the startling conclusions of that book were certainly held by him at the earlier date, though his tendency to pessimistic forecast seemed to me to have grown stronger in the interval.[74]

Of the book, Sidgwick had written to Pearson:

> I am much obliged to you for sending me your book which I am reading with much interest. When I find myself too depressed by it, I console myself by thinking that sociology is not yet an exact science, so that the powers of prediction possessed by the wisest intellect are limited. / I am glad to see that the reviews are giving you justice – so far as I see them.[75]

Sidgwick's own review primarily objected to the underdeveloped state of the social sciences, while remaining perversely silent on issues of race; he devoted half the review to skewering a different book.

Whatever Millian agnosticism Sidgwick may have shared concerning innate racial differences, his agnosticism was apparently broad enough to credit in the strongest terms Pearson's claims about race and national character, and the possibility that greater knowledge in this area would provide deeper cause for concern about the direction of civilization. The sweeping optimism of Comtean positivism, or even of a Herbert Spencer or a Marx, never tempted Sidgwick, and his anxieties about the future of civilization and its possible degeneration were often inflected with Pearsonian thoughts. After all, he did allow that if, regrettably, evidence of racial "debasement" from interracial marriage were forthcoming, then segregation should be maintained, as it should also be in cases where the "inferior races" supplied most of the manual labor.[76] And he insisted that "Civilised nations, so long as they are independent, have to fight; and, in performance of their legitimate business – for it is their legitimate business on utilitarian principles – of civilising the world, they have to commit acts which cannot but be regarded as aggressive by the savage nations whom it is their business to educate and absorb."[77] But, as events demonstrated, this "business" was a very tough sell.

Such views were also voiced by his brother-in-law Balfour. Balfour worried publicly that if cultural advance in Europe "is some day exhausted, who can believe that there remains any external source from which it can be renewed? Where are the untried races competent to construct out of the ruined fragments of our civilisation a new and better habitation for the spirit of man?" His answer was: "They do not exist: and if the world is again to be buried under a barbaric flood, it will not be like that which fertilised, though it first destroyed, the western provinces of Rome, but like that which in Asia submerged for ever the last races of Hellenic culture."[78] Power and prejudice, it seems, came with severe anxiety attacks and no little depression.

Alarmingly enough, Sidgwick's *Elements* simply proceeds from utilitarian assumptions, without revisiting the effort to defend them found in the *Methods*. But if that book represents Sidgwick's take on what utilitarianism means for politics, then the project of decolonizing utilitarianism has its work cut out for it. As previously explained, one aspect of that project simply involves acknowledging historical realities and unlearning the mythic narratives about the progress of liberalism, utilitarian or whatever. There is more to come, of course, but the simple commitment to theorizing, practicing, and teaching utilitarianism in a more historically and politically honest and interdisciplinary way is a basic step in the critical process.

The Upshot

> The emphasis on colorblindness without addressing the inherited impacts of structural and systemic racisms just reiterates what critical race analysts … have been calling out as "raceless racisms" for the past twenty-five years. (David Theo Goldberg, *The War on Critical Race Theory*)

These snapshots of the canonical utilitarian patriarchs have been deliberately schizoid, switching from a softer light to a harsher one for purposes of interrogation on matters of utilitarianism and empire. The contrasts reflect with surprising accuracy the different academic constituencies engaged with these figures, the admiring ethicists working to repair versus the anti- and postcolonial decolonizing critics working to displace. The aim here is to keep both sides in view, and to determine what survives the critical process.

The emphasis has mostly been on an admittedly narrow cast of characters. This is in part because, for all the admirable feminist philosophers and radicals from Wollstonecraft to Harriet Taylor Mill, women, with the possible exception of Queen Victoria, played a lesser role in the very gendered, "manly" enterprise of building and enforcing Greater Britain. Besides, the purpose here is to take the very figures highlighted in the all too exclusionary canons and problematize them, after giving them all they deserve by way of charity in interpretation. Many lesser-known figures could have made an appearance here, from Thomas Cooper, the American utilitarian who defended slavery, to Michael Macmillan, whose 1890 book *Promotion of General Happiness* took the forms of racism to be found in Mill and Sidgwick and made them more explicit and dogmatic. There is an enormous amount to be learned from analyzing such figures, by way of larger historical context and just how often utilitarianism has gone insanely wrong, but within the realms of academic philosophy they are too often and easily dismissed as not representing utilitarianism at its best. The sketches given above, however, should leave little doubt that, if this is utilitarianism at its best, then there is a lot of reparative apologizing and decolonizing to do with respect to utilitarianism and the ideological purposes to which it has been put, including more recent ones.

Hopefully, however, the internal, dialectical conflicts and incoherencies to be found in this company of classical utilitarians also open up possibilities for constructive critique, for demonstrating how even in their times and places there were alternative possibilities and options that were or were not understood or explored, for better or worse (or no) reasons, in ways that can teach us more about just what current utilitarians are trying to reconstruct or deconstruct when it comes to the classical utilitarians. Simple historical accuracy can be a very painful thing, disconcerting to those invested in mythic histories that erase the violence and domination that brought their world into being. But there is no going back.

Much could be inserted at this point about the problems of an increasingly professionalized Eurocentric, Anglo-American academic philosophy over the course of the twentieth century, how ethical and political philosophy sank from sight during the reign of logical positivism and other analytical philosophical orientations, or how the cult of Wittgenstein and ordinary language shrank the world, or how the Continental successors to Nietzsche yielded the Nazi Heidegger, or how things took a radical turn in the 1960s. There were bright spots, of course, but the overall story was and is, as Charles Mills famously complained, one of "blinding whiteness," and ideology presenting itself as expertise, richly deserving of all the radical scorn heaped on it by anti-establishment social movements. Whether in philosophy departments or economics departments, medical schools or law schools, the order of things was in fact set by male, often WASP-ish whiteness, and a familiar clubbiness or old boys' network, the effects of which are still being felt, as with the reign of Gilbert Ryle at Oxford. It is perhaps no surprise that Sidgwick's *Elements* remained in the Cambridge University curriculum well into the twentieth century. But not in academic philosophy, which for the most part followed the example of G. E. Moore and studiously dispensed with any serious effort to come to terms with the unsavory side of its ethical and political past through patterns of departmentalization and canonization that made ignorance and evasion easy. And, more generally, as Olivette Otele demonstrates:

> The absence of black stories in most British history books prior to the Second World War sheds some light on the question of racism by omission. Utilitarian views on the usefulness of imperial subjects and black and brown bodies demonstrate that they were not seen as part of the national experience. They were useful, and then they were forgotten. One could argue that given the low number of black Britons, they were likely to be excluded from grand narratives. Yet one could also argue that there was a relatively low number of white Britons in comparison to indigenous populations across the British Empire, and yet their stories have been widely researched and shared.

> The historical amnesia of these omissions is in fact a blanket which hides a history of violence.[79]

Witness the silences noted in the previous chapters, and in this one. Silences, even as the elite institutions of higher education grew ever more steadily into support systems for white supremacy and empire. As Symonds contended, in the case of Oxford, the ample funds from Cecil Rhodes and the army of Rhodes Scholars they supported, along with institutions such as the Round Table, went far to help Oxford continue the work, if not the formal organization, of the Imperial Federation League of the 1880s into the twentieth century.[80]

And, of course, as Dipesh Chakrabarty and many others have insisted, as the twentieth century unfolded, across much of the world the peoples in the "waiting room of history" opted to throw off the Millian and Sidgwickian strictures about the unreadiness of peasants for self-rule,[81] though it was not until the 1960s that Anglo-American academic philosophers actually started wondering if they themselves might learn something from such events.

For present purposes, however, and to move the story along, consider the ways in which classical utilitarianism was continued in, or revived in, certain English-language academic contexts – spottily at first, but picking up with the early work of the Australian philosopher J. J. C. Smart and the extensive defenses from Richard Brandt, John Harsanyi, and other familiar names, before launching more rapidly with the work of Peter Singer and his early mentors R. M. Hare, James Griffin, Jonathan Glover, and of course Parfit, though these figures were more guarded in their defenses than Singer.[82]

The overarching themes of these early works had everything to do with utilitarianism as against deontological, rights-based ethical frameworks, debates over act versus rule utilitarianism, reconstructions in terms of preference satisfaction accounts of the good or well-being, or game theory, and lots and lots of contrived puzzle cases and dilemmas, from burning palaces to lifeboat survival tactics, to supposedly felicific lynchings or executions, though Smart had been quite prescient in bringing in issues related to biological engineering, future generations, and factory farms. They had, in ways reflective of the currents of academic fashion and the hostility to the history of philosophy that positivism left in its wake, almost nothing to do with even a marginal historical awareness of the actual views and contexts of the classical utilitarians, and/or anything having to do with settler colonialism, colonialism, and imperialism, which was left in the abstract, as with Williams on Government House utilitarianism.

Recalling Mulgan's ideal outlook utilitarianism, one could say that these years set the format for the general answer to the question of how to teach utilitarianism to the next generation – namely, by cultivating political amnesia about its checkered historical record. Focusing on private ethics and concocted puzzle cases made this easy as well as fun.

It was above all with the practical ethics of the early Peter Singer that something closer to classical utilitarianism found a champion capable of speaking to both academic audiences and a broader, indeed global, public, much like the Philosophical Radicals of old, whose work he treated with a respectful yet astute historical awareness informed by a wide philosophical diet that included Hegel and Marx. For purposes of understanding what a serious return to classical utilitarianism looks like today, but with more open, decolonizing possibilities, the work of Singer is the obvious starting point and surprisingly fertile ground. It is precisely because of the many strengths of Singer's claims that he is singled out here as playing a pivotal role in the transition from the work of the classical utilitarian patriarchs to that of their admirers today, and the opportunities afforded for a decolonizing approach.

An Australian, Singer was educated at Melbourne University, where he was converted to utilitarianism by the anti-utilitarian arguments of his teacher H. J. McCloskey. He continued his education at Oxford, where he was strongly influenced by such fellow students and friends as Richard Keshen, and Stanley and Roslind Godlovitch, who first sparked his interest in vegetarianism and animal liberation, and by Parfit, Glover, and, above all, Hare, who supervised his work and persuaded him to accept universal prescriptivism, the view that moral judgments are not cognitive or descriptive statements but rather prescriptions, though made from a universal point of view. Metaethically, Singer for decades defended Hare's prescriptivist (and noncognitivist) interpretation of how the beginning of ethical thought comes with the language of universalizability:

> essentially that a moral judgment cannot be based on individual properties, such as proper names or personal pronouns. If I think that it is wrong for you to cheat on your taxes, then I must also hold that if I am in similar circumstances, it would be wrong for me to cheat on my taxes. I cannot claim that because it is I who benefit when I cheat on my taxes, the cases are different.[83]

Singer is certainly one of the most influential and prolific philosophers and public intellectuals of the last half-century, having been a key figure in launching the global animal liberation movement, establishing the field of practical or applied ethics (especially bioethics), advancing the Australian Green Party, and directing attention to crucial issues of global justice and world poverty. Possessed of an uncanny talent for exposing the incoherencies of traditional Judeo-Christian morality, he has challenged the basic conceptions of moral personhood, dignity, and duty cherished by most non-utilitarian ethicists, religious or secular. As noted, his philosophical hero is none other than Sidgwick, to whom he has steadily grown ever more philosophically indebted, despite their profound differences over the significance of religion and belief in an afterlife (not to mention parapsychology).

Many aspects of Singer's utilitarianism have stayed remarkably consistent, despite changes in his metaethics and view of the good. Indeed, he denies that there is anything extraordinary about the basic premises of the thinking that has led him to challenge so much of traditional morality. In addition to the factual premise that "humans are not the only beings capable of feeling pain, or of suffering," the following three moral premises have frequently served as the ground for even his most controversial positions:

1. Pain is bad, and similar amounts of pain are equally bad, no matter whose pain it might be.
2. The seriousness of taking a life depends, not on the race, sex, or species of the being killed, but on its individual characteristics, such as its own desires about continuing to live or the kind of life it is capable of leading.
3. We should consider ourselves responsible both for what we do, and for what we refrain from doing.[84]

From this modest basis, initially fleshed out in the terms of preference utilitarianism rather than the classical hedonistic utilitarianism he now favors, he has developed arguments to show the moral irrelevance (or, at best, derivative value) of national boundaries, of species boundaries, and of traditional views of the sacredness of life. Thus, to use one of his chief examples, if one were walking by a shallow pond and noticed a small child apparently drowning, and if one could rescue the child at little cost, getting a bit muddy, then surely rescuing the child would be the right thing to do.[85] From this homely example, which is in fact in line with the "Good Samaritan" laws adopted in various legal systems, Singer develops his case that aiding desperate individuals across the globe is a precisely parallel situation ethically, despite the various informational and strategic issues that might make it seem quite different. Globally, some 22,000–24,000 children die daily as a result of preventable poverty-related causes. Failing to save lives in distant places by, say, giving to the Against Malaria Foundation is no different from walking by the drowning child. Although, given the pervasiveness of the notion in commonsense morality, some distinction might be made, for utilitarian purposes, between killing and letting die, this should have much less force than deontological approaches to ethics suggest. Even if we allow some difference in the appropriate degrees of censure or punishment attached to acting versus omitting to act, the salient moral point is that the consequence is an unnecessary death, and the world in general would be a happier place if people did not absolve themselves of responsibility on the ground that they did not throw the child in the pond, produce famines in distant lands, and so on.[86]

Relatedly, Singer has been remarkably consistent in his detestation of Rawls's theory of justice as fairness: "When I first read this book [*A Theory of Justice*], shortly after its publication in 1971, I was astonished that a book with that title, nearly 600 pages long, could utterly fail to discuss the injustice of the extremes of wealth and poverty that exist between different societies." Rawls's work, early and late, "remains firmly based on the idea that the unit for deciding what is just remains something like today's nation-state. Rawls's model is that of an international order, not a global order."[87] Part of the problem, Singer claims, is the way in which Rawls's method of reflective equilibrium credits ordinary intuitions that should carry no epistemic weight whatsoever.

A bigger problem would seem to be the way Rawls's vision really was a descendant of a Kantian cosmopolitan vision of a world order of nations dominated by a Eurocentric philosophy and legal order, and still giving too much credit to patriotism. For Singer, an excess of partial attachment to one's own nation and fellow citizens, such that their plight always takes priority, is as indefensible as a racist attachment to one's own race or a sexist attachment to one's own gender. He argues that, although some partial attachments can, within limits, be justified from an impartial point of view – for example, attachments to friends and family – many partial attachments are profoundly suspect and morally arbitrary, especially in an interconnected world headed for environmental crisis. A US citizen who helps the relatively affluent poor in the US, or who ignores the impact the US has on global climate change, on the ground that fellow Americans come first, is demonstrating a lethal prejudice rather than the type of humanity that figures in any plausible utilitarian approach.

The upshot of Singer's argument is that individual citizens across the globe, but especially in the more affluent countries, ought to be contributing much more to the relief of severe suffering, either through direct individual giving to effective anti-poverty and other aid organizations, or through the creation and support of effective, global institutional structures for eliminating severe suffering. Singer has been making this argument ever since his seminal 1972 article "Famine, Affluence, and Morality," and it has increasingly come to the fore in his activist efforts, especially with the publication of *The Life You Can Save*, and the consequent Effective Altruism (EA) movement.[88] Even Singer's more Rawlsian opponents give him credit for making a very powerful case.[89]

Parallel arguments figure in Singer's case for animal liberation, which he debuted in 1973 in the *New York Review of Books*.[90] The contributors to the work he reviewed were, he claimed, launching a new liberation movement, demanding "that we cease to regard the exploitation of other species as natural and inevitable, and that, instead, we see it as a continuing moral outrage." He made the case at length shortly thereafter, with the book *Animal Liberation* in 1975, a work that became the manifesto of the movement, inspiring such organizations as People for the Ethical Treatment of Animals.[91] In essence, the point was that "speciesism" was not unlike racism or nationalism or any other unjustifiable, morally arbitrary boundary condition underwriting prejudicial treatment.

To be sure, this did not entail that non-human animals and human ones ought always to be accorded equal or similar treatment, or that all lives were of equal worth:

> While self-awareness, the capacity to think ahead and have hopes and aspirations for the future, the capacity for meaningful relations with others and so on are not relevant to the question of inflicting pain – since pain is pain, whatever other capacities, beyond the capacity to feel pain, the being may have – these capacities are relevant to the questions of taking life. It is not arbitrary to hold that the life of a self-aware being, capable of abstract thought, of planning for the future, of complex acts of communication, and so on, is more valuable than the life of a being without these capacities. To see the difference between the issues of inflicting pain and taking life, consider how we would choose within our own species. If we had to choose to save the life of a normal human being or an intellectually disabled human being, we would probably choose to save the life of a normal human being; but if we had to choose between preventing pain in the normal human being or the

> intellectually disabled one ... it is not nearly so clear how we ought to choose.[92]

Thus, by virtue of their capacities for pleasure and pain, non-human animals have moral standing, and some non-human animals, such as the great apes or dolphins, might share human capabilities in ethically relevant ways, might be "persons" – that is, rational and self-aware beings, taking the life of which would be especially serious, given their preferences for continued existence. For example, Singer has helped advance the Great Ape Project, which calls for extending the "community of equals" to the great apes, guaranteeing at the least their rights to life, liberty, and freedom from torture. Of course, on Singer's utilitarian account, unlike that of rights-based approaches to animal liberation, non-human animal rights, like human rights, have a derivative, utilitarian justification. And in good utilitarian fashion he believes in the possible justifiability of civil disobedience – his first book, based on his Oxford thesis, was *Democracy and Disobedience*.[93] He has urged that the movement follow the examples of Gandhi and Martin Luther King, Jr. in adopting a non-violent approach to protesting such things as factory farming and animal experimentation and testing.

Already evident in Singer's arguments regarding animal liberation were many of the considerations that he would bring to the field of bioethics, where, he holds, claims about the sanctity and sacredness of human life are mostly both hypocritical and inimical to societal well-being. *Rethinking Life and Death: The Collapse of Our Traditional Ethics* challenged traditional morality with something close to Bentham's vigorous acrimony. Singer even frames a set of alternative basic commandments. Thus, instead of "treat all human life as of equal worth," he would urge "recognize that the worth of human life varies," the better to avoid the costly absurdity of prolonging the life of individuals in, for example, persistent vegetative states. "Never intentionally take innocent human life," would be replaced by "take responsibility for the consequences of your decisions," even if these are simply foreseen rather than intended. "Never take your own life" would give way to "respect a person's desire to live or die," and "be fruitful and multiply" should be rejected in favor of "bring children into the world only if they are wanted." And, of course, rather than holding that we should "treat all human life as always more precious than non-human life," we should refrain from discriminating on "the basis of species."[94]

No doubt it is Singer's willingness to demonstrate just how important his philosophical arguments are to public policy and everyday life, to the decisions that are made every day in hospitals and research facilities across the world, that has generated the at times intensely hostile reaction to him. In *Rethinking Life and Death* and *Should the Baby Live?* (with Helga Kuhse), he defended the justifiability of not only euthanasia and abortion, but also infanticide in cases of severe disability, and this has made him the target of protests by such groups as Not Dead Yet. But his careful arguments against the inconsistency, hypocrisy, and presumption of a medical profession that would inflict sustained suffering on, for example, spina bifida infants in the name of allowing nature to "take its course," rather than allowing parents to opt to end the life that would soon, after greater suffering, be ended anyway, were scarcely recognizable in the charges of his critics.

Beyond these important contributions, Singer has steadily rethought and reworked his metaethical commitments and claims about human nature. He has long sought to develop his arguments in line with the latest research in sociobiology and other fields, defining what he calls a "Darwinian Left." In *The Expanding Circle: Ethics, Evolution and Moral Progress*, he argued that

> our ability to reason developed because it conferred advantages on us, but reason is like an escalator, in the sense that once you step on it, it carries you onwards, whether or not you wish to go to the end. Some elements of our ethics – especially ideas of impartiality and equality – may therefore be the outcome of our reasoning capacities and hence less directly under the influence of our genes than more emotional or intuitive responses.[95]

And it was in the second edition of *The Expanding Circle* that Singer made official what he had been hinting at for a number of years: namely, that he had abandoned the noncognitivist metaethic imbibed from Hare in favor of the nonmetaphysical moral rationalism defended at length in Parfit's *On What Matters*. Put precisely, the "judgement that 'one's own interests are one among many sets of interests' can be accepted as a descriptive claim about our situation in the world, but to add that one's own interests are 'no more important than the similar interests of others' is to make a normative claim. If I deny that normative claims can be true or false, then I cannot assert that this claim is true."[96] But on Parfit's account:

> Unless we are to fall into skepticism about knowledge as well as skepticism about ethics, we must accept that there are normative truths about what we have reason to believe, as well as about

> what we have reason to want, and reason to do. Consider, for example, the statement: "When we know that some argument is valid, and has true premises, we have decisive reasons to accept this argument's conclusion" … That statement, Parfit argues, is neither a tautology nor an empirical truth. It is a true normative statement about what we have reason to believe."[97]

Parfit's work is, for Singer, "a worthy successor" to Sidgwick's *Methods of Ethics*. Indeed, it is now roundly accepted that Sidgwick's brand of non-naturalistic and non-reductive, but also non-metaphysical and non-ontological, fallibilistic metaethical cognitivism has been given a brilliant makeover in Parfit's *On What Matters*.[98] And Singer's foundational work with Katarzyna de Lazari-Radek, *The Point of View of the Universe: Sidgwick & Contemporary Ethics*, mobilizes Parfit's account of objective irreducible normative reasons in an even more ambitious effort to defend, as Parfit did not, a Sidgwickian hedonistic utilitarianism, through the evolutionary debunking of the alternatives. Singer had always done much to carry on Sidgwick's legacy even before his metaethical change of heart, but with *The Point of View of the Universe* and *Does Anything Really Matter?* he has expressly foregrounded Sidgwickian metaethics.[99]

It is not surprising that Singer's utilitarian ethics and politics could remain fairly constant, despite dramatic changes in his metaethics. People have often come to a utilitarian outlook via very different metaethical and metaphysical worldviews. But the point of this review of his work is to explore fissures in his ongoing arguments allowing for a more decolonizing approach. Singer, like Sidgwick, has often introduced critical considerations that might take one in a different direction, away from the legacy of empire, rather than in perpetuation of it.

Consider how Singer often introduces Sidgwick on impartiality. Addressing the issue of how the popular view that "we may or even should favor those of 'our own kind' conceals a deep disagreement about who our own kind are," he introduces this passage from the *Methods*:

> We should all agree that each of us is bound to show kindness to his parents and spouse and children, and to other kinsmen in a less degree: and to those who have rendered services to him, and any others whom he may have admitted to his intimacy and called friends: and to neighbors and to fellow-countrymen more than others: and perhaps we may say to those of our own race

> more than to black or yellow men, and generally to human beings in proportion to their affinity to ourselves.[100]

He continues by provocatively bringing in Heinrich Himmler's confession that "Whether the other races live in comfort or perish of hunger interests me only in so far as we need them as slaves for our culture; apart from that they do not interest me."

Singer's purpose, of course, is to open up an examination of just which partial or special attachments might be justifiable from an impartial utilitarian point of view, Sidgwick's Point of View of the Universe, and he suggests that these examples should subvert the belief that it is "self-evident that we have special obligations to those nearer to us." He then proceeds to introduce the drowning child case, arguing how by extension it demonstrates our "obligation to help strangers in distant lands" and that the mere fact of distance should not matter in considering an obligation to aid. From there, he goes on to consider Godwin's burning palace dilemma and later softening of his at first severely impartialist effort to dispel the "magic in the pronoun 'my'" (Singer has long recognized the importance of Godwin and Wollstonecraft). He then introduces another constant in his approach, namely Hare's two-level theory:

> To guide our everyday conduct we need a set of principles of which we are aware without a lot of reflection. These principles form the intuitive, or everyday, level of morality. In a calmer or more philosophical moment, on the other hand, we can reflect on the nature of our moral intuitions and ask whether we have developed the right ones, that is, the ones that will lead to the greatest good, impartially considered. When we engage in this reflection, we are moving to the critical level of morality which informs our thinking about what principles we should follow at the everyday level. Thus the critical level serves as a testing ground for moral intuitions.[101]

With this critical perspective, Godwin's rethinking can be reaffirmed:

> Given the unavoidable constraints of human nature and the importance of bringing children up in loving homes, there is an impartial justification for approving of social practices that presuppose that parents will show some degree of partiality toward their children.
>
> It is even easier to find an impartial reason for accepting love and friendship. If loving relationships and relationships of

> friendship are necessarily partial, they are also, for most people, at the core of anything that can approximate to a good life. Very few human beings can live happy, fulfilled lives without being attached to particular other human beings. To suppress these partial affections would destroy something of great value and therefore cannot be justified from an impartial perspective.[102]

Hence the retort to Bernard Williams, to the effect that, if there are times when the problem is having one thought too many, there are also times when the problem is having one thought too few, and no matter how widely shared or deeply held, say, racist convictions might be, they are subject to critique because they cannot be justified from an impartial utilitarian point of view, which in Singer's hands is informed by relevant evidence from evolutionary biology, psychology, etc.

What is more, Singer, with de Lazari-Radek, offers a robust defense of Sidgwick on how an esoteric morality might possibly be justified on utilitarian grounds, thus rejecting the demand, common to Kant, Rawls, and many others, that moral rules or principles must meet a publicity condition to be counted as moral at all. Following Parfit, they maintain that a self-effacing theory is not necessarily a self-defeating one, or incompatible with being true. Following Toby Ord, they agree that the "requirement that 'thought in the world' *is* conducted in such a way as to lead to the best outcome is a way of determining how it is conducted," even if everyone is deploying a decision procedure such that they follow public moral rules that are non-utilitarian, at least in the small. For global utilitarians, especially, everything is up for assessment in terms of consequences – decision procedures, acts, rules, character, etc. – and Singer and de Lazari-Radek agree that decision procedures are subject to such considerations, given how the number of felicific acts in the long-run strategy needs to be considered in such a connection, not simply one-off acts. Finally, they agree with Parfit that it is unrealistic to suppose that utilitarianism – or rather, consequentialism generally – could insist that "no one would try to act in accordance with its criterion of rightness," and that at most utilitarianism might be partly self-effacing. Sidgwick was correct in thinking that utilitarianism might lead to recommending an esoteric morality, and that fact might in itself best be kept secret.[103] But realistically, it is important on utilitarian grounds to consider the benefits of a shared public code and open discussion, and to recognize the potential dangers of elitism in this connection – if not Government House paternalism, perhaps other forms of exploitative hierarchy.

But the case for an impartial defense of partial attachments, and this extending perhaps even to a more or less esoteric utilitarian morality, opens up many questions. As Singer runs through Sidgwick's list of candidate partialities, considering what does or does not pass impartial muster, he recognizes that considerable flexibility is called for in the case of kinship relations. Consider:

> Kin networks can be important sources of love, friendship, and mutual support, and then they will generate impartially justifiable reasons for promoting these goods. But if that cousin you have not heard from in decades suddenly asks for a loan because she wants to buy a new house, is there an impartially defensible ground for believing you are under a greater obligation to help her than you would be to help an unrelated, equally distant acquaintance? At first glance, no, but perhaps a better answer is that it depends on whether there is a recognized system of cooperation among relatives. In rural areas of India, for example, such relationships between relatives can play an important role in providing assistance when needed and thus in reducing harm when something goes awry. Under these circumstances there is an impartial reason for recognizing and supporting this practice. In the absence of any such system, there is not. (In different cultures, the more impersonal insurance policy plays the same harm-reduction role and thus reduces the need for a system of special obligations to kin, no doubt with both good and bad effects.)[104]

Such a line of argument, only sketched by Singer, calls for a much fuller range of empirical and historical evidence. Of course, Singer's treatment of nationalism and patriotism is appropriately harsher, and he argues that we "should reject racist immigration policies, for the same reason that we should reject racism. Neither race nor ethnicity should be a requirement for citizenship … Citizenship and kinship are distinct." And the notion of reciprocity is not terribly plausible as a rationale for favoring fellow citizens either. Invoking Benedict Anderson on "imagined communities," Singer allows that if

> Anderson is right, and the modern idea of the nation rests on a community we imagine ourselves to be part of rather than one that we really are part of, then it is also possible for us to imagine ourselves to be part of a different community. That fits well with the view I have defended … the complex set of developments we

> refer to as globalization should lead us to reconsider the moral significance we currently place on national boundaries. We need to ask whether it will, in the long run, be better if we continue to live in the imagined communities we know as nation-states or if we become more open to the idea that we are members of an imagined community of the world.... Our problems are now too intertwined to be well resolved in a system consisting of nation-states, in which citizens give their primary, near-exclusive loyalty to their own nation-state rather than to the larger global community.[105]

There is much open to question here, about the contours of political community and the justifiable role of kinship. Obviously, Singer is no relativist, moral or conceptual. He does not say much about the history or culture of imperialism, but what he does say sounds unapologetic:

> Acts of the kind carried out by Nazi Germany against Jews, Gypsies, and homosexuals, by the Khmer Rouge against Cambodians they considered to be their class enemies, by Hutus against Tutsis in Rwanda, and by cultures that practice female genital mutilation or forbid the education of women are not elements of a distinct culture that are worth preserving, and it is not imperialist to say that they lack the elements of consideration for others that is required of any justifiable ethic.[106]

What does Singer mean by "imperialist" then? He never delves into the actual history of utilitarianism and empire in any historical detail, though his politics are anti-racist and anti-sexist (he has always supported women in philosophy), as well as anti-speciesist. Certainly, he sides with the resistance movements to twentieth-century colonialism, settler colonialism, and imperialism. Though not an absolute pacifist, he strongly leans that way, and he has carried the utilitarian case for animal liberation and veganism further than any previous utilitarian, tying it to climate politics as well. Moreover, he has been exemplary in insisting that there were non-Western utilitarians long before there were Western ones, typically singling out the ancient Chinese philosopher Mozi as a case in point. In other work, including important forthcoming work, he has engaged in an illuminating dialogue with Buddhist philosophers about the possible filiations with utilitarianism.[107] There is a lot to admire in all this.

But with his analysis of the failings of the international system of nation-states, his sketch of the open justificatory horizons for kinship networks, his defense of the impartial justification of partial attachments – even to a possibly esoteric degree – and his recognition of the significance of non-Eurocentric, non-Anglo-American approaches to utilitarianism, he has opened the door to a more thoroughgoing critical decolonizing project. For all we know, it may no longer be utilitarian to invoke the model of Western utilitarianism, or at least to center it in the way that it has been centered. And if, to recall Mulgan's ideal outlook utilitarianism, it is indeed an open question how to teach utilitarianism to the next generation, and what the effects of teaching it in the familiar ways might be, then a dilemma forces itself on us – how can one actually pronounce on such matters as how self-effacing utilitarianism should be without considering all the evidence from its past as well as its present and likely future? Obviously, an impartial assessment would require considering the consequences of utilitarianism's problematic past, and how it might be perceived by peoples who have suffered from that past. The alternative of maintaining that the world will be made better by continuing to downplay, hide, or obscure that past seems both false and utterly unrealistic, even more so than Sidgwick's position on the value of deploying evasive tactics with regard to the truth of religion.

And really, when it comes to insisting that "it is unrealistic to suppose that utilitarianism, or rather consequentialism generally, could insist that 'no one would try to act in accordance with its criterion of rightness,' and that at most utilitarianism might be partly self-effacing,"[108] the affirmations seem more like matters of faith than of evidence. How could they not, when so much of the relevant evidence is being ignored or erased? We need only take Singer at his word about the utilitarian importance of considering the consequences of teaching and practicing utilitarianism in one way or another to be directed to the histories considered earlier and the issue of decolonization. Utilitarianism, and consequentialism in general, could potentially be especially good at reflexive critique, at their own critical self-interrogation, as a matter of addressing the very problems they seek to solve. The most enduring epistemological parts of Sidgwick's work have to do with his self-doubts and epistemic humility, not with his quest for certainty as an individual knower. Coherence, consensus, and certainty were for him aspirations for ethics, with the first two often compromising the third.

Perhaps Singer and de Lazari-Radek might update and adapt one more thought from Sidgwick, who, in his 1898 collection of essays on *Practical Ethics*, would lament (albeit in gendered terms) that if

> we are to frame an ideal of good life for all … we can only do this by a comprehensive and varied knowledge of the actual opportunities and limitations…. And this knowledge a philosopher – whose personal experience is often very limited – cannot adequately attain unless he earnestly avails himself of opportunities of learning from the experience of men of other callings. But … even supposing him to have used these opportunities to the full, the philosopher's practical judgement on particular problems of duty is liable to be untrustworthy, unless it is aided and controlled by the practical judgement of others who are not philosophers.[109]

Such concerns, read in connection with the dialogical, communicative demands of achieving a coherent consensus of experts as set out in Sidgwick's criteria, might well seem to support a drive to derive light from a great many other minds, as incorporated in today's academic attempts to achieve greater diversity, equity, and inclusion, given that "expertise" can be a very widely dispersed thing and perhaps only confidently achieved through political educational processes informed by a much wider and richer range of experiences, including those born of struggle.

4

Different Places, Different Voices, Different Virtues

> Mainstream political philosophy textbooks sanitize and mystify the actual record of the past few hundred years by constructing the West as if white racial domination had not been central to the history of the West. We go from Plato to Rawls without a word being uttered about the racist views of the leading modern Western political theorists and the role of these views in justifying Western political domination over the rest of the World. Acknowledging the racial exclusions in these thinkers' ideologies provides a far more honest and illuminating political framework, since it unites the anti-feudal (white) politics of the standard narrative of modernity with the 'other' (nonwhite) politics of the alternative narrative of modernity: the anti-colonial, anti-slavery, anti-imperialist, and anti-segregationist struggles of people of color against racialized liberalism and for the recognition of equal nonwhite personhood. They can be discussed together rather than in separate Jim-Crowed conceptual spaces. (Charles W. Mills, *Black Rights/White Wrongs*)[1]

The above passage first appeared in Mills's 2005 essay "Kant's *Untermenschen*," and it was reprinted without change in his 2017 book *Black Rights/White Wrongs*, which analyzes how white ignorance "has been able to flourish all these years because a white epistemology of ignorance has safeguarded it against the dangers of an illuminating blackness or redness, protecting those who for 'racial' reasons have needed not to know."[2]

Mills's critique obviously applies to the classical utilitarian philosophers, though he himself mostly called out the racism pervading the social contract tradition, from its beginnings to Rawls and beyond. His *The Racial Contract*, from 1997, made the case, and he continued to make the case until his death, too soon, in 2021. His late work acknowledged how there were changes for the better, but even shortly before his death he observed that, at meetings of the American Philosophical Association, "you have to put on dark glasses, or else you'll get snow blindedness from the expanse of white faces."[3] He had not compromised his belief that "White supremacy is the unnamed political system that has made the modern world what it is today," or that there is a pervasive epistemology of ignorance, "the learned aversion of white people to the racism inherent in their own privilege."[4]

Mills rarely mentioned Sidgwick, but the critique presented here resonates with his approach, though the utilitarian side of the story suggests different cautionary lessons for today – not only how systemic racism and other injustices have been and are perpetuated by the academic epistemology of ignorance contorting the teaching of classical utilitarianism, but also how a decolonized utilitarian critical theory might emerge from all the critique, aligning with projects like The Red Deal, the Indigenous Environmental Network, or Amazon Frontlines, rather than the neoliberal orders they oppose. The more implosive parts of the outlook developed by de Lazari-Radek and Singer might hint at what needs to be done, what epistemologies of ignorance, what affirmations and forgettings, are playing against the decolonization of utilitarianism. The danger of continuing the hubristic overreach of the nineteenth-century figures is an obvious concern, along with a too limited awareness of the significance of racism and the violence of capitalism, or of the how and why of movements resisting such forces. Where are the academic utilitarians in all those environmental movements working "from the ground up" rather than from the blindingly white top down? For some environmental activists, the East India Company has, among its offspring, groups such as The Nature Conservancy and big philanthropy.

Different directions are possible, inspired in part by the combined force of Godwin's thoughts on the violence of states and the value of relationships, Bentham's on non-anthropocentrism, John Mill's on pursuing happiness by putting it out of our minds, and Sidgwick's speculation that the same might go for utilitarianism itself. Why not look to a wider world of experiments in living, alternative decision procedures and virtues, different visions of kinship (less fixated on the bourgeois nuclear family), critical theories of happiness, economies of care and gifting, anarchist or abolitionist perspectives on the state and policing, emergent strategies for decentralized movement building, more radically anti-anthropocentric outlooks, and the cultural formations that the long history of liberalism seeks to erase? The Iroquois

Confederacy was much better at practicing democracy and freedom than ancient Athens, but its contributions do not figure in the canons of Western Civ courses in anything like the manner of the latter. And as Graeber and Wengrow ask in *The Dawn of Everything*, which incorporates a sharp critique of Steven Pinker's *The Better Angels of Our Nature*:

> why then insist that all significant forms of human progress before the twentieth century can be attributed only to that one group of humans who used to refer to themselves as "the white race" (and now, generally, call themselves by its more accepted synonym, "Western civilization")? There is simply no reason to make this move. It would be just as easy (actually, rather easier) to identify things that can be interpreted as the first stirrings of rationalism, legality, deliberative democracy and so forth all over the world, and only then tell the story of how they coalesced into the current global system.[5]

Perhaps Godwin would have admired Graeber and Wengrow's history, which is consistently supportive of anarchist beliefs, and among other things makes the following point, helpful for thinking about Singer's famous child drowning in a pond example:

> there's another way to use the word "communism"; not as a property regime but in the original sense of "from each according to their abilities, to each according to their needs". There's also a certain minimal, "baseline" communism which applies in all societies; a feeling that if another person's needs are great enough (say, they are drowning), and the cost of meeting them is modest enough (say, they are asking for you to throw them a rope), then of course any decent person would comply. Baseline communism of this sort could even be considered the very grounds of human sociability, since it is only one's bitter enemies who would not be treated this way. What varies is just how far it is felt such baseline communism should properly extend.[6]

The argument continues with a brilliant account of how the supposed traveler's tales of Baron de la Hontan, featuring the Native American character "Adario," were probably based on the life of Kandiaronk, a statesman of the Wendat known for his oratorical skills, who had in fact visited Europe. In Lahontan's work, thanks to Kandiaronk, there are "all the familiar criticisms of European society that the earliest missionaries had to contend with – the squabbling, the lack of mutual aid, the blind submission to authority – but with a new element added in: the organization of private property." On Lahontan's candid account: "They think it unaccountable that one man should have more than another, and that the rich should have more respect than the poor. In short, they say, the name of savages, which we bestow upon them, would fit ourselves better, since there is nothing in our actions that bears an appearance of wisdom."[7]

Curious Dialogues with a Savage of Good Sense Who Has Travelled was published in 1703, and although the European perspective is for the most part given the last, very Christian word, and the liberatory gender and sexual practices of the Wendat, which were admirably non-binary and non-coercive or hierarchical, came in for special outrage, it is evident from the text that Kandiaronk was the wisest person in the room, so to speak. Indeed, as Graeber and Wengrow point out, most educated, liberal college students today would enthusiastically side with Kandiaronk, on everything from LGBTQ+ issues, to religion, to marriage, to democracy, and on and on. At that point, Europe was very far from taking "equality" seriously, though in publicly rejecting it there was perhaps less hypocrisy than in the next centuries.

From such anthropological – admittedly, radical anarchist anthropological – research, the broad-band absurdities of the grand narratives of Western liberalism, of the supposed birthing of religious toleration and liberal representative democracy, stand out in frightening relief.[8] The "Doctrine of Discovery," the Inter Caetera, was a Papal Bull issued in 1493 by Pope Alexander VI, and it stated that any land not already inhabited by Christians could be claimed by Christian rulers. But it was widely appropriated and used to facilitate the removal (and genocide) of Indigenous peoples even by non-Catholics, being famously legitimated in the US legal system in the trio of Marshall cases in the 1820s that essentially opened the way to, and legally sanctioned, the forced removal of Native Americans from their traditional homelands. The Catholic Church never repudiated this doctrine until early in 2023, and in practice it can be said that the outlook reflected in the Doctrine of Discovery is not dead, so much as transmuted by changing political and economic structures, such as the reservation system that came about as the result of the displacement and genocide condoned in the application of the Doctrine.[9] There was, contra John Stuart Mill, never anything in the least bit "noble" in the US government's treatment of Native North Americans, or in that of the Canadian government, part of the British Commonwealth.[10]

And the injustices endure. As Estes, Yazzie, Denetdale, and Correia put it, in *Red Nation Rising: From Bordertown Violence to Native Liberation*:

> In the specific context of present-day US bordertowns, Christianity and its ethos of charity still uphold and reproduce the genocidal, racist intent of the Doctrine of Discovery. One need only drive by a church-run soup kitchen setting up in the early morning hours in a place like Gallup, New Mexico, to see a familiar scene: so-called vagrants and transients, in the words of police, streaming in from their encampments to get a bite to eat. Those serving them, usually white churchgoers and volunteers, appear clean and well-dressed – upstanding US citizens. Those seeking food are usually required to participate in conversion activities (also known as proselytizing) to receive the "selfless" charity of the church. They sing for their supper by receiving moral uplift from Christ for their failings. In this scene, there are two classes of people: Indians, who represent the barbarous nations, and white Christians, who do the virtuous work of US nationalism by dutifully spreading Christianity and caretaking the souls of dirty savages.
>
> Bordertowns are thick with churches. Dozens of denominations compete for funding and visibility to do "charity work" for Native people. Their sole function is to distribute charity through philanthropy and social uplift and, in return, collect souls. But mostly what they collect is money. Churches and nonprofits rake in millions of dollars to "help" Native people under the auspices of charity, yet leave in place the inequity and suffering of Native people. Instead, these institutions and organizations (and the people who work for and worship at them) make a living off the misery of Native people. Rather than practicing a genuine form of equality and love, which Native concepts of kinship express, these institutions profit socially, economically, and culturally off the permanent subjugation of Native people. So long as these purveyors of charity maintain a monopoly on resources and power in bordertowns, so too will the colonial relationship between Native peoples and the United States remain intact. Their relevance – indeed, their very existence – is premised on the permanence of US occupation of Native lands – a performance of the Doctrine of Discovery that never ends. Anyone who espouses decolonization must, therefore, address the inherent colonialism of charity and denounce the churches and nonprofits that benefit from it.[11]

These passages from Graeber, Estes et al. do not invoke romanticized notions of the "noble savage" or simpler ways of life "in harmony with the earth." There is, to be sure, an enormous amount to learn from Indigenous peoples and cultures – so much so that there is no need to bury them in myths. There are crucial lessons to be drawn from this complicated area of activist scholarship, which bears so importantly on matters of kinship, reciprocity, resistance, and practices that might challenge the idea that, say, Singer's Effective Altruism, as currently conceived, is the correct way of living the utilitarian life. Given the complexity and diversity – linguistic, cultural, historical, etc. – of Indigenous communities around the world, what follows should be regarded as grounded in specific histories and contexts, rather than a sweeping universalism that would render the term "Indigenous" analogous to the term "Oriental" in obscuring differences in racialized and political ways.[12] The drift shares much with Andrea J. Richie's claims for emergent strategies that "focus on starting small and making space for and learning from uncertainty, multiplicity, experimentation, adaptation, iteration, and decentralization."[13]

But, as with anarchism and same-sex love, utilitarianism is often something that dare not speak its name, or at least might not see the need to.

All Our Relations

In *Braiding Sweetgrass: Indigenous Wisdom, Scientific Knowledge, and the Teachings of Plants*, Robin Wall Kimmerer talks of love:

> No one would doubt that I love my children, and even a quantitative social psychologist would find no fault with my list of loving behaviors:
> *nurturing health and well-being
> *protection from harm
> *encouraging individual growth and development
> *desire to be together
> *generous sharing of resources
> *working together for a common goal
> *celebration of shared values
> *interdependence
> *sacrifice by one for the other
> *creation of beauty
> If we observed these behaviors between humans, we would say "She loves that person."[14]

It is a beautiful list, though, as with utilitarianism, much remains to be filled in when it comes to such things as "health and well-being."

But Kimmerer, an accomplished writer and botanist, and an enrolled member of the Citizen Potawatomi Nation, is not addressing only the human world. She adds that if she acted this way toward a garden, we would say that she loves that garden. But why, then, "would you not make the leap to say that the garden loves her back?"

Kimmerer's book helps us enter our world in a very different way, one of radical reciprocity, kinship, and the gift relationship, with these presented in non-anthropocentric – that is, non-human-centered – ways. For her, "to become native to this place, if we are to survive here, and our neighbors too, our work is to learn to speak the grammar of animacy, so that we might truly be at home." The language of animacy reveals a different world, and is very unlike English, say, in which you are either "a human or a thing." Thus, grammar "boxes us in by the choice of reducing a nonhuman being to an *it*, or it must be gendered, inappropriately, as a *he* or a *she*." But saying "*it* makes a loving land into 'natural resources.' If a maple is an *it*, we can take up the chain saw. If a maple is a *her*, we think twice."[15]

But what if "it" is exchanged for "ki" and the plural form "kin" – a broad pronoun, adapted from the better but longer Potawatomi word "Bemaadiziiaaki," to refer to a being of the living Earth. As Kimmerer explains in another work, these are "revolutionary pronouns" that can help counter the linguistic imperialism, a correlate of settler colonialism, that replaces "the language of nature as subject with the language of nature as object," with consequences we see "all around us as we enter an age of extinction precipitated by how we think and how we live."[16] By contrast, in "Potawatomi and most other indigenous languages, we use the same words to address the living world as we use for our family. Because they are our family."[17]

Consider, for example, the gift relationship with wild strawberries:

> our human relationship with strawberries is transformed by our choice of perspective. It is human perception that makes the world a gift. When we view the world this way, strawberries and humans alike are transformed. The relationship of gratitude and reciprocity thus developed can increase the evolutionary fitness of both plant and animal. A species and a culture that treat the natural world with respect and reciprocity will surely pass on genes to ensuing generations with a higher frequency than the people who destroy it. The stories we choose to shape our behaviors have adaptive consequences.[18]

Kimmerer has heard all the objections, from students complaining that this talk would be anthropomorphizing, unscientific, etc., but she is unfazed. She is a brilliant scientist, and can speak that language as well – the language of a formal training in botany. But she recognizes how important it is to speak more than one language, and derives much support from learning the Potawatomi of her ancestors, a language that, like other Native American languages, is far less noun-centered and affords a grammar of animacy that can reinforce her sense of kinship with a much wider range of beings. The Anishinaabe peoples, including the Potawatomi or Bodewadmi, have far more verbs in their language than nouns, and find active beingness everywhere. But, as with Jane Goodall and her chimpanzees, this improves her science rather than compromising it. New possibilities are opened up:

> I have heard our elders give advice like "You should go among the standing people" [trees] or "Go spend some time with those Beaver people." They remind us of the capacity of others as our teachers, as holders of knowledge, as guides.... We don't have to figure out everything by ourselves: there are intelligences other than our own, teachers all around us. Imagine how much less lonely the world would be.[19]

This is more than a heuristic device, but even as simply that, the value is clear.

To be sure, Kimmerer has a discerning respect for traditional ecological knowledge, while recognizing that the prescriptions for sustainable living often come in the shape of practices and stories – stories, say, of Nanabozho, the Original Man, who so often learns the hard way. Instead of listening to the wise heron, Nanabozho fishes and fishes in a lake until it is overfished, depleted. "When Nanabozho got home to his lodge, he learned a key rule – never take more than you need. The racks of fish were toppled in the dirt and every bite was gone."[20] She seeks to learn from both sources, though she does spend more time worrying and wondering "if much that ails our society stems from the fact that we have allowed ourselves to be cut off from that love of, and from, the land." Like many Native American environmental activists and Indigenous people elsewhere, she does not regard land as a mere commodity or property, so much as an integral part of herself. Land is part of the relationships that form the self. "The currency of a gift economy is, at its root, reciprocity. In Western thinking, private land is understood to be a 'bundle of rights,' whereas in a gift economy property has a 'bundle of responsibilities' attached."[21] More fully,

> The moral covenant of reciprocity calls us to honor our responsibilities for all we have been given, for all that we have taken. It's our turn now, long overdue. Let us hold a giveaway for Mother Earth, spread our blankets out for her and pile them high with gifts of our own making. Imagine the books, the paintings, the poems, the clever machines, the compassionate acts, the transcendent ideas, the perfect tools. The fierce defense of all that has been given. Gifts of mind, hands, heart, voice, and vision all offered up on behalf of the earth. Whatever our gift, we are called to give it and to dance for the renewal of the world.
>
> In return for the privilege of breath.[22]

Kimmerer's words can resonate with the "Land Ethic" of Aldo Leopold, the ethic, famously formulated in *A Sand County Almanac and Sketches Here and There*, which also viewed the Land in a very local bioregional fashion, as a community of which we are a part, not a commodity, not something without moral standing.[23] For Leopold, "we can only be ethical in relation to something we can see, understand, feel, love, or otherwise have faith in." Famously put, "A thing is right when it tends to preserve the integrity, stability, and beauty of the biotic community. It is wrong when it tends otherwise." This was explained as part of a long human history of expanding the circle of ethical concern, with the next needed step being a holistic, ecocentric relationship with Land.[24]

Kimmerer has in fact collaborated with the Leopold-influenced Center for Humans and Nature, co-editing and contributing to the five-volume set on "Kinship." Also contributing to these volumes is the brilliant Potawatomi philosopher Kyle Powys Whyte, who concludes his essay as follows:

> While simple, my final questions suggest the possibility of a society with multiple spheres of kinship that go beyond just our closest family and friends. The level of intimacy varies across relationships, from plants to human neighbors, but we can certainly imagine and practice social relationships where our work, political, religious, and environmental responsibilities embody the qualities of consent and reciprocity – not only with our fellow humans but also with the diverse animacies with whom we share the land.[25]

There is much to admire about Leopold, but his mindset (and forestry background) did reflect a far more Eurocentric perspective than the works of Kimmerer or Whyte, who are not embedded in the racist histories and legacies of the American environmental movement. Lauret Savoy has demonstrated how Leopold's work also has its erasures and exclusions, particularly with respect to women and peoples of color.[26] As with the history of utilitarianism, the nineteenth- and early twentieth-century forms of conservation and environmentalism were entangled in the "scientific racism" and eugenicism of imperialism, with their epistemologies of ignorance. Even such admirable environmental activists as Bill McKibben, with his collection of environmental writings from Thoreau to the present, *American Earth*,[27] studiously avoid diving into or confronting this side of environmentalism, the side that celebrated the triumph of Anglo-Saxon civilization, as with Teddy Roosevelt, who did so much for the National Park system. For *The Red Deal*, "settler state conservation policies stem from 'protecting' slivers of nature by killing and removing Indigenous peoples from the land to create nature reserves, national and state parks, and 'public lands.'"[28]

These points need amplification.

The Limits of Academic Environmentalism and Environmental Philosophy

The racist moral hygiene of these early, conservationist environmental initiatives, which has led to much recent renaming, reached a peak in Madison Grant's *The Passing of the Great Race*.[29] Grant was a pillar of the white establishment, a zoologist and anthropologist as well as a lawyer and friend of Roosevelt and Hoover. He was certainly in his day regarded as a co-founder of the American conservation movement, and he worked energetically to save the redwoods and the bison, to found the Bronx Zoo, and to establish various parks. But in addition to serving on the board of the Museum of Natural History, he was very active with the American Eugenics Society and the Immigration Restriction League. It was Grant who put the Congolese Mbuti man Ota Benga on display at the Bronx Zoo, and who won a great admirer in Adolf Hitler, who confessed to Grant that *The Passing of the Great Race*, with its Nordic supremacism, was his favorite book. Grant and his followers returned the compliment, praising Hitler and his eugenicist programs. As Jonathan Peter Spiro summarizes it, in his comprehensive work on Grant, *Defending the Master Race: Conservation, Eugenics, and the Legacy of Madison Grant*, "the history of the eugenics movement, from its origins with Sir Francis Galton to its flowering under the Big Four in the United States to its apotheosis under the Nazis, was embodied by the presidency of the International Federation of Eugenic Organizations, which passed from England (Leonard Darwin, 1921–27) to the United States (Charles Benedict Davenport, 1927–32) to the Third Reich (Ernst Rudin, 1932–36)."[30] Eugenicists were everywhere, in this telling trajectory, as was an obsession with a morally hygienic "pristine" wilderness. Grant was in the thick of it, a key player in the white supremacist version of environmentalism that has echoed down to the present, sparking the resistance found in the movements for environmental justice that in some (only some) ways started gaining momentum in the 1980s.

Although Leopold was no Grant, his Land Ethic was oblivious to the environmental racism figuring in everything from wilderness "preservation" to siting toxic waste dumps disproportionately in communities of color. A virtue of the environmentalisms of Kimmerer, Whyte, and many other Indigenous activists is that they do not carry that baggage. They recognize the realities of environmental racism and sexism, while also recognizing the problems of speciesism and consistently adhering to non-anthropocentric perspectives reflecting a much larger, non-Eurocentric, non-Anglo-American historical framing of environmental philosophizing and activism.

Admittedly, some insightful philosophizing has happened in narrower Eurocentric contexts, concerning the most defensible types of non-anthropocentrism. As Marion Hourdequin explains,

> Environmental philosophers diagnosed the problem with anthropocentrism as a failure to value nonhuman organisms and other aspects of the natural world. Thus, questions of value have been at the core of discussions of anthropocentrism and non-anthropocentrism. The issue is not that anthropocentrism fails to acknowledge that the nonhuman realm has *any* value. Even anthropocentric theories grant that animals, plants, wetlands, meadows, and the like can have value of some kind. But according to anthropocentric ethics, other-than-human things have value only *instrumentally*, as means to the ends of those things that have *intrinsic* value, which is more fundamental. One can think of intrinsic value as value that a thing has in its own right, or for its own sake. It is sometimes referred to as *inherent* value, suggesting that intrinsic value is value contained within the entity that possesses it, not value bestowed from the outside. The trouble with valuing organisms and the environment only instrumentally,

> or extrinsically, according to nonanthropocentrists, is that these modes of valuing are too contingent on human interests and desires.[31]

A famous thought experiment from Richard Routley, the "last man" case, asked whether, if there were only one remaining person on Earth, and that person, presumably soon to perish himself, had it in his power to destroy all remaining living creatures, it would be ethically objectionable for him to do so. If so, that suggested that there was more to the value making for ethical standing than being a human person.

There ensued much debate, much of it highly relevant to Singer's version of animal liberation, over the merits of such non-anthropocentrisms as biocentrism, sentiocentrism (Singer's Benthamite/Sidgwickian view), ratiocentrism, being the "subject-of-a-life," and ecocentrism, that last finding inherent value or standing in such ecological wholes as natural communities, bioregions, or perhaps the entire Earth, Gaia. One can imagine endless riffs on the Routley thought experiment – the last man might have the option of destroying all living creatures, or all conscious creatures, or all sentient creatures, or all reasoning creatures, etc., and the choice of options that we would morally censure would reveal the bounds of ethical standing, as we see it. These debates opened up important divisions between one form or another of animal liberation and ecocentrism, which seemed separated by a holistic firewall. The tenor of the division was captured by Dale Jamieson in a bold essay "Animal Liberation Is an Environmental Ethic":

> In the early 1980s it seemed clear that environmental ethics and animal liberation were conceptually distinct. To be an environmental ethicist one had to embrace new values. One had to believe that some non-sentient entities have inherent value; that these entities include such collectives as species, ecosystems, and the community of the land; and that value is mind-independent in the following respect: even if there were no conscious beings, aspects of nature would still be inherently valuable. What remained to be seen was whether any plausible ethic satisfied these conditions.... Once it became clear what was required for membership in the club of environmental ethicists, most animal liberationists did not want to join.[32]

As Jamieson explained, some in the animal liberation movement, notably Tom Regan, charged ecocentrists such as Leopold and Callicott with courting "environmental fascism," since it was not clear why humans might not be, say, culled like other animal populations for the sake of the health of the biotic community. Leopold held that the Land Ethic comes after the circle of ethical consideration has expanded to cover the protection of human rights, but that highly suspect developmental perspective raised many questions about just when and why the interests of individual humans could be overridden for the sake of the biotic community.

Jamieson ingeniously sought to bridge the contested terrain. Suspicious of the notion of intrinsic value, he reconstructed it as a difference in the process or structure of valuing, between valuing something for its own sake and valuing it instrumentally. He also set out distinctions between: (1) the "source and content of values…. Were there no sentient beings there would be no values but it doesn't follow from this that only sentient beings are valuable"; and (2) "primary and derivative value": "Creatures who can suffer, take pleasure in their experiences, and whose lives go better or worse from their own point of view are of primary value. Failure to value them involves failures of objectivity or impartiality in our reasoning or sentiments." But non-sentient "entities are not of primary value because they do not have a perspective from which their lives go better or worse. Ultimately the value of non-sentient entities rests on how they fit into the lives of sentient beings. But although non-sentient entities are not of primary value, their value can be very great and urgent."[33]

Armed with these distinctions, Jamieson tried to demonstrate that "the content of our values may include our intrinsically valuing an entity that is of derivative value, and that this valuing may be urgent and intense, even trumping something of primary value." Works of art might be one case in point, as when human lives are sacrificed to save great works of art, which happened in World War II. But non-sentient parts of the environment might be another, such that they are of derivative value, but "can be of extreme value and can be valued intrinsically." Thus, "animal liberationists can value nature intrinsically and intensely, even though they believe that non-sentient nature is of derivative value." They can therefore "join environmental ethicists in fighting for the preservation of wild rivers and wilderness areas. … rightly understood, they can even agree with environmental ethicists that these natural features are valuable for their own sakes."[34] What animal liberationists cannot do, however, "is claim the moral high ground of the mind-independent value of nature which, since the early days of the movement, environmental ethicists have attempted to secure." For Jamieson, that was no loss since there is no high ground to secure, though he did admit that "someone who fails to value deserts lacks sensitivity while someone who fails to value people or gorillas lacks objectivity. Although in both cases the dispute involves how we see ourselves in relation to the world, to a great extent different considerations are relevant in each case."[35]

Given these conflicts within animal liberation philosophy, and between it and ecocentric forms of environmental (or, better, ecological) philosophy, Jamieson admitted that differences would remain, differences over such matters as "wilderness" protection, biodiversity maintenance, population control, etc. But he added a puzzling note in his conclusion:

> Part of the reason for the divisions within both the environmental and animal liberation movements is that contemporary Western cultures have little by way of positive images of how to relate to animals and nature. Most of us know what is bad – wiping out songbird populations, polluting water ways, causing cats to suffer, contributing to smog, and so on. But when asked to provide a positive vision many people turn to the past, to their conception of what life is like for indigenous peoples, or what it is to be "natural". None of this will do. So long as we have a paucity of positive visions, different views, theories, and philosophies will compete for attention, with no obvious way of resolving some of the most profound disagreements.[36]

What with the range of controversies here, Jamieson's conclusion was perhaps understandable.[37] But it will not do either. Indeed, it betrayed a baffling Eurocentric epistemology of ignorance, such that the whole world of environmental thinking and practice was shrunken down to a set of academic controversies in US colleges and universities since the 1960s, as if there were nothing to count as environmental ethics at any other time or place in the history of the world. His sweeping dismissal, in this article, of any possible contributions from Indigenous peoples – or any other peoples, with the possible exception of China – was worthy of James Mill. There was no recognition or acknowledgment of the fact that Native Americans and other Indigenous peoples have always been on the front lines of environmental activism, as with the Indigenous Environmental Network and many other organizations. The water protectors, climate activists, and protectors of sacred sites share a much bigger and broader history, and one "rooted in struggle, in what we do, what we observe, and the relationships we make … It is thoroughly grounded in the material world we inhabit. It does not come from thought experiments or philosophical debates. Our writing and thinking quite literally emerge from the ground up; they are always grounded in our relationship with land and with people."[38]

Morality's Progress seems an unfortunately apt title, like *Pilgrim's Progress* calling to mind how it is a microcosm of that longer and profoundly problematic Eurocentric narrative of the birth of liberalism and the expanding circle of Enlightenment reason, even if it is post-theological reason being singled out for praise. As Glen Sean Coulthard puts it, taking Marx as a focal point of his critique:

> Marx propagated within his writings a typically nineteenth-century modernist view of history and historical progress. This developmentalist ontology provided the overarching frame from which thinkers as diverse as Immanuel Kant, Georg W. F. Hegel, John Stuart Mill, and Adam Smith sought to unpack and historically rank variation in "human cultural forms and modes of production" according to each form's "approximation to the full development of the human good." … this modernist commitment often led Marx (along with Engels) to depict those non-western societies deemed to be positioned at the lower end of this scale of historical or cultural development as "people without history," existing "separate from the development of capital and locked in an immutable present without the capacity for historical innovation…. He suggests that, although vile and barbaric in practice, colonial dispossession would nonetheless have the "revolutionary" effect of bringing the "despotic," "undignified," and "stagnant" life of the Indians into the field of capitalist modernity and thus onto the one true path of human development – socialism.[39]

Except for the socialism bit, what difference Marx or Mill?

Furthermore, like Leopold, Jamieson invoked "wilderness" as an object of an environmental ethic, without acknowledging the settler colonial history of that singularly lethal social construction. As so many Indigenous environmental activists have taken great pains to show, "wilderness" has often been deployed like the notion of "terra nullius," opening the way for the application in some fashion of the Doctrine of Discovery. In the US, the National Park system and other wilderness protection areas, celebrated by some as "America's Best Idea," illustrates the same settler colonial history of forced displacement of Native Americans as many other parts of the country. From Yosemite to Mt. Rushmore, the protected areas were never uninhabited, "untrammeled," but only became relatively so after the forced removal of the inhabitants. For just such reasons, even the Sierra Club, founded by John Muir, has decided to drop the name of its founder in much the way that the name of Cecil Rhodes has been dropped from public monuments.

All of this might seem to reaffirm that Kimmerer and Whyte represent an ecological political ethic that needs to be teased apart from the too insular and self-celebratory stories told by Eurocentric academic philosophers. But just as utilitarianism can self-efface and urge its adherents to look elsewhere, Jamieson's call for alternative visions could be taken seriously, and considered in connection with his climate ethics to open up another path to a critical utilitarianism, one rivaling that of de Lazari-Radek and Singer.

In his 2007 article "When Utilitarians Should Be Virtue Theorists," Jamieson argued that:

> Utilitarianism is a universal emulator: it implies that we should lie, cheat, steal, even appropriate Aristotle, when that is what brings about the best outcomes. In some cases and in some worlds it is best for us to focus as precisely as possible on individual acts. In other cases and worlds it is best for us to be concerned with character traits. Global environmental change leads to concerns about character because the best results will be produced by generally uncoupling my behavior from that of others. Thus, in this case and in this world, utilitarians should be virtue theorists.[40]

Jamieson prefaced his argument with a well-taken warning about "the problem" – namely, that humans "are transforming Earth in ways that are devastating for other forms of life, future human beings, and many of our human contemporaries," referring to biodiversity loss, greenhouse gas emissions, etc., and rightly noted that philosophers, presumably the academic ones, "in their professional roles have by and large remained silent about the problem."[41] No surprise there, since "it is hard to know what to say [about these issues] from the perspective of the reigning moral theories: Kantianism, contractarianism and commonsense pluralism"[42] – Kantian obtuseness in denying that "the business of morality is to *bring something about*" and obsessing over the purity of the will to obey the moral law is matched by the contractarian willingness to exclude "from primary moral consideration all those who are not parties to the relevant agreements" (say, future generations, non-human animals, women, those lower on the scale of civilization, etc.). Commonsense pluralism, like the Victorians' commonsense morality, is stuck in an "inherent conservatism" and unwilling to accept that our everyday moral beliefs and actions might be seriously problematic.[43] By contrast, utilitarianism, "with its unapologetic focus on what we bring about, is relatively well positioned to have something interesting to say about our problem … for utilitarians, global environmental change presents us with a moral problem of great scope, urgency and complexity."[44]

How so? Jamieson's argument carries forward themes from Sidgwick and Singer (and Mulgan), but with important twists. For him, utilitarianism is a singularly fluid approach, so much so that it "is not wedded to any particular account of what makes outcomes good, of what makes something an outcome, or even what makes something an action." It simply requires us to bring about the best outcomes, "to do what is best," which may or may not involve consumerism, individual utility maximization, etc. Moreover, he thinks he is in line with the classical utilitarians in focusing on the moral psychology of the utilitarian agent. Bentham and Mill were "strangers to this doctrine" of act utilitarianism as currently understood:

> They were promiscuous in their application of the principle of utility to acts, motives, rules, principles, policies, laws, and more besides. Rather than beginning with the principle of utility and then demanding that people become gods or angels in order to conform to it, they start from a picture of human psychology which they then bring to the principle. While conforming to the principle of utility is supposed to make us and the world better, embedding the principle in human psychology is what makes the principle practical … the world comes to people in chunks of different sizes: sometimes we must decide between acts, at other times between rules or policies. Indeed, acts can express rules and policies, and rules and policies are instantiated in acts. One of the most difficult problems we face as moral agents is trying to figure out exactly what we are choosing between in particular cases. Yes, textbook act-utilitarianism is a non-starter as an answer to our question, but who would have thought otherwise?[45]

Thus, rather than taking a "local" approach insisting on just one focal point for utilitarian assessment, "we should be 'global' utilitarians and focus on whatever level of evaluation in a particular situation is conducive to bringing about the best state of affairs." Here he quotes from none other than Parfit – "Consequentialism covers, not just acts and outcomes, but also desires, dispositions, beliefs, emotions, the color of our eyes, the climate and everything else. More exactly, C [consequentialism] covers anything that could make outcomes better or worse."[46]

And it is with this in mind that Jamieson urges that, given "the problem" – better termed "*The Big problem*" – part of a promising utilitarian strategy could be a selective "non-contingency," requiring or teaching "agents to act in ways that minimize their contributions to global environmental change" by specifying "that acting in this way should generally not be contingent on an agent's beliefs about the behavior of others." Many environmental problems such as climate change are often construed in stock game-theoretical terms as huge, complex collective action problems, though of a spectacularly challenging (even "wicked") variety. All the familiar (and not so familiar) free rider problems arise, especially since any single individual's harmful contributions – say, from driving to the store or enjoying a fire in the hearth in winter – seem minuscule as contributions to the Big problem, even while being not so minuscule as individual benefits. As with the paradox of voting, one's individual contribution to the general outcome seems not to make much difference to that outcome, except in very rare circumstances. But of course, the bad outcomes of "what we together do" or "what we together do not do" are what make for the Big problem, the "back of the invisible hand" where supposedly self-interested behavior (or even what is taken for morally acceptable behavior) produces catastrophically sub-optimal rather than optimal results.

Any such version of individual utility maximization is, for Jamieson, as faulty as Kantian or commonsense moral action, when it comes to what utilitarianism should prescribe:

> Together we produce bad outcomes that no individual acting alone has the power to produce or prevent. Moreover, global environmental change often manifests itself in ways that are quite indirect. The effects of climate change (for example) include sea level rises, and increased frequencies of droughts, storms, and extreme temperatures. These effects in turn may lead to food shortages, water crises, disease outbreaks, and transformations of economic, political and social structures. Ultimately, millions may die as a result, but climate change will never be listed as the cause of death on a death certificate. Because our individual actions are not decisive with respect to outcomes, and we are buffered both geographically and temporally from their effects, many people do not believe that their behavior has an effect in producing these

> consequences. Even when people do see themselves as implicated in producing these outcomes, they are often confused about how to respond, and uncertain about how much can reasonably be demanded of them.[47]

But utilitarianism can do better. Or at least a global green utilitarianism promoting the green character virtues:

> Given our nature and the nature of our problem, non-contingency is more likely to be utility-maximizing than contingency. This is because contingency is likely to require calculation, and calculation is not likely to generate utility-maximizing behavior. Thus, in the face of our problem, utilitarians should take virtues seriously. Focusing on the virtues helps to regulate and coordinate behavior, express and contribute to the constitution of community through space and time, and helps to create empathy, sympathy and solidarity among moral agents.[48]

The virtues in question, however, are of a revisionary nature. They are green virtues, those "that utilitarians should try to exemplify in themselves and elicit in others, given the reality of global environmental change." Jamieson breaks these down in terms of their degree of revisionism with respect to existing values – either preservation, rehabilitation, or creation. Humility, especially with respect to nature, might be an example of the first; temperance, with some updating, might be a case of the second, if it could be turned to reining in overconsumption and promoting moderation; and, with the third, Jamieson recommends mindfulness: a

> virtuous green would see herself as taking on the moral weight of production and disposal when she purchases an article of clothing (for example). She makes herself responsible for the cultivation of the cotton, the impacts of the dyeing process, the energy costs of the transport, and so on. Making decisions in this way would be encouraged by the recognition of a morally admirable trait that is rarely exemplified and hardly ever noticed in our society.[49]

"Mindfulness" usually carries rather different connotations, as Jamieson (a very sixties-ish person) well knows. But this presentation of utilitarianism as an ongoing research project, with the specific call to recognize how big environmental problems lead to a concern with character because of the need to "uncouple" one's individual actions from the problematic collective actions (or inactions) of others, and how utilitarians "need to develop a catalog of the green virtues and identify methods for how best to inculcate them," are salubrious reminders of how flexible and self-effacing utilitarianism can be, and how, as with Mulgan's ideal outlook utilitarianism, concrete questions about how to teach it can sharpen the focus. Utilitarianism could and should bring – and, in fact, always has brought – a lot of psychology to the table, developing an account of virtue in terms of character traits that reflect enduring dispositions of thought *and feeling* that can in the relevant contexts trump calculative generators of action. In some contexts, more calculative approaches may be called for, when non-complacency is obviously demanded, and there are many complications that come with balancing these factors, as with the two-level approach in general. Perhaps it might help, Jamieson speculates, to relax the demands of non-complacency, going with a "progressive consequentialism" that merely seeks to progressively produce a better world, without the maximizing requirement. There might still be conflicts, however, and there simply is "no algorithm for designing the optimal utilitarian agent. Nor is there an algorithm for constructing the perfect constitution, which constrains majority rule when it should but does not prevent its expression when it should not."[50] Utilitarian judgment, on this account, demands a lot of practical wisdom.

Nonetheless, overall, Jamieson remains unmoved by the familiar challenges:

> If utilitarianism really implied that I should throw tequila bottles out of the window while commuting to work in my SUV, this result would not on the face of it be any more shocking than some other possibilities that utilitarianism can countenance in various hypothetical situations: for example, that in some cases I might be morally obliged to hang innocent people, torture prisoners or carpet-bomb cities. The reason that these objections do not sway anyone with utilitarian sympathies is because, by hypothesis, all of these cases presuppose that my acting in these horrific ways would produce the best possible world. If the world is in such a deplorable state that hanging innocent people would actually constitute an improvement, that is surely not the fault of utilitarian theory. On the other hand, if the assumption that the contemplated act is optimal is not in play, then the critic is making the ubiquitous error … of purporting to show that

> utilitarianism directs agents to act in ways that make the world worse or less good than it could be.[51]

If there were overwhelming evidence that such collective action via green virtue really was futile, given how far gone the world was, then this rationale would fail, and the Dark Mountain Project might look like the best option.[52] But, frightening as the evidence is, it is not that damning – and one might wonder just what kind of person the "last man" would have to be to even countenance the further destruction of the world.

Jamieson's recent article with Marcello Di Paola, "Climate Change, Liberalism, and the Public/Private Distinction," adds an analysis of how the various features of climate change make it extremely difficult to maintain the classic, core liberal distinction between a public sphere and a private sphere of supposedly nonpolitical individual action: "Many of the GHG-emitting behaviors that contribute to the disruption of the climate system – such as using computers, taking hot showers, eating this or that, driving cars, investing here or there, and having children – are traditionally regarded as private. Yet today, through climate change, these apparently private behaviors can have very public consequences, however indirect, across spatial, temporal, and genetic boundaries."[53] Here, again, consequentialist political theories have an advantage over rigid rights-based or deontological views, in recognizing how the boundaries of the public sphere are historically contingent and always up for negotiation in light of changing circumstances. Changes in legal and ethical norms regarding cigarette smoking are a case in point.

But it is in his *Reason in a Dark Time: Why the Struggle against Climate Change Failed – and What It Means for Our Future* that Jamieson has argued his case at greatest length, and with a much fuller and thoroughly damning account of the failures of policy action on climate change, and of the economistic and stock ethical theoretical approaches to it. His hopes for a global climate deal have dimmed, and although his basic line of argument remains constant, he has shifted his terminology somewhat, substituting "consequentialism" for "utilitarianism." The picture of the green virtues has expanded to stress cooperativeness and an attitude of non-domination and respect toward nature – respect that could take various forms, but might include ideas of "nature as a partner in a valuable relationship," even being at home in it, or nature as crucial background to giving life meaning, or part of a concern for "psychological integrity and wholeness."[54] Furthermore, for Jamieson, "there is important truth in the claim that humans are part of nature." This can take shifting shapes, from more physical or ecological to a sense of how "nature has brought us into existence and sustains us, but it also constitutes our identity." As he sums it up:

> it is because of these perspectives from which we see ourselves as part of nature that we cannot fully reduce nature to competing baskets of distributable goods, at least not without radically changing our own self-understandings. We are hesitant about markets in kidneys and more than hesitant about markets in brains, in part because we see these organs as partly constitutive of who we are. Even if we allow such markets we will not be tempted to think that everything that is important about a kidney or a brain is expressed by its market value. It would be strange for someone to do a benefit–cost analysis of a brain as if its value in a shadow market were its most important feature. The same sort of strangeness attaches to attempts to assess in market terms "the value of the world's ecosystem services and natural capital." A residue remains of our relations to nature that cannot be fully expressed in the language of economics. This dimension is primordial, and occurs in various traditions around the world. It cannot easily be dismissed.... Respect for nature is an important virtue that we should cultivate as part of an ethics for the Anthropocene. Respect can be manifest in many different ways within a single person, sometimes simultaneously. Nature itself is not a single thing and we can respect elements or dimensions of nature while expressing contempt for others. Respecting nature is respecting ourselves.[55]

Sounding a note resonating with Kimmerer's grammar of animacy, he observes how the mistreatment of nature can lead to a downward spiral of increasing disrespect, leading to more mistreatment and more disrespect, etc. And he also shows a healthy recognition that the work of moving people to adopt the green virtues is probably not best done by academic philosophers, though they have a role to play.

As a reconstruction of classical utilitarianism, Jamieson's account is laudable. But the evidence he assembles, from such impeccable sources as the Intergovernmental Panel on Climate Change, demonstrates the disastrous failures of the international system that Sidgwick envisioned and helped legitimate, the neoliberal world order, and of all those well-meaning (or not so well-meaning) political and policy functionaries squirting the perfume of expertise on it to deflect attention from how the Concert of Europe and the Anglo-American alliance have a long history of greenhouse gas emissions to atone for. All this is bleak. But the open-ended project of the green utilitarian virtues (in contrast with the egoistic Aristotelian ones), and the at least glancing recognition that other "traditions around the world" and non-academics may have something to contribute to it, are less depressing.

As with his essay on animal liberation, Jamieson only gestures in the direction of alternative worldviews, and his notions of "nature" and the "Anthropocene" need to be interrogated, just as his notion of "wilderness" did. He continues to express an uncritical indebtedness to the canon of *American Earth*, with no evident awareness of the seriousness of its erasures and exclusions. The expressions "racism" and "environmental racism" are not in his index, and are largely absent from his analysis, for all its virtues. The basics of critical race theory and critical race studies – to the effect that racism affects every part of society and culture, is systemic rather than merely individual prejudice, and is embedded in social systems from education to economics to law – never flicker into view in his writings. There is no acknowledgment of the possible importance and relevance of Indigenous peoples, even as climate activists, or possible exemplars of green virtues.[56]

There is indeed something reminiscent of John Stuart Mill in this – the Mill who waxed eloquent about his love of open green spaces and the dangers of carrying economic growth and competition too far. In *Paradise Now: The Story of American Utopianism*, Chris Jennings explains how Mill and the utopian socialist Robert Owen challenged the claim that communism invariably undermined "productivity and innovation by diminishing competition, thrift, and personal incentive."[57] Much is said about Oneida and other utopian projects. But as with Mill and Jamieson, nothing is said about those Indigenous peoples who have so often successfully practiced communism.

In fact,so successfully in some cases that, as Graeber and Wengrow show in detail, the "colonial history of North and South America is full of accounts of settlers, captured or adopted by indigenous societies, being given the choice of where they wished to stay and almost invariably choosing to stay with the latter. This even applied to abducted children.... By contrast, Amerindians incorporated into European society by adoption or marriage ... almost invariably did just the opposite: either escaping at the earliest opportunity, or ... returning to indigenous society to live out their last days." By the standard of free market ideologues insisting that one should be "free to choose," this seems like a particularly severe indictment. What explains such decision procedures? The choosers themselves often left a record of their clear reasons:

> Some emphasized the virtues of freedom they found in Native American societies, including sexual freedom, but also freedom from the expectation of constant toil in pursuit of land and wealth. Others noted the "Indian's reluctance ever to let anyone fall into a condition of poverty, hunger or destitution. It was not so much that they feared poverty themselves, but rather that they found life infinitely more pleasant in a society where no one else was in a position of abject misery.... Still others noted the ease with which outsiders, taken in by "Indian" families, might achieve acceptance and prominent positions in their adoptive communities, becoming members of chiefly households, or even chiefs themselves. Western propagandists speak endlessly about equality of opportunity; these seem to have been societies where it actually existed. By far the most common reasons, however, had to do with the intensity of social bonds they experienced in Native American communities: Qualities of mutual care, love and above all happiness, which they found impossible to replicate once back in European settings. "Security" takes many forms. There is the security of knowing one has a statistically smaller chance of getting shot with an arrow. And then there's the security of knowing that there are people in the world who will care deeply if one is.[58]

"Above all happiness," with security, love, and less of a policing state to inflict violence. A baffled Bentham should have loved it, and a gentle Godwin surely would have loved it. What epistemologies of ignorance keep Jamieson and so many others from considering, or thinking there is any need to consider, such histories, or how those histories are playing out in environmental activism? Avoidance of this evidence was a problem for Mill and it is a problem still. This is unfortunate, and odd in the extreme, given the need for additional research proposals about the green virtues that utilitarianism might deploy to good effect to address the Big problem of environmental destruction in a way that other political/ethical approaches cannot. Plausibly, utilitarianism should self-efface in this direction, with greater green humility than its predecessors were apt to display, despite their receptiveness to animal liberation. Relationships do matter, and only a very parochial view, impervious to decades of research in gender studies, assumes that the only relationships that matter, or that can be impartially justified, are those of the bourgeois family as it has evolved in recent centuries. Having opened all these vistas, all these pathways to learning from other ways of life, rather than dominating or obliterating them from a distance, utilitarians need to follow their own advice more.

All Our Allies

To be sure, many other academic environmental philosophers, for example Deep Ecologists and ecofeminists, have taken a more receptive approach to Indigenous environmental or ecocentric political ethics. Hourdequin comments on the exasperation some have felt with the debates over sentiocentrism, biocentrism, ecocentrism, etc., and notes the shift in interest to valuing attitudes and an emphasis on the quality of relations. Such an approach supposedly shifts from an emphasis on maximizing value or acting in accord with the moral law to a concern with how to relate well, and with that shift in mind, Hourdequin moves beyond a Eurocentric perspective to a consideration of Confucianism and Daoism, as well as such movements as Deep Ecology and ecofeminism, including Vandana Shiva's ecofeminism.

However, as with Jamieson, Singer, and so many others, Hourdequin seems reluctant to address the violence, racism, and brutality of colonialism, settler colonialism, and imperialism. But in theorizing and practicing the green virtues, why not center those character traits and relationships that come out in global environmental or ecological activism confronting the heavy-handed oppressions of the neoliberal global order?[59] Consider:

> In the United States, Indigenous caretakers have been the most confrontational arm of the environmental movement by blocking the construction of extractive infrastructure. They have therefore also been the most heavily targeted and criminalized. Following the Standing Rock protests, eight states passed American Legislative Exchange Council (ALEC)-inspired "critical infrastructure" laws criminalizing the protesting of oil pipelines. Legislation pushed by the Trump administration would make "inhibiting the operation" of an oil pipeline, such as simply standing in the way of construction, an offense punishable by twenty years in prison. Water protectors and land defenders are the new generation of political prisoners.... The intense criminalization of caretaking reveals the extent to which the ruling class will go to protect its interests and keep capitalism in place. If we're going to have a chance at defeating the fossil fuel industry and preserving the Earth, which keeps us alive, the decriminalization of caretakers and caretaking labor

> – Indigenous caretakers, in particular – must be a fundamental priority.[60]

Some of the key issues here concern how, as with Kimmerer and Whyte, the challenge is to present a non-anthropocentric vision of environmental justice, which in some contexts has been framed in overly anthropocentric terms, as though a concern with the non-human world meant obscuring the injustices of the human one[61] – for example remaining oblivious to the carcinogenic toxics being dumped on the Blacks of Louisiana's "Cancer Alley." In such contexts, animal liberation and ecocentric environmentalisms have sometimes appeared to be affluent white indulgences reflecting an epistemology of ignorance about racial injustices.

That this is a distortion of the theory and practice of environmental justice has been demonstrated by research on the history of African American environmentalism. Against *American Earth*, one might set Camille T. Dungy's edited volume *Black Nature: Four Centuries of African American Nature Poetry*, or Stefanie K. Dunning's *Black to Nature: Pastoral Return and African American Culture*, or Dianne D. Glave's *Rooted in the Earth: Reclaiming the African American Environmental Heritage.*[62] These works often lean non-anthropocentric in ways that are not apparent in Robert Bullard's classic exposé of environmental racism, *Dumping in Dixie: Race, Class, and Environmental Quality*.[63] Although her argument is complex, doing justice to the distinctive issues of the injustices inflicted on African Americans throughout history, Kimberly K. Smith concludes that, even if a strong environmental ethic demands the recognition of intrinsic value in nature, "the black tradition ... is not hostile to such nonanthropocentric perspectives."[64]

Moreover, the complex interweavings of activist movements for animal liberation and ecocentric bioregionalisms or Earth Liberation are scarcely captured in the abstract arguments of Jamieson or Hourdequin. In his extraordinary work, grounded in a wealth of empirical research on such movements as the Animal Liberation Front and the Earth Liberation Front, David Naguib Pellow argues:

> As a scholar and activist who has spent many years working in the field of environmental justice (EJ) studies and in the EJ movement, I hold dear the hope that advocates of earth and animal liberation and advocates of EJ will recognize and build upon the many generative links and possibilities between them. The EJ movement is largely composed of people from

> communities of color, Indigenous communities, and the working class. They are focused on combating environmental inequality, racism, and injustice – the disproportionate burden of environmental harm facing those populations.... I demonstrate that many ideas at the root of EJ movements are consonant with total liberation. In fact, the ideas that radical animal and earth liberation activists express in their public and internal movement conversations are almost entirely reflective of concepts contained at the heart of the Principles of Environmental Justice – a sort of founding document of the U.S. EJ movement.
>
> Activist delegates to the First National People of Color Environmental Leadership Summit adopted the Principles in 1991. The Preamble reads, in part,
>
>> WE, THE PEOPLE OF COLOR, gathered together at this multinational People of Color Environmental Leadership Summit, to begin to build a national and international movement of all peoples of color to fight the destruction and taking of our lands and communities, do hereby re-establish our spiritual interdependence to the sacredness of our Mother Earth.
>
> Principle 1 affirms "the interdependence of all species," while principle 5 supports "the fundamental right to political, economic, cultural, and environmental self-determination of all peoples. The delegates ... set forth their opposition to racism and ecological destruction, recognized the inherent and cultural worth of nonhuman natures, and explicitly acknowledged the inseparability of humans and the more than human world.[65]

The Summit reflected the early influence of the Indigenous Environmental Network, devoted to Indigenous environmental/ecological activism throughout the Western hemisphere and the world. The Indigenous activists, with "the experiences of centuries of struggle for self-determination and resistance to resource-extractive land use," brought to the Summit, and the movement in general, a much wider lens and one that was strongly non-anthropocentric and often ecocentric.[66] As with the 2010 People's Agreement drafted in Cochabamba, Bolivia, the principles resonated with "ecofeminism, ecosocialism, and anti-imperialism infused with traditional Indigenous ecological knowledge," which is to say, non-anthropocentrism.[67]

In *What Is Critical Environmental Justice?*, Pellow reframes environmental justice as Critical Environmental Justice, a paradigm more attuned to intersectionality and how "multiple social categories of difference are entangled in the production of, and in challenges to, environmental injustice, including race, gender, sexuality, ability, class, and species." He also stresses the need for multiscalar methodologies and questioning how "transformative analyses and visions of environmental justice might seek to function ... beyond the state, capital, and the human through a broad anti-authoritarian perspective." And, crucially, he supports "articulating a viewpoint that all humans and more-than-human actors are *indispensable* to the present and for building sustainable and just resilient futures." Critical Environmental Justice thus redefines environmental justice and in doing so approximates "the concept of ecological justice, which engages more deeply with the uneven relationships of human beings to the broader nonhuman world and embraces a more respectful and egalitarian relationship between the two." Ecological justice "destabilizes the notion of the human as a biological category at the pinnacle of a human/nature hierarchy and, instead, embraces it as a political category that engages with the broader ecological community." Alas, what passes for environmental justice with so many governments today, including the US, remains stubbornly anthropocentric.[68]

Pellow is right to underscore the deep problems with the extractivist capitalism exercising so much sinister influence over even the government departments supposedly dedicated to environmental protection and justice.[69] And he would be the first to admit that Critical Environmental Justice is not news to the communities with the longer histories sympathetic to it. Kimmerer tells the story of how the Onondaga Nation, which during the revolutionary era was nearly annihilated by a genocide-bent George Washington, took on the Allied Chemical Corp. that had severely polluted the vast Lake Onondaga. The Onondaga "took a stance that reversed the usual equation in which economics take priority over well-being." They sued for a complete restoration of the Lake. The goal was not anthropocentric, not casinos or revenue or revenge. Kimmerer quotes Clan Mother Audrey Shenandoah on how the point was justice: "we seek justice. Justice for the waters. Justice for the four-leggeds and the wingeds, whose habitats have been taken. We seek justice, not just for ourselves, but justice for the whole of Creation."[70]

At any rate, the point is that, both on the ground and in theory, locally and globally, there are strong currents of environmentalism that combine environmental justice and ecological justice in ecocentric platforms bringing together Indigenous activists, animal liberationists, ecofeminists, ecosocialists, ecoanarchists, anti-imperialists, anti-capitalists, and more. Indeed, as *The Red Deal* explicitly states, although "Indigenous people are, and have always been, at the forefront of the struggle for climate justice," non-Indigenous allies are needed and welcome too. Becoming native to a place, as Kimmerer allows, can be an open process. Furthermore, we

> should all be looking to grassroots Indigenous and frontline organizations in the Global South who are calling for far more visionary, militant, creative, and comprehensive climate justice programs than those the Global North environmentalists can offer. These movements tend to also have a strong ethical foundation when it comes to capitalism and US imperialism. We can contribute to and draw from these movements by educating and organizing to permanently halt fracking, mining, and all types of resource extraction in Indigenous communities.... We can unconditionally support Indigenous-led movements and grassroots organizations that protect air, land, and water.[71]

But tragically, all over the world, the "state responds to water protectors – those who care for and defend life – with an endless barrage of batons, felonies, shackles, and chemical weapons. If they weren't before, our eyes are now open: the police and the military, driven by settler and imperialist rage, are holding back the climate justice movement."[72] And all other critical environmental/ecological justice movements. *Don't Look Up* – or Down, Ahead, Sideways, Wherever.

Beyond the physical infrastructures of oppression, there is more to remove. The "infrastructures we must dismantle are not only those that manifest in pipelines, bulldozers, smokestacks, concrete dams, or man camps – the material infrastructure of extractivism. Rather, the critical infrastructure we must undo is the philosophy that drives these material conditions" – the ideology of extractivist capitalist "growth."[73]

Michi Saagiig Nishnaabeg activist, author, and artist Leanne Betasamosake Simpson advances the critique of capitalism in ways especially helpful for thinking of green virtues and Indigenous environmental movements:

> When Nishnaabeg are historicized by settler colonial thought as "less technologically developed," there is an assumption that we weren't capitalists because we couldn't be – we didn't have the wisdom or the technology to accumulate capital, until the Europeans arrived and the fur trade happened. This is incorrect.

> We certainly had the technology and the wisdom to develop this kind of economy, or rather we had the ethics and knowledge within grounded normativity to *not develop* this system, because to do so would have violated our fundamental values and ethics regarding how we relate to each other and the natural world. We chose not to, repeatedly, over our history.[74]

Simpson's anti-capitalism is more intersectional and encompassing than such remarks convey, and very much part of her active involvement in such movements as Land Back and Idle No More, in opposition to the politics of recognition promoted by the Canadian government. She is an outstanding example of critical environmental/ecological justice theorizing arising from practices of resistance.

> I want to use the pain and anger that heteropatriarchy strikes to reject the replication of settler colonial gender violence within our bodies, communities, and nations. We need all genders to do this, and we all need to think critically about how we replicate this in our communities and in our daily lives. Placing the interrogation of heteropatriarchy at the center of our nation-building movements ensures that our nation building counters the impact the settler colonial political economy has on Indigenous bodies, intimacies, sexualities, and gender. It counters the continual violent attack on bodies, intimacies, sexualities, and gender as a dispossessing force. We have a choice. We can choose to uphold white, heterosexual, masculine control over Indigenous bodies, or we can choose to collectively engage in the dismantling of heteropatriarchy as a nation-building project. Nation building in Indigenous contexts is a collective effort, and in critically undoing the gender hierarchy, what happens to Indigenous women, children, and 2SQ bodies is the measure of our success as nations.[75]

These concerns with the fluidities of gender and sexual identities recall the views of Kandiaronk, and compare favorably to Mill's view that the status of women was the key indicator of a nation's success, though needless to say, the "nations" in question are not those "imagined communities" of delusional nation-states that Singer criticized, but ones with actual grounded practices of reciprocity. Of key importance here are the notions of consent and non-domination, fundamental to this grounded normativity of reciprocity and care for all beings. It figures throughout Nishnaabeg education:

> Coming to know also requires complex, committed, *consensual* engagement. Relationships within Nishnaabewin are based upon the consent – the informed (honest) consent – of all beings involved. The word *consensual* here is key because if children learn to normalize dominance and nonconsent within the context of education, then nonconsent becomes part of the normalized tool kit of those with authoritarian power. Within the context of settler colonialism, Indigenous peoples are not seen as worthy recipients of consent, informed or otherwise, and part of being colonized is engaging in all kinds of processes daily that given a choice, we likely wouldn't consent to. In my experience of the state-run education system, my informed consent was never required. Learning was forced on me using the threat of emotional and physical violence. In postsecondary education, consent was coercive: if you want these credentials, this is what you have to do, and this is what you have to endure. This is unthinkable within Nishnaabeg intelligence. In fact, if there isn't a considerable amount of demonstrated interest and commitment on the part of the learner, learning doesn't occur at all. Raising Indigenous children in a context where their consent, physical and intellectual, is not just required but valued goes a long way to undoing the replication of colonial gender violence.... Being engaged – deeply and consensually – in the physical, real-world work of resurgence, movement building, and nation building is the only way to generate new knowledge on how to resurge from within Nishnaabeg intellectual systems. We cannot just think, write, or imagine our way to a decolonized future. Answers to how to rebuild and how to resurge are therefore derived from a web of consensual relationships that is infused with movement (kinetic) through lived experience and embodiment. Intellectual knowledge is not enough on its own.[76]

The above passage is from a chapter entitled "Land as Pedagogy." Filled with wonderful stories of Nanabush and Binoojiinh, models of learning by doing (and often failing), Simpson weaves her way to the point that the "academic industrial complex does not and cannot provide the proper context for Nishnaabeg intelligence without the full, valued recognition of the context within which Nishnaabeg intelligence manifests itself: the practice of *Aki* – freedom, sovereignty, and self-determination over bodies, minds, and land." It is very hard to see how this might work, in the familiar educational systems of the Western world (and other parts of the world as well).

> I imagine myself talking about postsecondary education with Nanabush right now, and he immediately asking me why I think spending sixty hours a week indoors in a classroom or on a computer is Indigenous education at all. Point taken. I've just spent several hours writing all of this down when my Ancestors have always understood this, and in fact, I think my kids understand most of it. Several Nishnaabeg elders are embodying all of these teachings right now, and any Indigenous person with motivation to learn to think inside the land should be interacting with their own elders and experts in their own homelands instead of reading me. So while I could ask Nanabush what Nishnaabeg education is, I'd have to be ready for him to flip the table. He's not known for his patience, for one thing, and for another, he's spent eternity trying to demonstrate that with his own life. It's not Nanabush's fault we aren't paying attention.[77]

Nanabush is another name for Nanabozho, the same Original Man who appears so often in Kimmerer's writing. Indeed, Simpson's Nishnaabeg heritage is closely related to Kimmerer's Anishinaabe one, the Ojibwe and the Potawatomi. Both share, with Whyte as well, an enormous amount when it comes to the grammar of animacy, a relational grounded ethics of care and reciprocity, non-anthropocentrism, and a sense of how academic forms of knowledge production may be neither the first nor the last word. Simpson's activism is somewhat more in the foreground, but the politics of Land Back, Idle No More, Keep It in the Ground, Standing Rock, Pachamama, Resurgence, Emergent Strategies, and most everything in *The Red Deal* emerge in these collective works as well. What do the green virtues look like now? Not the Aristotelian or Millian ones, not the ones featured in the Great Chain of Being or the scale of civilization, but rather the ones figuring in resistance to those forces. The identification with Land and all our relations, human and more, is so powerful, fundamental, and consistent throughout that there is no sharp dichotomy between green virtues and other virtues, just as there is no artificial dualism of altruism versus self-interest.[78] The webs of one's meaningful relationships are too tangled, like a mycorrhizal network in the forest, to compartmentalize them.

What would Nanabush say to Bentham, Godwin, the Mills, and Sidgwick? What about to de Lazari-Radek, Singer, Jamieson et al.? It is no stretch to think that he would ask: Are your ways of life really the best ways to teach the next generation about what matters?

Allies and Altruists: Ways to and from EA

Suppose we are inclined to agree with the utilitarian outlooks associated with Jameson, Mulgan, de Lazari-Radek and Singer, whatever their differences. Suppose that, with them, we admit that accelerating environmental destruction is *the Big problem*, albeit one linked with the vast food production systems that inflict endless suffering on non-human animals and massively contribute to a wide range of environmental disasters, the bigotries and prejudices associated with nationalism, the refusal to confront the consequences of our actions for future generations or the global poor, and, frustratingly, the blinkered and all too frequent inability, courtesy of traditional ethical-political perspectives, to so much as recognize that there are serious ethical issues about what we together and individually do that are involved in all these.[79]

Why, then, would we ignore the work of the most dedicated champions of environmental and ecological justice, and remain oblivious to the grim realities that they confront when it comes to the forces opposing effective action to address the Big problem? Has the utilitarian or consequentialist nothing to learn from the political and personal risks they take, or from the histories and cultures that lead them to the frontlines of these movements of resistance and resurgence? If one is looking for the virtues needed to steer the world away from impending disaster, why not look to the relationships built in resistance movements?[80]

It is far from obvious why this would be inconsistent with the utilitarian or consequentialist call to explore the possibilities for the green virtues, with greater respect for nature, relationships with and in nature, and so on, though the obstacles to living lives in line with such virtues are greater than Jamieson recognizes. *The Red Deal* is right to stress the continuities between imperialisms old and new, the still present civilizing mission with its attendant violence and extractivist capitalism, its assaults on women and LGBTQ+ communities, especially in BIPOC communities – communities where one can often find the lived practices of non-anthropocentric orientations as part of the very quest for environmental and ecological justice.

Jamieson, Mulgan, de Lazari-Radek and Singer, Parfit, and many others[81] allow for indirect, possibly self-effacing utilitarian approaches, for working with and around core partial attachments, for some uncertainty about the exact nature of sentience and how ecological wholes might be valued, for the need for a greater range of perspectives about the histories and filiations of utilitarianism in all its varieties and the consequences of promoting it, and, in fact, for movement building. On grounds of epistemic humility alone, not to mention Sidgwick's consensus of experts criterion, there should be more open-mindedness about non-Judeo-Christian ways to inculcate green virtues. If only for purposes of figuring out the odds of political mobilization being successful, and a better possible strategy than the Effective Altruist one of devoting one's resources to direct aid to distant suffering strangers, now or in the future, such resistance efforts should be of keen interest. Where is the Singer of *Democracy and Disobedience*?

Singer might reply to Nanabush that he is not Nishnaabeg and does not have the relationships or identities in question. How can he learn from him? There are certainly tough questions here about the roles of white allies. Simpson is especially suspicious of non-BIPOC allies, and for good reason. As Kyle Powys Whyte has explained:

> The resilience of settler privilege is a barrier. Gestures toward allyship can quickly recolonize Indigenous peoples. Some people have tried to create bonds of allyship by believing that Indigenous wisdom and spirituality are so profound that Indigenous people have always lived in ecological harmony. This is the romantic approach. Other allies have tried to create solidarity through claiming that Indigenous and non-Indigenous environmentalists should not distinguish their efforts. In this view, environmental issues threaten us all, and we should converge around common problems that affect all humanity, instead of wasting dwindling time on environmental racism. This is the same-boat approach.... Subscribers to the romantic view are unprepared to respond to criticisms of supposed Indigenous hypocrisies, like the alleged contradiction of tribally sanctioned coal industries. Responding to these critiques requires an understanding of colonialism, yet some romantics are unwilling to take the time to learn how the U.S. forcefully re-engineered tribal governments to facilitate extractive industries. This understanding is key if one's goal is to undermine the levers of power that undermine Indigenous self-determination and well-being today....
>
> The same-boat approach also misses the colonial context. The conservation movement has been as damaging to Indigenous peoples as extractive industries. National parks, ecological restoration projects, conservation zones, and even the uses of certain terms – especially "wilderness" – are associated with forced displacement of entire communities, erasure of Indigenous histories in education and public memory, economic

> marginalization, and violations of cultural and political rights. Though certain sectors of conservation have improved greatly, newer movements, such as the international UN-REDD+ Programme, still repeat harms of the past. Almost every environmental achievement in the U.S. – such as the Clean Air or Clean Water acts – has required Indigenous peoples to work hard to reform these laws to gain fair access to the protections.
>
> A decolonizing approach to allyship must challenge the resilience of settler privilege, which involves directly facing the very different ecological realities we all dwell in. Sometimes I see settler environmental movements as seeking to avoid some dystopian environmental future or planetary apocalypse. These visions are replete with species extinctions, irreversible loss of ecosystems, and severe rationing. They can include abusive corporations and governments that engage in violent brainwashing, quarantining, and territorial dispossession of people who stand in their way.
>
> Yet for many Indigenous peoples in North America, we are already living in what our ancestors would have understood as dystopian or post-apocalyptic times. In a cataclysmically short period, the capitalist–colonialist partnership has destroyed our relationships with thousands of species and ecosystems.[82]

Clearly, this is a key part of the case for the more comprehensive program of decolonization. What, then, does Whyte suggest by way of being a good ally? The role is demanding:

> One can't claim to be an ally if one's agenda is to prevent his or her own future dystopias through actions that also preserve today's Indigenous dystopias. Yet how many environmentalists do just this? I do not see much differentiating those who fight to protect the colonial fantasy of wilderness from those who claim the Dakota Access pipeline does not cross Indigenous lands. Indigenous environmental movements work to reject the ancestral dystopias and colonial fantasies of the present. This is why so many of our environmental movements are about stopping sexual and state violence against Indigenous people, reclaiming ethical self-determination across diverse urban and rural ecosystems, empowering gender justice and gender fluidity, transforming lawmaking to be consensual, healing intergenerational traumas, and calling out all practices that erase Indigenous histories, cultures, and experiences.

> Perhaps these goals and values are among the greatest gifts of Indigenous spirituality and wisdom. I want to experience the solidarity of allied actions that refuse fantastical narratives of commonality and hope. Determining what exactly needs to be done will involve the kind of creativity that Indigenous peoples have used to survive some of the most oppressive forms of capitalist, industrial, and colonial domination. But above all, it will require that allies take responsibility and confront the assumptions behind their actions and aspirations.[83]

If one is serious about movement building to solve the Big problem, how can one ignore the virtues involved in being a good ally? In being able to acknowledge that other peoples need to be centered in the effort to make this world a better place? And that we need courage, cooperation, sensitivity, perceptiveness, love, humility, creativity, responsibility, and a capacity for a reflexive, critical theoretical take on our own enabling (or disenabling) circumstances, whether in allying with the Indigenous Environmental Network, or considering Effective Altruism or the menu of green virtues?

So, what *would* Nanabush say about Effective Altruism as an alternative?

Recall that the Effective Altruism (EA) movement, which owes much to Singer, claims to be a rational, evidence-driven effort to reform philanthropy to make it maximally effective, to do the most good, save the most lives, and neutralize the ineffective, often sentimental charitable giving that is widely deemed to be virtuous. If that means neutralizing the Christian missionaries of the bordertowns – so far, so good.

EA has attracted thousands of very idealistic and well-meaning people, with a disproportionate number of EAs identifying as utilitarians, out to do the most good. Still, EA remains to a very great extent a network of elite academic enclaves of privileged white men. Christopher Sebastian, in his contribution to *The Good It Promises, the Harm It Does*,[84] complains that EA is "mind-blowingly white ... Data compiled from EA sources illustrate the whiteness of the community.... A total of 87 percent of survey participants were white, 10 percent were Asian, 5 percent Latin American or Spanish origin, 1 percent were Black, and 4 percent were of other racial identities."[85] Moreover, normative whiteness is "cooked into the ideological foundation, because it focuses on maximizing the effectiveness of donors' resources, which entrenches power in the hands of donors and further reinforces a power imbalance." Amia Srinivasan, in her Foreword to the volume, observes that "contradictions between what a movement 'says' and 'does' reveal something deep about how the movement practically works – and why it is successful. In turn, such revelations can tell us something about the limits of what such a movement can plausibly achieve."[86] This is not to say that EA is successful, though it has surely done much good in some sense. To the contrary, her point is that we should question EA about its downsides: "What if Effective Altruism, whatever the intentions of its leaders and followers, systematically harmed those it promised to help, eroding democratic decision-making, creating perverse incentives, and reinforcing the very structures that produce the suffering it purports to target?" The wide-ranging contributions to the volume, mostly (even admirably) by non-philosophers, combine to make just such a case, often by drawing on the experiences of activists of color working in low-income communities who have suffered from the top-down, metrics-obsessed, deep-pocketed mandates being generated by EA via the institutions of the "philanthropy industrial complex." The philosophy fronted here is from the ground up, born of struggle, rather than from the academic and social top down, and takes into account factors that EA tends to ignore, especially with respect to grassroots community organizing (though Singer is far less guilty of that than others). The Gates Foundation, a big player in the EA fanbase, has a very mixed record, and at any rate is plainly not in the vanguard of the movement for a more inclusive democratic culture and global decision-making process.[87]

This lesson obviously applies more broadly, not just to the failings of inclusivity with EA – which extend to class, gender, and sexual identity as well – but to most of the efforts academic philosophers are pursuing to try to steer the world to a happier future. It is no good to insist that whatever the real-world failings or misapplications, whatever the limitations of the social institutions and practices producing them, whatever the blinding whiteness and epistemologies of ignorance of its practitioners, the principles of, say, utilitarianism remain untouched and persuasive, easily reapplied in better ways without any taint. Any such defense is, at best, premature, even on Sidgwickian grounds of the need for coherence and consensus (and a historical as well as analytical approach), and, at worst, part of the very practices of erasure that, as with the Lockean principles on display in the US Declaration of Independence, have done more to deflect attention away from the historical realities of racism than to confront them. Utilitarians do need to worry a lot more about being somehow party to what is effectively the teaching of white supremacism.

Nanabush might well wonder – we all should – why EAs do not worry more about this, and what kind of allies they could possibly be, if they have so little to say about settler colonialism, racial capitalism, grassroots community building, etc., even as reflected in their own house. How do these factors affect the projects and results of EA? How do EAs inculcate the EA mindset and love of all our relations? And how could the related program of 80,000 Hours (the cumulative hours of a career), with its prioritizing of lucrative careers yielding more income to be given away to EA-sanctioned causes, comport with the green virtues and/or a decolonizing resistance movement?

Admittedly, it is not easy to put into practice the protest chant "Nothing about Us without Us." But how can we proceed, without building deep, non-dominating relationships with human and non-human worlds, with a grounded, practice-based normativity allowing for relationships of love and friendship that are themselves experiments in living, in living the green virtues, but without the green-washing? We cannot, like the two Mills, stay distant but dominating, relying largely on the words of people sharing our politics and prejudices to guide us in "doing good" for distant strangers. The degree to which neoclassical development economists have fallen prey to a version of the domination of strangers is well known, from both radical critiques such as the collection *Paradigm Wars: Indigenous Peoples' Resistance to Economic Globalization* and more mainstream ones, for example *Poor Economics: A Radical Rethinking of the Way to Fight Global Poverty*. The first helps document the ways in which development economics has continued the colonial project of extraction and exploitation; the second shows how the excessive abstract modeling of neoclassical economic theory has taken a disastrous a priori approach to policies aimed at alleviating global poverty and requires actual empirical research on the cultural and political contexts the policies are impacting.[88] The second informs the work of Singer and some of the Effective Altruists. The first does not. As with Effective Altruism in relation to *The Red Deal*, the resistance movements, from the Zapatistas to Standing Rock, are not part of the calculation.

EA was introduced in the previous chapter in connection with Singer's famous "save the drowning child" example. The case and associated argument have appeared in many of Singer's works, but one of the fullest treatments is in *The Life You Can Save*, the title of both the book and the organization based on it, which, like the Centre for Effective Altruism at Oxford, practices and promotes EA.[89] The argument has remained remarkably consistent:

> First premise: suffering and death from lack of food, shelter, and medical care are bad.
> Second premise: if it is in your power to prevent something bad from happening, without sacrificing anything nearly as important, it is wrong not to do so.
> Third premise: by donating to effective charities, you can prevent suffering and death from lack of food, shelter, and medical care, without sacrificing anything nearly as important.
> Conclusion: therefore, if you do not donate to effective charities, you are doing something wrong.[90]

The drowning child case is only an illustration of a case in point to which the argument applies. Singer wants to do more than pull "at your heartstrings by focusing on a single child in need" – he wants to appeal to your reason and win "your assent to an abstract but compelling moral principle." He argues that it is difficult, and not just from a utilitarian perspective, to deny these premises, which comport with the Golden Rule and other mainstays of ethical theory, religious or not.[91] Who would claim that the mere accident of distance matters morally? Or time? But then we are led down a slippery slope to a conclusion that is as demanding as the Deep Ecology lifestyle, with no escape in sight from that old friend (or nemesis) commonsense morality:

> We tend to assume that if people do not harm others, keep their promises, do not lie or cheat, support their children and their elderly parents, and perhaps contribute a little to needier members of their local community, they've done well. If we have money left over after meeting our needs and those of our dependents, we may spend it as we please. Giving to strangers, especially those beyond one's community, may be good, but we don't think of it as something *we have* to do. But if the basic argument presented above is right, then what many of us consider acceptable behavior must be viewed in a new, more ominous light. When we spend our surplus on concerts or fashionable shoes, on fine dining and good wine, or on holidays in faraway lands, we are doing something wrong.[92]

In running through the world religions on the duty of charitable giving, Singer shows how often such giving is considered a matter of basic justice, not supererogatory, or above and beyond the call of duty. Thus, for some Christians, "sharing our surplus wealth with the poor is not a matter of charity but of our duty and their rights. Aquinas even went so far as to say 'It is not theft, properly speaking, to take secretly and use another's property in a case of extreme need: because that which he takes or the support of his life becomes his own property by reason of that need.'"[93] Singer agrees that such giving is a duty of justice, or at least a stringent moral duty. And he adds, with a bow to Thomas Pogge, that we not only have a serious positive obligation to help others, but, in the world today, also an urgent duty to refrain from harming them, since affluent countries are actively harming the global poor through everything from GHG emissions to predatory lending and trade policies, extractivism, etc. Refraining from active harm is something that even libertarians recognize as an obligation, however complex this gets to be in "One World." Although Singer rejects the distinctions between acts and omissions, doing and allowing to happen, he also recognizes how, given pervasive belief in them, utilitarian policy may need to accommodate them.

Such arguments do set Singer apart from others involved in EA, such as Will MacAskill and the Centre for Effective Altruism at Oxford. MacAskill is less inclined to stress the strict duty to give, appealing instead to the attractive, empowering life that comes with giving. In fact, he has been at some pains to deny that EA equates with utilitarianism or is about a normative duty or obligation, positive or negative, to self-sacrifice in a demanding way for the greater good. Singer is good at inducing guilt; MacAskill's strength is in cheerleading for change, so to speak. And at least in his earlier work, MacAskill, as Elizabeth Ashford has argued, tended to bracket the structural background institutions defining the choice options for giving in the way that so many economists tend to do, failing to see the extent to which "choice" is defined and limited in a world of structural, negative externalities, such that millions of people even in affluent countries can scarcely be said to be free even to "choose" sufficient and healthy (and slavery-free) food options, or having some type of home.[94] Thus, larger questions about challenging the whole system defining the feasible set of options tend to fall out of the picture, with a more limited sense of "systemic" change.[95]

That is much less the case with Singer:

> I am open-minded about the best way to combat poverty. Some organizations – Oxfam for example – are engaged in emergency relief, development aid and advocacy work for a fairer deal for low-income countries. Suppose, however, that after investigating the causes of global poverty and considering what approach is most likely to reduce it, you conclude that the only way to end

> extreme poverty is a systematic transformation of the global economic order. Does that imply that you should not donate to effective charities working to help people in extreme poverty, and instead should put all your resources into bringing about that systematic transformation? No, it does not, or at least not without first answering some crucial questions. What kind of transformation would you like to see? Not, presumably, the alternatives to capitalism that were tried in the Soviet Union, China, Cuba, Cambodia, or any of the other 20th-century regimes that set out to abolish capitalism, for none of them has worked out well.... Next, if you can describe what kind of transformation you would like to see, can you describe a feasible path to it? More important still, is there anything you can do that will make that path more likely to be taken, and the transformation achieved? Only if you can answer these questions affirmatively would it make sense to put your time, energy, and money into organizations promoting the desired transformation to the global economic system ... After all, if you can't heal the wound, that's not a reason for refusing a band-aid.[96]

This is Singer's set reply to those who complain that his EA does not get at the systemic roots of the problems, the global systems and structures that create the poverty in the first place, a critique that Angus Deaton and William Easterly have pushed forcefully.[97]

But this defense concedes that if the facts line up on the side of political activism and movement building for radical change, so be it. And the choice is hardly a binary one between capitalism and the state socialism of the former Soviet Union or China under Mao. The evils of certain types of capitalism, particularly that of the US but in other extractivist economies as well, are far worse than anything promoted by The Red Deal, much less the socialism of Bernie Sanders, which has been a visible and viable possibility in the US. And trying to tell the activists involved in seeking justice for murdered and missing Indigenous women that poverty is worse in sub-Saharan Africa is surely a waste of time, and not something Singer or other EAs spend time on, which suggests the limited horizons of the EA community. Why are they so confident that building up an EA community is likely to succeed as a whole, even supposing the beneficent impact of the individuals promoting it?

To be sure, Singer does a marvelous job of assembling data on global poverty and the options for alleviating it, mobilizing a wealth of research on how highlighting "identifiable victims" generates more support, and on the importance of creating a "culture of giving." His analysis of that last indicates how he would reply to some of the worries expressed above:

> The growth of effective altruism … has led to the formation of EA groups all over the world: I've spoken to many of them, often over a videolink. There are groups in the United States, Canada, Australia, and New Zealand, in every major European country, and in places like Abu Dhabi, Hong Kong, and Singapore, providing venues for people to come together to discuss and act upon ideas like those in this book. Local Effective Altruism Network (LEAN) supports over 350 groups that aim to use reason and evidence to guide their efforts to do as much good as possible.[98]

He does worry about the coercive norm of self-interest, which contorts people much as Ahmed claims the coercive norm of happiness does. The odd masculinism of a supposedly tough-minded Hobbesian "realism" is indeed damaging, and Singer seeks a more high-minded moral:

> there is both a broad and a narrow sense of self-interest. The long-running debate about whether humans are capable of genuine altruism is, in practical terms, less significant than the question of how we understand our own interests. Will we understand them narrowly, concentrating on acquiring wealth and power for ourselves? Do we think that our interests are best fulfilled by conspicuously consuming as many expensive items as possible, so that everyone knows that we are rich? Or do we include among our interests the satisfactions that come from helping others?[99]

Singer can and often does live up to the anti-consumerist demands of something like the deep green lifestyle.

In fact, the research he cites suggests various complications – for example, how asking for less can sometimes yield more, and in good utilitarian fashion he follows the evidence where it leads, proposing various tiers of reduced asks that might yield more. There is a whiff of esoteric morality here. Singer thinks that, ethically speaking, everyone, himself included, ought to give more. But, also ethically speaking, he needs to go with what works best. He admits that he does not always live up to his own standards, though he gives away a lot. Echoing Godwin, he doubts that his partiality toward his ailing mother was really justifiable by strictly impartial standards. But, of course, he did support her.

And when it comes to marshaling the best available metrics to crush ineffective giving strategies – such as saving a single child, or whale, when the funds could save many more – he is willing to stretch a point. After all, he has given a great deal to Oxfam, despite the complexity of the organization precluding the clear evidence of efficacy that one sees with the Against Malaria Foundation. As he explains, "Oxfam is an advocate for policy change, as well as doing direct aid projects, and these attempts to change policy also have unique contexts that preclude randomized controlled trials." But examining "two of Oxfam's successful advocacy efforts will enable us to see the judgments we need to make to decide if such efforts are worthwhile."[100]

The two cases do seem like excellent examples of effective advocacy work, though in neither case do they meet the "gold standard" of the *Poor Economics* research program, the randomized, controlled trials run by the Jameel Poverty Action Lab. The first concerns Oxfam's support for a women's coalition in Mozambique organized to battle various injustices, such as widows and divorced women having no claim to their husband's property and being left destitute, and fathers having no obligation to support their children. Oxfam supported advocacy training and a media campaign, and in fact there was successful legislation passed to rectify these problems. Oxfam's continued support to see that the laws are enforced and that women know their rights has Singer's seal of approval, even though it "isn't possible to quantify the impact of Oxfam's work." Another case concerned Oxfam's support for groups in Ghana "seeking transparency and public accountability for the oil revenues" that were recently coming in. Oxfam devoted some $200,000 to the cause, and Ghana ended up budgeting $116 million for agriculture, especially "poverty-focused agriculture" benefiting the little guys. But, Singer asks, can "we then say that spending $200,000 led to $116 million in benefits for the poorest Ghanaian farmers in just one year, with sums on the same scale continuing to flow for a number of years? That may be the case, but it is also possible that the government would have reached the same desirable outcome without Oxfam's involvement." Still, even without clear evidence, the enormity of the pay-off seems to have justified the risk of the investment.[101]

Another case concerns Oxfam Australia assisting the ragpickers of Pune, India – "women who make their living by sifting through the town garbage dump to collect not just rags but anything else that can be recycled." These women, Dalits, "had been isolated and held in contempt as the lowest of the low, exploited economically and sexually harassed by the dealers to whom they sold their gleanings."[102] Laxmi Narayan, who had been offering a literacy program for the ragpickers, won support from Oxfam to help the women organize a Registered Association of Ragpickers. The effort blossomed and produced more resources, such as "running a savings scheme and a microcredit facility," with earnings used to "provide scholarships and school texts for members' children." In fact, they were able to tell Oxfam that, much as they appreciated the support, they no longer needed it.[103]

With these cases, Singer is surely exercising an impressive practical wisdom, allowing the special contingencies of the case to justify support even in the absence of the hard data demonstrating effectiveness. These may not be cases of resistance on the scale of The Red Deal, but they show how, even with a founding father of EA, the case for political advocacy and mobilization aimed at structural change can be compelling. And, of course, there is also the case for animal liberation and other causes to be considered.

In *Doing the Most Good: How Effective Altruism Is Changing Ideas about Living Ethically*, Singer explains more fully that EAs all agree that "a world with less suffering and more happiness in it is, other things being equal, better than one with more suffering and less happiness," and, moreover, that EAs

> do not discount suffering because it occurs far away or in another country or afflicts people of a different race or religion. They agree that the suffering of animals counts too and generally agree that we should not give less consideration to suffering just because the victim is not a member of our species. They may differ, however, on how to weigh the type of suffering animals can experience against the type of suffering humans can experience.[104]

Where does Singer himself stand? His remarks make it clear, as does the new edition of his classic *Animal Liberation Now*, that he has not changed his stripes in light of recent EA developments. He seems predictably sympathetic, with many other EAs, to the belief "that even if we think farmed animal like chickens, pigs, and cows have less capacity to suffer than human beings, the huge numbers involved and the relatively low cost of making a difference to those numbers by encouraging people to cut down or eliminate the consumption of animal products makes this the most cost-effective way of reducing suffering."[105] And, of course, there are the ramifications of veganism for helping reduce GHG emissions. Interestingly, he brings in Leopold's Land Ethic to explain how EAs "have not shown much interest in the intrinsic value of nature. Just as they tend to view values like justice, freedom, equality and knowledge not as good in themselves but good because of the positive effect they have on social welfare, so they do not value nature as good in itself but instead ask whether preserving nature will be good or bad for animals and humans." And he reasserts his view that "intrinsic value is to be found only in conscious experiences (not all conscious experiences but only in positive ones)."[106]

Significantly, however, in his more archly philosophical work with de Lazari-Radek, *The Point of View of the Universe*, more doubts and qualifications arise when considering non-human animals. They review the familiar ground, going over Sidgwick's candidate circles of possible partiality to argue against the claim that speciesism is impartially justifiable. But they also consider the significance of population ethics and average v. total utility. They side with Sidgwick, whose plumping for the Total View "remains a straightforward and consistent way of handling these questions, even if it has a deeply counter-intuitive consequence" – namely, the Repugnant Conclusion (concerning a ridiculously overpopulated world of marginally happy individuals that sums to the most total happiness), which, however, they doubt we have very clear intuitions about. But they add, with reference to the Victorians Leslie Stephen and Henry Salt:

> Stephen's argument [is] that killing some animals is justifiable when it makes it possible for others to exist, if those animals have good lives and everything else is equal. We can now see that Salt, who rejected this view as "nonsense" because it takes into account the interests of beings who may never exist, assumes the prior existence view, whereas Stephen takes the total view. Our inability to resolve the issue between these two views means that we are also unable to reach a decision on the defence of eating meat in the circumstances described, in which animals lead good lives and would not exist if it were not for the practice of killing them for meat. Here arguments from moral uncertainty do not help us either, because there are risks on both sides. If we eat meat from animals who have led good lives, we are risking killing a sentient animal and depriving it of further life. Some philosophers have advanced strong arguments for thinking that this is wrong. On the other hand we will be supporting a system that gives good lives to many animals, as well as to humans who want to combine farming with concern for animal welfare. Some philosophers and other thinkers have argued that such a system of farming benefits animals and humans, and that without it, important values will

> be lost. If we cannot be completely confident about the choice between these two views, that uncertainty does not point us in one direction rather than the other.[107]

The suggestive distinction in the above passage between the argument made by "some philosophers" and that made by "some philosophers and other thinkers" hints at a broader buy-in for the latter, which is probably correct. Here again a way has opened to a very different outlook, a serious alliance between some animal liberation activists and some ecocentric activists, including Kimmerer, Whyte, and Simpson. The principles of the "Honorable Harvest," of subsistence, and of that wider and vastly more inclusive form of reciprocity voiced by Kimmerer might fit here, in meaningful ways of life fostering grounded relationships benefiting both humans and animals in respectful interaction with each other. Regenerative agriculture, permaculture, community gardens, Traditional Ecological Knowledge with various Indigenous peoples – all could make a good case, with a beautiful greening of the Repugnant Conclusion. Perhaps, given these possibilities, the uncertainty does point us in this direction.[108]

But it is difficult to claim certainty about the EA views on such matters, or on, say, the Indigenous Environmental Network, when there is so little in their literature betraying any serious awareness of the global movements of resistance and those leading them.

Past Present

Extending the green virtues to incorporate the virtues or traits of being a good ally is important, but difficult. Kimmerer is more willing to line up with those white environmentalists Whyte criticizes, and she speaks to a broad and mostly non-Indigenous audience. Her recommendations about adopting the grammar of animacy are freely given, and she would like to see that grammar spread, even at the risk of some cultural appropriation. She is not alone in being more receptive to less activist, less radical audiences, working with the heirs of Leopold.

But the legacy of Leopold also included other, edgier options, such as Deep Ecology, with its own form of ecocentrism and an extended self-identifying with a wider world of beings. It had its failings, a too manly obsession with the "cult of wilderness" among them, but it also reflected the influences of Native American practices, Gandhian non-violence, Buddhism, and, in later phases, ecofeminism. It also tells a story about possibilities for cultivating and inculcating green virtues with good allies.

Consider how Deep Ecology evolved from the lifestyle principles as formulated by its famous champion the Norwegian philosopher Arne Naess to the ecofeminism of Freya Mathews. The lifestyle, or outlook (see the Appendix), provides the practical takeaways of the basic perspective of Deep Ecology, reflecting an emphasis on living lightly, bioregionalism, local ecosystems, and ecocentrism, which makes for a "deep" sense of ecological justice rather than shallow anthropocentric approaches to sustainability. In the 1970s, Naess and many of his followers, including Gary Snyder, Bill Devall, and George Sessions, developed an account of the "ecological self" as one of radical interrelatedness, a function of its relations, and, in some formulations, able to overcome the limits of an anthropocentric ego identity in an expanded sense of self incorporating all one's relations.

But the recent phases of Deep Ecology have distanced it from a masculinist celebration of "wilderness" – what Freya Mathews has called the "cult of wilderness." Mathews argues that "wilderness and wildness are valued in deep ecology not only as sources of biodiversity but as sources of authentic experience, the kind of experience that will enable us to achieve ecological selfhood, in Naess's sense. / From a postcolonial point of view, this valorization of wilderness can be problematic .... 'idealizing' indigenous peoples as simply part of nature, deep ecologists are in fact perpetuating racist misunderstandings." As Mathews indicates, Indigenous people often deny that they were living in a wilderness rather than a "managed estate"; their claim is simply that "this managed estate was ecologically intact at the time of colonization." Furthermore,

> Feminists might ask why deep ecologists do not regard the subsistence traditions of settled horticultural communities as furnishing experiential sources of ecological selfhood. To work with nature via the domestic activities of growing food and husbanding animals is to enter into a relationship with nature arguably as profound as that of the hunter-gatherer. For the farmer or gardener becomes a nurturer of non-human life, as well as a consumer of it, and is likely to develop a profound identification with the plants and animals that she has tended.... The fact that subsistence practices throughout prehistory and the less-developed world today are predominantly the province of women tends to support the case that in excluding these practices as a source of ecological selfhood, male deep ecologists (where most deep ecologists, whether self-appointed or appointed by those who take it upon themselves to make such appointments,

> *are* male) are privileging their own masculine experience and the lifestyle ideals to which it gives rise.[109]

Mathews urges that the principle of subsistence, "articulated for the West in the theories of permaculture and bioregionalism," provides a better path to "begin the process of becoming native again, reinhabiting our homeplaces, even when they lie in the degraded hearts of cities." Or, as Kimmerer puts it, "Restoring land without restoring relationship is an empty exercise. It is relationship that will endure and relationship that will sustain the restored land."[110] She too recommends gardening. After all, breathing in "the scent of Mother Earth stimulates the release of the hormone oxytocin, the same chemical that promotes bonding between mother and child, between lovers. Held in loving arms, no wonder we sing in response."[111]

Mathews is right about the notion of wilderness – hence, "non-interference" must be reconceptualized in terms distinct from "wilderness protection," as it is in the work of Kimmerer, Whyte, and Simpson. And the prescient warnings of Ramachandra Guha, who foresaw how radical environmentalism, too, could be turned to imperialist purposes, should be kept in mind:

> I by no means wish to see a world completely dominated by human beings … I have time for the tiger and the rainforest, and wish also to try and protect those islands of nature not yet fully conquered by us. My plea rather is to put wilderness protection (and its radical edge, deep ecology) in its place, to recognize it as a distinctively North Atlantic brand of environmentalism whose export and expansion must be done with caution, care, and above all with humility. For in the poor and heavily populated countries of the South, protected areas cannot be managed with guns and guards. Rather, conservation must take full cognizance of the rights of the people who lived in (and oftentimes cared for) the forest before it became a National Park or a World Heritage Site.[112]

Guha cites Raymond Bonner's *At the Hand of Man*: "Livingstone, Stanley and other explorers and missionaries had come to Africa in the nineteenth century to promote the three C's – Christianity, commerce, and civilization. Now a fourth was added: conservation. These modern secular missionaries were convinced that without the white man's guidance the Africans would go astray"; "The World Wildlife Fund professed to care about what the Africans wanted, but then tried to manipulate them into doing what the Westerners wanted."[113] Coming in the aftermath of the colonial violence that "was a fact of life in postwar Britain," linked to the two decades of uprisings that "threatened British rule in colonies across the world, in Palestine, Malaya, Kenya, Cyprus, and Aden," the formation of the World Wildlife Fund, with its British and US leadership, was bound to be treated with understandable suspicion by those who had been resisting an empire that continued to deploy the brutal tactics of the nineteenth century. The problem was much bigger than Deep Ecology, but Deep Ecologists did not grasp the issues with any real awareness, political and historical, of how the organizations they supported might be perceived, received, and rejected.[114] The oppressive sense of "unity" can be a problem for Naess as well as for Mill, if it is in fact simply a mechanism for the culture of imperialism because the self-realization of the expanded ego is merely the inflated ego of the patriarchal white environmentalist.[115]

Yet it is also true that living the Deep Ecology lifestyle, replacing "vegetarian" with "vegan" and "wilderness" with better alternatives, is a plausible way to realize Jamieson's green virtues.[116] Although much elaboration is needed, the alignment with the green virtues is striking: the Deep Ecology lifestyle would clearly do wonders, if widespread, for staying within the nine planetary boundaries, reducing pollution and GHG emissions, saving biodiversity, and cultivating the relationships with other beings and non-human natural communities and bioregions that facilitate alliances of resistance to environmental destruction. As many of the communications of the Earth Liberation Front urged, "Earth liberation, animal liberation, and human liberation are all intertwined into one revolutionary struggle."[117] Jamieson, Singer, and the rest of us could well take comfort in the fact that in practice such activist movements often work it out, even if they have had to learn a lot about how where they are coming from and who they are matters.

Recall too that Sidgwick, despite his intuitionism, was hardly suggesting that moral reflection always proceeds from the Point of View of the Universe – to the contrary, that point of view was only potentially reached after exhaustively working through common (and evolving) moral views in all their messy reality, a sustained effort to figure out what "we" really think, with the "we" in question being admittedly too limited. Jamieson had a point when he confessed: "in the end it is difficult to live at a level as general and abstract even as the American fight for civil rights and animal rights."[118]

One can still legitimately worry, with the contributors to *The Good It Promises, the Harm It Does*, that the EAs (and Jamieson) do not go far enough in considering radical movements and alternatives. Gruen approvingly quotes the courageous environmental activist Gus Speth to help make the point:

> After over forty years of working in the environmental movement in international development, I have come to the conclusion that our largest problems – from climate change to inequality and poverty – are deeply rooted in the fundamentals of our political-economic system. Working within that system to achieve incremental changes, however valuable, will never be enough. The current system is simply not programmed to secure the well-being of people, place, and planet.... If we are to escape the crises now unfolding all around us, we must create a new system.[119]

Insofar as some utilitarians support a system perversely impacting those doing the real work of ecological justice, they are not worrying enough about how their own positions of privilege might make for reification, and how the support, data, and research methods available to them might be ideologically skewed by the very system that needs to be interrogated – matters on which there is too much unfortunate continuity with the classical utilitarians.

But even MacAskill, the apostle of "Longtermist" EA concern for the distant future, can compromise his own case. He allows that, despite the familiar facts about the drop in a bucket impact of, say, an individual going vegetarian (as he himself did at age 18) as compared to supporting such things as clean air technologies:

> There are good reasons to become and stay vegetarian or vegan: doing so helps you be a better advocate for climate change mitigation and animal welfare, more able to avoid charges of hypocrisy; and you might reasonably think that avoiding causing unnecessary suffering is part of living a morally respectable life. But if your aim is to fight climate change as much as possible, becoming vegetarian or vegan is only a small part of the picture.
>
> Emphasizing personal consumption decisions over more systemic changes is often a convenient move for corporations. In 2019 Shell's chief executive, Ben van Beurden, gave a lecture in which he instructed people to eat seasonally and recycle more, lambasting people who eat strawberries in winter. In reality, in order to solve climate change, what we actually need is for companies like Shell to go out of business. By donating to

> effective nonprofits, we can all make this kind of far-reaching political change much more likely.[120]

That is partly true, though again there is that worry about the master's tools never dismantling the master's house.[121] Effecting nonreformist reform through nonprofits is itself a too limited perspective, and adding the rest of the Deep Ecology lifestyle, along with pipeline protests and The Red Deal, would probably go far to put the fossil fuel industry out of business.

And MacAskill goes even further, explaining that there are reasons to avoid some events that would undermine the ability "to keep our options open as much as possible" – things like "the formation of a world government, the development of AGI [Artificial General Intelligence], and the first serious efforts at space settlement." These would risk a serious locking in of values disenabling value responsiveness to emerging threats, existential and catastrophic ones in particular. And we also have reasons to

> [p]revent smaller-scale lock-ins – for example, by supporting conservation efforts. Even if we don't know whether some species or work of art or language is valuable, there is an asymmetry between preserving it and letting it be destroyed. If we preserve it and conclude later that it's not worth holding on to, then we can always change our minds. If we let it be destroyed, we can't ever get it back.[122]

That last point is reminiscent of Jamieson's arguments for animal liberation as an environmental ethic. Moreover, MacAskill agrees with Singer that, even if "the probability of any one individual having an impact on some major event like an existential catastrophe is small," that is also "true for many ordinary sorts of morally motivated actions. If you join a protest, or vote, or sign a petition, then the chance that your action will make a difference to the outcome is very small. Nonetheless, these are actions that we often should take, because the probabilities aren't tiny and the gains are very great if we *do* make a difference."[123]

In the spirit of the canonical Mill, he adds a pitch for "a morally exploratory world" that "would favour political experimentalism – increasing cultural and intellectual diversity, if possible … we might already be on the way to a single global culture. If we are aiming to get to the best possible society, we should worry about premature convergence, like a teenager marrying the first person they date."

One case he cites is the diversity that "enabled one community, the Quakers, to develop their own views on the morality of slavery; after they had come to see its immorality, that idea had the potential, under the right conditions, to spread."[124] But another, more current example, is that of "charter cities: autonomous communities with laws different from their surrounding countries that serve as laboratories for economic policies and governance systems." The Chinese city of Shenzen was one such example, but a limited one – "there could be Marxist charter cities and environmentalist charter cities and anarchist communitarian charter cities," and "in addition to creating a diversity of formal institutions, we could try to cultivate a diversity of cultures, too."[125]

Yes, indeed, especially the Indigenous cultures that might save the world, and experiments in the Deep Ecology lifestyle and outlook attuned to The Red Deal.

Thus, with MacAskill, as with Singer, Jamieson, and company, the critical material needed for decolonizing, de-centering, and transcending utilitarianism is often given in the course of developing utilitarianism itself,[126] indicating how it can assimilate notions of relational virtue, value nature, self-efface, be effectively turned in different directions to face new challenges, support lifestyles not apparently utilitarian, facilitate alliances, comport with different metaethical views, and, even when foundationalist (in aspiration), point to the need for a much wider dialogue and set of relationships. If junking "economic man" would make the world a better, happier place – and it probably would – the utilitarian can be down with it. In the end, there is no single or decisive account of human nature or moral psychology at play in utilitarianism, and little agreement even about the nature of happiness or well-being. It is all an open field when it comes to inquiry and change. Controlled, randomized experiments are not enough, when the need is for social, communal experiments in living and resistance. There is no algorithmic logic of inquiry for those, only imagination and openness, including an openness to different vocabularies for relating to the non-human world.

Suggestively enough, Jamieson, in his co-authored work with Bonnie Nadzam, *Love in the Anthropocene*, invokes Iris Murdoch to help describe the emerging threats to love and care: "Love is the extremely difficult realization that something other than oneself is real." Although they do need to absorb Whyte's critique of the term "Anthropocene," the moral they draw is important: "The Anthropocene threatens to give us a narcissist's playground – a nature that is only the extension of ourselves and our desires, without independent meaning or sustenance.

Loving relationships are not possible in a world that consists only of oneself and one's projections."[127]

Part of the task, as always, is to "get the dear self out of the way enough to be able to really see and come to know … the world of other people, plants, animals, oceans and rivers around us." But as the devastation wears on, "as the world and technology change, some familiar human experiences of love and the natural world, even modest ones, may become increasingly unthinkable, even lost." And in "losing nature as a fully independent partner, we will have lost our best teacher for learning that something other than ourselves is real and thus a profound opportunity for learning how to love." How "will love arise in a world without nature as we have known it?"[128]

A revisionary Deep Ecology and other ecocentric outlooks can help. Plausibly, one can think one's way there out of utilitarian concerns, and then happily live there without ever much thinking about utilitarianism, confident that, on reflection, such an outlook, such an experiment in living, is justifiable as part of a serious, collective movement to deal with the Big problem. The green virtues, by their very non-contingency, put one in that company, with the hope that they will be shared and reciprocated in real and rich relationships, improving the smaller worlds in which we mostly live.

After all, it is not as though Deep Ecology or the Indigenous perspectives considered here are opposed to promoting happiness. Quite the contrary.

Appendix

In light of the fact that it would take four planet Earths to support a global population living at the same level of GHG-emitting affluence as Americans, the lifestyle in the box below might seem the best fit for the green virtues.

1. Use simple means; avoid unnecessary, complicated instruments and other sorts of means.

2. Choose activities most directly serving values in themselves and having intrinsic value. Avoid activities that are merely auxiliary, have no intrinsic value, or are many states away from fundamental goals.

3. Practice anti-consumerism. This negative attitude follows from trends 1 and 2.

4. Try to maintain and increase the sensitivity and appreciation of goods on sufficient supply for all to enjoy.

5. Eliminate or lessen neophilia – the love of what is new merely because it is new.

6. Try to dwell in situations of intrinsic value and to act rather than being busy.

7. Appreciate ethnic and cultural differences among people; do not view the differences as threats.

8. Maintain concern about the situation in developing nations, and attempt to avoid a standard of living too much higher than that of the needy (maintain a global solidarity of lifestyle).

9. Appreciate lifestyles that can be maintained universally

– lifestyles that are not blatantly impossible to sustain without injustice toward fellow humans or other species.

10. **Seek depth and richness of experience rather than intensity.**
11. **Appreciate and choose, when possible, meaningful work rather than just making a living.**
12. **Lead a complex, not complicated, life, trying to realize as many aspects of positive experiences as possible within each time interval.**
13. **Cultivate life in community rather than in society.**
14. **Appreciate, or participate in, primary production – small-scale agriculture, forestry, fishing.**
15. **Try to satisfy vital needs rather than desires.**
16. **Attempt to live in nature rather than just visiting beautiful places; avoid tourism (but occasionally make use of tourist facilities).**
17. **When in vulnerable nature, live "light and traceless."**
18. **Appreciate all life-forms rather than merely those considered beautiful, remarkable, or narrowly useful.**
19. **Never use life-forms merely as means. Remain conscious of their intrinsic value and dignity, even when using them as resources.**
20. **When there is a conflict between the interests of dogs and cats (and other pet animals) and wild species, try to protect the wild creatures.**
21. **Try to protect local ecosystems, not only individual life-forms, and think of one's own community as part of the ecosystem.**
22. **Besides deploring the excessive interference in nature as unnecessary, unreasonable, and disrespectful, condemn it as insolent, atrocious, outrageous, and criminal – without condemning the people responsible for the interference.**
23. **Try to act resolute and without cowardice in conflicts, but remain nonviolent in words and deeds.**
24. **Take part in or support nonviolent direct action when other ways of action fail.**
25. **Practice vegetarianism.**

Notes

Introduction: Decolonizing Utilitarianism

1 See, for example, Toby Ord, *The Precipice: Existential Risk and the Future of Humanity* (Hachette Books, 2021); Johan Rockström and Owen Gaffney, *Breaking Boundaries: The Science of Our Planet* (DK, 2021); James Gustave Speth, *The Bridge at the Edge of the World: Capitalism, the Environment, and Crossing from Crisis to Sustainability* (Yale University Press, 2009); and David Theo Goldberg, *Dread: Facing Futureless Futures* (Polity, 2021).

2 Herman Daly's critical approach is summed up in his July 27, 2022 *New York Times Magazine* interview, "This Pioneering Economist Says Our Obsession with Growth Must End." For details, see Jon D. Erickson, *The Progress Illusion: Reclaiming Our Future from the Fairytale of Economics* (Island Press, 2022), and Matthias Schmelzer et al., *The Future Is Degrowth: A Guide to a World beyond Capitalism* (Verso, 2022). Scott Galloway's *Adrift: America in 100 Charts* (Portfolio, 2022) chronicles a wide range of social ills, including the isolation, loneliness, and diminished intimacies of Americans, along with their sharply declining trust in government. Even life expectancy has been shortening in recent years, though it varies greatly with race and class (especially education level).

3 For an illustrative study, see Aryeh Neier, *The International Human Rights Movement* (Princeton University Press, 2020). Obviously, there are many variations on, and scholarly industries built on, the metanarratives, depending on whether the orientation is premodern, modern, or postmodern.

4 See Glen Coulthard, *Red Skin, White Masks: Rejecting the Colonial Politics of Recognition* (University of Minnesota Press, 2014), and Leanne Betasamosake Simpson, *As We Have Always Done: Indigenous Freedom through Radical Resistance* (University of Minnesota Press, 2017).

5 Lisa Lowe, *The Intimacies of Four Continents* (Duke University Press, 2015), pp. 2–3. Amy Allen's *The End of Progress: Decolonizing the Normative Foundations of Critical Theory* (Columbia University Press, 2017) offers a congenial approach to decolonizing critical theory, as do Olivette Otele's *African Europeans* (Basic Books, 2023) and David Theo Goldberg's *The War on Critical Race Theory* (Polity, 2023). Also important for framing what follows here are Duncan Bell's *Dreamworlds of Race: Empire and the*

Utopian Destiny of Anglo-America (Princeton University Press, 2020) and edited volume *Empire, Race and Global Justice* (Cambridge University Press, 2019), which offer helpful typologies of scholarly disagreements over whether liberalism and imperialism are necessarily connected or only contingently so (or whether the one must reject the other). But the fluid and shifting forms of not only liberalism, racism, and imperialism, but utilitarianism in connection with them, are hard to nail down.

6 Lowe, *The Intimacies of Four Continents*, pp. 196–8, note 54.

7 Ibid., p. 2.

8 Ibid., p. 46.

9 Ibid., pp. 112–13.

10 See also Shashi Tharoor, *Inglorious Empire: What the British Did to India* (Penguin Books, 2017), p. 54 and p. 193, for comments on the distancing bureaucratic structures that enabled Mill, as Examiner of Indian Correspondence, to play his part in the exploitation of India. Tharoor's work, along with William Dalrymple's *The Anarchy: The Relentless Rise of the East India Company* (Bloomsbury Publishing, 2022) and Sathnam Sanghera's *Empireland: How Imperialism Has Shaped Modern Britain* (Penguin Books, 2021) provide accurate accounts of the exploitations, atrocities, and pervasive, violent racism of the British Empire – see especially Sanghera's ch. 9, "On the Origins of Our Racism," which covers such examples as the British genocide in Tasmania in the early nineteenth century.

11 John Stuart Mill, *On Liberty*, in *The Collected Works of John Stuart Mill*, vol. XVII: *Essays on Politics and Society*, ed. J. M. Robson, introduction by A. Brady (University of Toronto Press, 1977), p. 224.

12 Mill, *Utilitarianism*, ed. Katarzyna de Lazari-Radek and Peter Singer (W. W. Norton and Company, 2022), pp. 10–11.

13 See my "Mill and Sidgwick, Imperialism and Racism," *Utilitas*, vol. 19, no. 1 (March 2007), and the extensive discussion in my *Henry Sidgwick, Eye of the Universe* (Cambridge University Press, 2004).

14 Or even a distinctively Millian utilitarianism or liberalism, as in the ambitious decolonizing reconstruction of Millian liberalism (but not utilitarianism) attempted by Inder S. Marwah in *Liberalism, Diversity and Domination: Kant, Mill and the Government of Difference* (Cambridge University Press, 2019).

15 Although there are some mentions of the two Mills and Bentham in Antoinette Burton and Isabel Hofmeyr, eds., *Ten Books that Shaped the British Empire: Creating an Imperial Commons* (Duke University Press, 2014), no major utilitarian work makes the list. Some, such as James Mill's *The History of British India*, should have, even if it is true that Evangelicals and Idealists were worse when it came to a missionary zeal for the Empire. Benjamin Jowett's Oxford was notoriously productive of ardent Idealist imperialists.

16 Parfit, *Reasons and Persons* (Oxford University Press, 1984), Part Three.

17 My article "Persons, Selves, and Utilitarianism" was part of the *Ethics* symposium on Parfit's book edited by Brian Barry – see *Ethics*, vol. 96, no. 4 (July 1986) – which also included Parfit's Comments on the contributions.

18 Edmunds, *A Philosopher and His Mission to Save Morality* (Princeton University Press, 2023); Singer, ed., *Does Anything Really Matter?* (Oxford University Press, 2017); McMahan et al., eds., *The Legacy of Derek Parfit*, vol. I: *Principles and Persons* (Oxford University Press, 2021), and vol. II: *Ethics and Existence* (Oxford University Press, 2023).

19 *The Happiness Philosophers* (Princeton University Press, 2017), *Henry Sidgwick, Eye of the Universe*, and, with Georgios Varouxakis, *Utilitarianism and Empire* (Lexington Books, 2005).
20 See Rawls, *A Theory of Justice* (Harvard University Press, 1971) and his introduction to Sidgwick's *Methods of Ethics*, 7th edition (Hackett, 1981). Rawls discusses Sidgwick in various other works as well, most importantly his *Lectures on the History of Political Philosophy* (Harvard University Press, 2008). For Williams, see his *Ethics and the Limits of Philosophy* (Harvard University Press, 1986); for Sandel, *Liberalism and the Limits of Justice*, 2nd edition (Cambridge University Press, 1998).
21 Pollan, *How to Change Your Mind: What the New Science of Psychedelics Teaches Us about Consciousness, Dying, Addiction, Depression, and Transcendence* (Penguin Books, 2019). Also Hilde Lindemann, *Holding and Letting Go: The Social Practice of Personal Identities* (Oxford University Press, 2014).
22 I mostly stand by the claims of that early article, although I wish that I had not excised the material in earlier drafts about Buddhism and esotericism. As my research on Sidgwick proceeded, I discovered that he had an extensive knowledge of psychology and parapsychology, knew William James and his theories, and addressed many of the questions about personal identity in fascinating ways that Parfit was unaware of. See Schultz, *The Happiness Philosophers*, ch. 4.
23 See Rorty's *Philosophy and the Mirror of Nature* (Princeton University Press, 1979). Cornell West's version of pragmatism also voiced deep reservations about philosophy as an academic discipline, but West and others did go further than Rorty or Foucault – see Leonard Harris, ed., *Philosophy Born of Struggle: Anthology of Afro-American Philosophy from 1917* (Kendall Hunt Publishing, 2000).
24 See Chomsky, "The Crimes of U.S. Presidents," www.youtube.com/watch?v=5BXtgq0Nhsc.
25 See also my "Bertrand Russell in Ethics and Politics," *Ethics*, vol. 102, no. 3 (April 1992). As with Mill (Russell's secular godfather), Russell must be read with a critical eye, though his mature views do illustrate how someone with deep utilitarian (even Sidgwickian) sympathies could end up a political radical and activist with strong anarcho-socialist tendencies.
26 At a minimum, academics should address the perils of impaired probing in their institutional environments as these were candidly set out in Charles Lindblom's *Inquiry and Change* (Yale University Press, 1992) and, more recently, in Angus Deaton's wise and welcome *Economics in America: An Immigrant Economist Explores the Land of Inequality* (Princeton University Press, 2023).
27 Vincent Lloyd's *Black Dignity: The Struggle against Domination* (Yale University Press, 2022) speaks to the limits of the diversity, equity, and inclusion framework.
28 See my *Henry Sidgwick, Eye of the Universe*, which includes an extensive and original account of the philosophically charged friendship between Sidgwick and Symonds and the significance of the circles in which they moved.
29 Mintz, "Decolonizing the Academy," www.insidehighered.com/blogs/higher-ed-gamma/decolonizing-academy.
30 Ibid.
31 See *Velvet Terrorism: Pussy Riot's Russia*, the exhibition and accompanying

catalog (Louisiana Museum of Modern Art and contributors, 2023). For the ongoing authoritarian threat in the US, see Stuart Stevens, *The Conspiracy to End America: Five Ways My Old Party Is Driving Our Democracy to Autocracy* (Twelve, 2023).

32 For the US, see Benjamin I. Page and Martin Gilens, *Democracy in America?* (University of Chicago Press, 2020), and Michael Sandel, *Democracy's Discontent: A New Edition for Our Perilous Times* (Harvard University Press, 2022). For the UK, see www.theguardian.com/commentisfree/2022/oct/19/uk-austerity-voters-brexit-cuts-chaos, and Simon Kuper, *Chums: How a Tiny Caste of Oxford Tories Took Over the UK* (IPS – Profile Books, 2022). Without the Electoral College, campaign financing tactics, gerrymandering, criminalization, incarceration, and various voter intimidation and disenfranchisement mechanisms, US electoral politics would be dramatically different.

33 The embeddedness of white supremacism in the US educational system at all levels is exposed by Donald Yacovone in *Teaching White Supremacy: America's Democratic Ideal and the Forging of Our National Identity* (Pantheon, 2022), though the State of Florida appears to be treating this work as a how-to manual.

34 See my "The New Chicago School of Philosophy," Rounded Globe (November 15, 2015); also Timuel D. Black, *Sacred Ground: The Chicago Streets of Timuel Black* (Northwestern University Press, 2019), and Danielle Allen, *Talking to Strangers: Anxieties of Citizenship since Brown v Board of Education* (University of Chicago Press, 2004).

35 See Arnold R. Hirsch, *Making the Second Ghetto: Race & Housing in Chicago, 1940–1960* (University of Chicago Press, 1983; new edition, 2021), or LaDale C. Winling, *Building the Ivory Tower: Universities and Metropolitan Development in the Twentieth Century* (University of Pennsylvania Press, 2017).

36 See https://freeexpression.uchicago.edu. The University has engaged in partisan political and economic interference time and again, not least with its pivotal role in the research and development leading to the nuclear arms race; it only presents a façade of neutrality by exempting its development, business and real estate / housing operations from the strictures of the Kalven Doctrine.

37 Baldwin, *In the Shadow of the Ivory Tower: How Universities Are Plundering Our Cities* (Bold Type Books, 2021).

38 Bunch, *After the Fall of the Ivory Tower* (William Morrow, 2022); Fleming, *Dark Academia* (Pluto Press, 2021); Ahmed, *Complaint!* (Duke University Press, 2021); García Peña, *Community as Rebellion* (Haymarket Books, 2022); and Patel, *No Study without Struggle* (Beacon Press, 2021). See also Riyad A. Shahjahan and Kirsten Edwards et al., "'Decolonizing' Curriculum and Pedagogy: A Comparative Review across Disciplines and Global Higher Education Contexts," *Review of Educational Research* (September 2021).

39 Olúfẹ́mi O. Táíwò, *Elite Capture: How the Powerful Took Over Identity Politics (and Everything Else)* (Haymarket Books, 2022). The same author's *Against Decolonisation: Taking African Agency Seriously* (Hurst & Company, 2022) rightly worries about the loose and increasingly pervasive use of the term. The psychology of decolonization is, as many years of postcolonial studies have demonstrated, rarely a matter of clear-cut binaries and oppositions.

40 I should candidly admit that the University of Chicago has always given me whatever freedom I needed. As they say, it's complicated.

41 And, given all the perversities of political history, the paradox of elite colleges and universities generating such fervent demands for decolonization and a more robust democratic culture in the face of (purported) popular resistance scarcely seems strange. Rorty had a keen eye for the paradoxes – see *What Can We Hope For?* (Princeton University Press, 2022). But on academic elite culture capture with negligible real-world political and material impact, see Fredrik deBoer's *How Elites Ate the Social Justice Movement* (Simon & Schuster, 2023).

42 See, for example, my "On Not Seeing in Philosophy," https://blog.apaonline.org/2016/09/29/on-not-seeing-in-philosophy/?amp, and "John Rawls's Last Word," *Philosophy of the Social Sciences*, vol. 39, no. 1 (March 2009). It is heartening to see such framings as that of Stephen Darwall, in his *Modern Moral Philosophy: From Grotius to Kant* (Cambridge University Press, 2023), acknowledging the limitations of previous Rawlsian-inspired work.

43 See Kimberle Crenshaw et al., eds., *Critical Race Theory: The Key Writings that Formed the Movement* (The New Press, 1996), and Richard Delgado, *Critical Race Theory: An Introduction*, 4th edition (New York University Press, 2023). See also Thomas C. Holt, *The Problem of Race in the 21st Century* (Harvard University Press, 2002), and various works by Goldberg, such as *The War on Critical Race Theory* and *The Threat of Race* (Wiley-Blackwell, 2009). As that last title puts it: "The mark of racist expression or belief, then, is not simply the claim of inferiority of the racially different. It is more broadly that racial difference warrants exclusion of those so characterized from elevation into the realm of protection, privilege, property, or profit. Racism, in short, is about exclusion through depreciation, intrinsic or instrumental, timeless or time-bound" (p. 5).

44 Said, *Culture and Imperialism* (Vintage, 1994), and Ahmed, *The Promise of Happiness* (Duke University Press, 2010).

45 The identification of utilitarianism with a crude economistic individualism is as common as the identification of it with a crude economistic aggregation. For the former, see Lewis R. Gordon, *Freedom, Justice, and Decolonization* (Routledge, 2021); for the latter, see Danielle Allen, *Justice by Means of Democracy* (University of Chicago Press, 2023). What follows here challenges both of these mischaracterizations.

46 Ramnath, *Decolonizing Anarchism: An Antiauthoritarian History of India's Liberation Struggle* (AK Press, 2011), p. 6.

47 Dale Jamieson argues as much in *Reason in a Dark Time: Why the Struggle against Climate Change Failed – and What It Means for Our Future* (Oxford University Press, 2014) – see chapter 4 below.

48 Some of the inversions of the familiar presented here will resonate with those of David Graeber and David Wengrow in *The Dawn of Everything: A New History of Humanity* (Farrar, Straus and Giroux, 2021). As should be evident from the sources cited here, the thinking back is a recipe not for nostalgia, but for imagining global futures – see Adom Getachew, ed., *Imagining Global Futures* (Boston Review, 2022).

49 A key work on these issues is The Red Nation's *The Red Deal: Indigenous Action to Save Our Earth* (Common Notions, 2021). In "Freedom Dreaming," Robin D. G. Kelley explains that *The Red Deal* "is a plan for decolonization that entails eliminating all forms of oppression and violence – racism, patriarchy, ableism, capitalism, imperialism, settler colonialism, and ensuring sexual and reproductive freedom. Grounded in Indigenous thought, *The*

Red Deal advances a vision of freedom based not on possession or anthropocentrism, but on balance, assembly, and mutuality. It makes no promise of triumph, but instead it promises a path for new ways of living and being together, where every life belongs, is valued, heard, respected, and protected under a system of justice that is nonpunitive, non-carceral, and transformative. It calls for nothing less than the reversal of colonial structures that have deliberately attempted to erase other ways of knowing through genocide": Kelley, "Freedom Dreaming," in Getachew, ed., *Imagining Global Futures*, p. 211.

1 Utilitarianism Now and Then

1 See Peter S. Goodman, *Davos Man: How the Billionaires Devoured the World* (Custom House, 2022) and Douglas Rushkoff, *Survival of the Richest: Escape Fantasies of the Tech Billionaires* (W. W. Norton and Company, 2022). In addition to Daniel Hausman's *Preference, Value, Choice, and Welfare* (Cambridge University Press, 2012) and other critiques of utility theory's use of preference satisfaction (and money) as a normative standard, there are many effective challenges to mainstream economics and the world the economists (especially American economists) have promoted – see Elizabeth Popp Berman, *Thinking Like an Economist: How Efficiency Replaced Equality in U.S. Public Policy* (Princeton University Press, 2022); Deaton, *Economics in America*; Binyamin Appelbaum, *The Economists' Hour: False Prophets, Free Markets, and the Fracture of Society* (Little, Brown, 2019); Robert Skidelsky, *What's Wrong with Economics?* (Yale University Press, 2020); and Gary Saul Morson and Morton G. Shapiro, *Cents and Sensibility: What Economics Can Learn from the Humanities* (Princeton University Press, 2017). For a far-reaching critique of neoclassical economics on the key matter of uncertainty, see John Kay and Mervin King, *Radical Uncertainty: Decision-Making beyond the Numbers* (W. W. Norton and Co., 2021).

2 On the "happiness industry," see Nicholas Hill, Sven Brinkmann, and Anders Petersen, eds., *Critical Happiness Studies* (Routledge, 2021), and William Davies, *The Happiness Industry* (Verso, 2016). The surge in "happiness studies" in recent decades has a downside, throwing more responsibility onto the individual and deflecting attention from systemic social and political issues in ways that lend themselves to the machinations of the corporate world. It is true that economic measures are not good indicators of happiness or well-being – see Richard A. Easterlin, *An Economist's Lessons on Happiness: Farewell Dismal Science* (Springer, 2021) – but the favored techniques and metrics of happiness studies, while an improvement, are also inadequate to the task, in part for the reasons given in Anna Alexandrova's *A Philosophy for the Science of Well-Being* (Oxford University Press, 2021). As Goldberg's *Dread* argues, the "counter to dread … involves co-developing a collective ecology of caring … crafting infrastructures of social care" (p. 210).

3 Deaton, *Economics in America*, p. 53. And "the increase in deaths of despair, around one hundred thousand every year since the mid-1990s, is confined to those without a college degree" (p. 220). Deaton's book, an incisive indictment of healthcare in the US and of much else besides, should be required reading for anyone contemplating a career in economics or public policy. For his more

extensive joint study, with Anne Case, see *Deaths of Despair and the Future of Capitalism* (Princeton University Press, 2020).

4 Nicholas Kristoff, "Why So Many Americans Are Feeling More Pain," *New York Times*, Sunday, May 7, 2023.

5 See The EAT–Lancet Commission on Healthy Diets from Sustainable Food Systems, January 16, 2019, and Walter Willet and Edward L. Giovannucci, *Eat, Drink, and Be Healthy: The Harvard Medical School Guide to Healthy Eating* (Free Press, 2017); also, Peter Singer, *Animal Liberation Now: The Definitive Classic Renewed* (HarperCollins, 2023).

6 See David Bandurski, "The 'lying flat' movement standing in the way of China's innovation drive" (Brookings, July 8, 2021, www.brookings.edu/articles/the-lying-flat-movement-standing-in-the-way-of-chinas-innovation-drive), and David Graeber, *Bullshit Jobs* (Simon & Schuster, 2018, and https://davidgraeber.org).

7 Galloway, *Adrift*, p. 222. Galloway's *Adrift*, like Putnam's *Bowling Alone* before it, charts how "Facebook is no substitute for face-to-face conversations or the deep connections we form working alongside others for the betterment of our communities" (p. 6), though such engagement, and even talking to neighbors, has been in steep decline, along with numbers of close friends, marriages, and even physical relationships. The rapidly accumulating evidence, and public conversations, about the deleterious impact of social media and innovations in AI are finally catching up with the research of Sherry Turkle in *Reclaiming Conversation: The Power of Talk in a Digital Age* (Penguin, 2016). And, of course, AI itself cries out for decolonization – see Kanta Dihal et al., at Decolonising AI (lcfi.ac.uk).

8 Again, see *Deaths of Despair* by Case and Deaton, though Richard Reeves's *Of Boys and Men* (Swift Press, 2023) amplifies a disturbing dimension of their account of current illfare – namely, the problems confronting young men without college degrees. The willingness of free-market enthusiasts to invoke a caricature of utilitarianism as they blame the victims of predatory corporations rather than the guilty corporations – such as Big Pharma – is amply documented; Deaton, in *Economics in America*, quotes Texas Republican Jeb Hensarling, on how "free market economics provided the maximum good to the maximum number" (p. 232).

9 Smith, *The Theory of Moral Sentiments*, ed. D. D. Raphael and A. L. Macfie (Liberty Classics, 1976), pp. 52–3.

10 A concise definition is given by Tim Mulgan: "The defining feature of utilitarianism is that it bases its moral evaluations on *impartial promotion of well-being*." See his primer *Utilitarianism* (Cambridge University Press, 2020), p. 1, also Crisp's "Taking Stock of Utilitarianism," *Utilitas*, vol. 26, no. 3 (September 2014).

11 See Alan Gibbard, "Five Girls on a Rock," *London Review of Books*, vol. 34, no. 11 (June 7, 2012); Dave Edmonds, *Would You Kill the Fat Man? The Trolley Problem and What Your Answer Tells Us about Right and Wrong* (Princeton University Press, 2013); and Katarzyna de Lazari-Radek and Peter Singer, *Utilitarianism: A Very Short Introduction* (Oxford University Press, 2017). For present purposes, it is sufficient to agree that, as de Lazari-Radek and Singer demonstrate (drawing on the psychological research of Joshua Greene), such cases are at best inconclusive and might even provide plausible support for a utilitarian perspective as the more thoughtful, reflective reaction

to such problems (pp. 32–41). Given how conflicting or incoherent people's intuitions are, with much swinging on the exact means by which one sacrifices the fat man (direct physical action or something less immediate), these cases are vulnerable to the type of debunking project that de Lazari-Radek and Singer apply to them, and to many other familiar thought experiments.

12 For a sampler, see de Lazari-Radek and Singer, *Utilitarianism: A Very Short Introduction*, and their *The Point of View of the Universe* (Oxford University Press, 2014); Ben Eggleston, ed., *The Cambridge Companion to Utilitarianism* (Cambridge University Press, 2014); James Crimmins, ed., *The Bloomsbury Encyclopedia of Utilitarianism* (Bloomsbury Academic, 2017); Tim Mulgan, *Understanding Utilitarianism* (Routledge, 2007) and *Utilitarianism.*

13 See John Broome, "Utility," *Economics and Philosophy*, 7 (1991), pp. 1–12. Ivan Moscati's *Measuring Utility: From the Marginal Revolution to Behavioral Economics* (Oxford University Press, 2019) provides a masterly review of developments in formal utility theory over a crucial historical stretch, though it is easy to agree with his conclusion that "the economists' struggle to measure utility, which began with the marginal revolution almost one hundred fifty years ago, is far from concluded" (p. 284).

14 As Martha Nussbaum neatly put it, in "Epistemology of the Closet," in her *Philosophical Interventions: Reviews 1986–2011* (Oxford University Press, 2012), p. 301. See also Donald Winch, *Wealth and Life: Essays on the Intellectual History of Political Economy in Britain, 1848–1914* (Cambridge University Press, 2009), and the works cited in previous notes.

15 Mulgan, *Utilitarianism*, pp. 3–4.

16 Ibid., p. 10.

17 Ibid., p. 15.

18 Ibid., p. 16. The chapters that follow here will highlight the importance of outlooks, ways of life, or portfolios of foci as the better options for utilitarianism and consequentialism in general.

19 Ibid., p. 17.

20 Ibid., pp. 18–19.

21 As argued in my book *The Happiness Philosophers*.

22 For the best account of the Auto-Icon, see James E. Crimmins's introduction to his edited work, *Jeremy Bentham's Auto-Icon, and Related Writings* (Thoemmes Press, 2002). For an early (albeit critical) canonization of Bentham, see Leslie Stephen's multi-volume *The English Utilitarians*, via Project Gutenberg: www.gutenberg.org/ebooks.

23 Bentham, "Article on Utilitarianism, Long Version," in *The Collected Works of Jeremy Bentham: Deontology, together with A Table of the Springs of Action and Article on Utilitarianism*, ed. Amnon Goldworth (Clarendon Press, 1983), p. 292.

24 See Philip Schofield, "Utilitarianism, God and Moral Obligation from Locke to Sidgwick," in W. Breckman and P. E. Gordon, eds., *The Cambridge History of Modern European Thought* (Cambridge University Press, 2019), pp. 111–30.

25 Michel Foucault, *Discipline and Punish* (Vintage Books, 1991), p. 201. As Foucault put it, "The threefold aspect of panopticism – supervision, control, correction – seems to be a fundamental and characteristic dimension of the power relations that exist in our society": "Truth and Juridical Forms," in Paul Rabinow, ed., *Power: Essential Works of Foucault, 1954–1984* (The New

Press, 2000), p. 70. See the notes below for correctives to the Foucauldian take.

26 Bentham, *The Collected Works of Jeremy Bentham: An Introduction to the Principles of Morals and Legislation*, ed. J. H. Burns and H. L. A. Hart, with a new introduction by F. Rosen (Clarendon Press, 1996, first published 1970). References to Bentham's works will mostly be to those edited by Philip Schofield and the Bentham Project's *Collected Works of Jeremy Bentham* (Clarendon Press, 33 volumes to date). The scholarly work of the Bentham Project is exemplary and has contributed enormously to the understanding of both Bentham and imperialism. For instance, the intricacies of the Panopticon project, and its relationship to Bentham's severe criticism of transportation to Australia as a method of punishment, are detailed in T. Causer, M. Finn, and P. Schofield, eds., *Jeremy Bentham and Australia: Convicts, Utility and Empire* (UCL Press, 2022).

27 Bentham despised a merely expository account of legal systems that described law as it was rather than as it ought to be, and he lamented the "relentless tyranny of the dead" evident in common law theory and practice.

28 Bentham, *The Collected Works of Jeremy Bentham: Rights, Representation, and Reform*, ed. Philip Schofield, Catherine Pease-Watkin, and Cyprian Blamires (Clarendon Press, 2002), p. 330.

29 W. V. O. Quine, "Five Milestones of Empiricism," in *Theories and Things* (Harvard University Press, 1986).

30 Mark Canuel, "Bentham, Utility, and the Romantic Imagination," in Stephen G. Engelmann, ed., *Jeremy Bentham: Selected Writings* (Yale University Press, 2011), p. 515. This essay offers a number of important corrections to the stock caricatures of Bentham.

31 Boralevi, *Bentham and the Oppressed* (Walter De Gruyter, 1984). But much work remains to be done on Bentham on race and racism.

32 Bentham, *Introduction to the Principles of Morals and Legislation*, p. 283.

33 But see Frederick Rosen, "Jeremy Bentham on Slavery and the Slave Trade," in Schultz and Varouxakis, eds., *Utilitarianism and Empire*, pp. 33–56, for a careful reading of Bentham that brings out how Bentham often used the word "slavery" in a general way, and how "there is no evidence that he emphasized security of property *over* abolition. Security was a complex idea and tended to preclude reform by force and violence. Bentham believed that 'to reform the world by force, you might as well reform the moon, and the design is fit only for lunatics.'" Reforming by example was better, a view he held for much of his life. This is what "stood behind his strategy of gradual reform, which included the abolition of slavery and other forms of injustice and oppression" (pp. 49–50).

34 Bentham, *The Works of Jeremy Bentham*, vol. IX: *Constitutional Code*, ed. John Bowring (William Tait, 1843), p. 110.

35 See, for a compelling account, James E. Crimmins, *Utilitarian Philosophy and Politics: Bentham's Later Years* (Bloomsbury, 2011).

36 Ibid., p. 2.

37 John Stuart Mill, "Whewell on Moral Philosophy," in *The Collected Works of John Stuart Mill*, vol. X: *Essays on Ethics, Religion, and Society*, ed. J. M. Robson (Liberty Fund, 2006, originally published by the University of Toronto Press in 1969), p. 173.

38 Bentham, *The Collected Works of Jeremy Bentham: Of Sexual Irregularities*

and Other Writings on Sexual Morality, ed. Philip Schofield, Catherine Pease-Watkin, and Michael Quinn (Clarendon Press, 2014).

39 Bentham, *Deontology*, ed. Goldsworth, pp. 256–7.

40 Peter J. Cain, "Bentham and the Development of the British Critique of Colonialism," *Utilitas*, vol. 23, no. 1 (March 2011).

41 Blake, *The Pleasures of Benthamism: Victorian Literature, Utility, Political Economy* (Oxford University Press, 2009), p. 196.

42 Ibid., p. 197.

43 See Lowe, *The Intimacies of Four Continents*, p. 45 and p. 112. But Lowe's remarks on Bentham are surprisingly spare, and what follows here draws on more extensive sources.

44 Schofield, *Utility and Democracy* (Oxford University Press, 2006), p. 220. At one point, Bentham even suggested that it would make more sense for Canada to unite with the United States.

45 Ibid., p. 200.

46 Jennifer Pitts, *A Turn to Empire: The Rise of Imperial Liberalism in Britain and France* (Princeton University Press, 2005), p. 103. Pitts records the famous anecdote about Lord Bentinck remarking to James Mill, "I am going to British India; but I shall not be Governor-General. It is you that will be Governor-General": ibid.

47 Stokes, *The English Utilitarians and India* (Oxford University Press, 1959), p. vii. Stokes's book is rich in archival research and an excellent resource on the details of administration, judicial reform, land tenure, and revenue policy, those last being crucial given how much funding came from land taxation. As he notes, only "in Ceylon, under the less authoritarian rule of the Colonial Office, did the Liberal wing of the utilitarian mind predominate" (p. 321). By contrast, James Mill was extremely authoritarian with respect to India, albeit in the name of "good government" (which for him meant government without any Indian participation).

48 Pitts, *A Turn to Empire*, p. 104.

49 Pitts, "Great and Distant Crimes: Empire in Bentham's Thought," in Engelmann, ed., *Jeremy Bentham: Selected Writings*, p. 485. This essay draws heavily on Pitts's earlier work, *A Turn to Empire*, but in this collection appears along with key writings by Bentham, including "Place and Time," a piece that some Bentham scholars would deny is one of his key writings on India.

50 Ibid., p. 491.

51 Pitts, *A Turn to Empire*, p. 121.

52 Pitts, "Empire in Bentham's Thought," p. 478.

53 Ibid., p. 492.

54 Ibid., pp. 489–91.

55 Jennifer Pitts, "Jeremy Bentham: Legislator of the World?" in Schultz and Varouxakis, eds., *Utilitarianism and Empire*, p. 80. See also Stephen G. Engelmann and Jennifer Pitts, "Bentham's 'Place and Time,'" *The Tocqueville Review*, vol. 32, no. 1 (2011).

56 Cain, "Bentham and the British Critique of Colonialism," p. 13. Note that the use of the term "Orientalism" is informed by the infamous debates between Orientalists, Anglicists, and Vernacularists when it came to Indian education, debates discussed in the following chapter. All sides were problematically imperialist.

57 Jon E. Wilson, *The Domination of Strangers: Modern Government in Eastern*

India, 1780–1835 (Palgrave Macmillan, 2010), p. 1. More needs to be said about the official or government intermediaries and their understanding of utilitarianism, about the colonial subjects who converted to the utilitarianism of the colonial systems, and about the colonized subjects who grew their own forms of utilitarianism. Again, much of the utilitarian influence came during Lord William Bentinck's governor-generalship. Bentinck was joined in his work by people with a mix of political perspectives: "Many of them believed in the Liberal ideas of 'peace, retrenchment and reform' (of the British franchise – there was no Indian franchise at this time), while others were attracted to utilitarian arguments that the government should promote 'the greatest happiness of the greatest number' of people through such measures as public education. Yet others … were evangelicals. What they all had in common was a belief that a government should do more than simply impose taxes and raise an army to defend the king, country and established church. The emergence of an educated middle class in Britain and the growth of the Company's empire, followed by a period of relative peace, encouraged the idea that in India the government had a responsibility to improve the material and moral lives of those it governed": Ian Barrow, *The East India Company 1600–1858: A Short History with Documents* (Hackett Publishing Company, 2017), pp. 106–7.

58 Javed Majeed, "James Mill's *The History of British India*: The Question of Utilitarianism and Empire," in Schultz and Varouxakis, eds., *Utilitarianism and Empire*, pp. 95–6. See also Majeed's unrivaled *Ungoverned Imaginings: James Mill's The History of British India and Orientalism* (Clarendon Press, 1992).

59 Stokes, *English Utilitarians*, p. 53.

60 Majeed, "James Mill's History," pp. 96–7. See also James Mill, "Colony," in the 1825 "Supplement" to the *Encyclopædia Britannica*, available at Colony: Online Library of Liberty (libertyfund.org). Mill analyzes the term "colony" as historically emphasizing either a people or a territory, and, in a fashion that would prove to be endlessly popular in imperialist theorizing, devotes a good deal of attention to the comparison of modern empires with those of ancient Greece and Rome.

61 Quoted in Stokes, *English Utilitarians*, p. 44.

62 Ibid., p. 56.

63 On the long history and global perils of undervaluing local community in relation to states and free markets, Raghuram Rajan's sobering account in *The Third Pillar: How Markets and the State Leave the Community Behind* (Penguin Press, 2019) offers a fund of insights, some drawn from his experiences as a former head of India's central bank.

64 Stokes, *English Utilitarians*, p. 320. As Stokes argues, the 1860s were also an important period for Benthamite influence in India. Indeed, the long history of Macaulay's proposed and often revised penal code is instructive. Drafted in 1834, it did not actually go into effect until 1862 (later in some areas). The code, which Macaulay drafted as part of his work with the East India Company's Indian Law Commission, in fact reflected Bentham's influence, among other influences (such as the Napoleonic Code), albeit modulated by more Whiggish caution when it came to social change. Still, John Mill gave it his blessing, and, as Stokes notes, the immediate implementation of it "would have tested the courage of the most intrepid Governor-General" – see Stokes,

English Utilitarians, p. 141, pp. 191–2. The code was extremely dismissive of Indian legal arrangements – see *Indian Penal Code, Prepared by the Indian Law Commissioners* (Pelham Richardson, Cornhill, 1838).

65 See Pitts, *A Turn to Empire*, p. 105 and pp. 118–21. Claims about India as a testing ground influencing change in London can be hazardous. In "Colonial Origins of Modern Bureaucracy: India and the Professionalization of the British Civil Service," *Governance*, 33 (Wiley Online Library, https://acrobat.adobe.com/id/urn:aaid:sc:US:8b15d83a-32fe-4356-aa9f-4c6b3cf982dd, February 2022), Agnes Cornell and Ted Svensson carefully consider the empirical evidence for the claim that merit reforms of the ICS were an influence on reform of the Home Civil Service, concluding that: "there is not much support for the view" that the former actually influenced the latter. They also conclude that this is not terribly surprising, since the "ICS as an institution was chiefly devoted to a despotic exercise of colonial rule, which neither sought to facilitate the emergence of a 'unitary, centralized state' nor to respond to the wants and wishes of colonial subjects … For the CSC, and other influential actors, to recognize the ICS as a precursor would have entailed the dual risk of having to admit to its less than noble role in India and to the ways in which the Home Civil Service similarly was detached from the concerns of the general public" (p. 547).

66 Blake, *Pleasures of Benthamism*, p. 202.

67 Ibid., p. 203.

68 Ibid., pp. 203–4. As Barrow notes, by the 1820s, "many British missionaries, government officials, and the public saw sati, or concremation as it was sometimes called at the time, as a symbol of the degraded state of Hindu society and a marker of the low moral standing of the Company's government. Although the vast majority of Hindu widows did not become satis – there were, on average, between five hundred and six hundred a year – evangelicals chose to focus on the practice because it was so emotive and therefore had the best chance of pushing the government to condemn an aspect of Hinduism. For reformers this was the first step in a larger civilizational battle: would the Company now disassociate itself from Hinduism and begin to promote values that reformers characterized as universal but were really Christian? When he issued his regulation abolishing sati in November 1829, Bentinck explained that his motivation was to benefit Hindus: 'I know nothing so important to the improvement of their future condition,' he wrote, 'as the establishment of a purer morality … and a more just conception of the will of God'": Barrow, *The East India Company*, p. 108.

69 Blake, *Pleasures of Benthamism*, pp. 224–5.

70 Citing the historian Angus Maddison, Tharoor notes, in *Inglorious Empire*, that at the beginning of the eighteenth century, "India's share of the world economy was 23 per cent, as large as all of Europe put together . . . By the time the British departed India, it had dropped to just over 3 per cent. The reason was simple: India was governed for the benefit of Britain" (pp. 2–3). See also Utsa and Prabhat Patnaik, *A Theory of Imperialism* (Columbia University Press, 2016), which mobilizes much new data to demonstrate just how wrong Bentham and the Mills were about the economic advantages Britain reaped by ruling India. And as Barrow notes, with reference to Rammohan Roy, "some Indians, like Roy and those who depended on the Company for their livelihoods, were supporters of the colonial government.…

However, Roy's assessment also reflects a patrician disdain for the peasantry. Peasants were very politically aware and, when faced with excessive or unfair taxes and revenue demands, sometimes rebelled against their landlords and the state. The British regarded these rebellions as law-and-order issues, but their frequency suggests that there was widespread hostility toward the revenue systems as well as the police and courts that enforced the revenue laws" (p. 115).

71 O'Flaherty, *Utilitarianism in the Age of Enlightenment: The Moral and Political Thought of William Paley* (Cambridge University Press, 2019), p. 2.
72 Ibid., p. 7.
73 William Paley, *The Principles of Moral and Political Philosophy* (Liberty Fund, 2002), pp. 137–8.
74 Le Mahieu, "Foreword" to Paley's *The Principles of Moral and Political Philosophy*, pp. xxiv–xxv.
75 Godwin, *An Enquiry Concerning Political Justice*, ed. Mark Philp (Oxford University Press, 2013), p. 53. Philp's edition of Godwin's collected works is a monument to Godwin scholarship, as is Pamela Clemit's edition of Godwin's letters.
76 Ibid., p. 54.
77 See Angela Y. Davis, *Freedom Is a Constant Struggle* (Haymarket Books, 2016).
78 Marshall, *Demanding the Impossible: A History of Anarchism* (PM Press, 2010), p. 203.
79 Peter Singer, *One World Now: The Ethics of Globalization*, revised edition (Yale University Press, 2016), p. 159.
80 Godwin, *Enquiry*, p. 461.
81 Ibid., pp. 25–6.
82 Ibid., p. 463.
83 For a sampler of the radical Godwin, see Peter Marshall's nicely curated collection *The Anarchist Writings of William Godwin* (Freedom Press, 1986).
84 Peter H. Marshall, *William Godwin* (Yale University Press, 1984), pp. 109–10. It is intriguing that, as Gabriel Palmer-Fernandez points out in his introduction to Cappelletti's valuable work on *Anarchism in Latin America* (AK Press, 2017), when European and Russian anarchists tried to spread the message in Latin and South America in the nineteenth century, many of the Indigenous peoples they met up with found little to disagree with in anarchism, having already practiced something of the sort for centuries.
85 Marshall, *Godwin*, p. 113.
86 Caroline Reitz, "Bad Cop / Good Cop: Godwin, Mill and the Imperial Origins of the English Detective," *Novel: A Forum on Fiction*, vol. 33, no. 2 (Spring 2000).
87 See Schofield, "Godwin and Bentham's Circle," *The Bodleian Library Record*, vol. 24, no. 1 (2001), which concludes that the two had surprisingly little direct contact, though Bentham seemed to think that when Godwin said "Justice," he should have said "Utility."
88 Paley, *Principles of Moral and Political Philosophy*, p. 200.
89 Godwin, *The Enquirer: Reflections on Education, Manners and Literature* (Augustus M. Kelley, 1965, originally published in 1797), pp. 113–14.
90 That Godwin continues to inspire radical anarchists is evident from Richard Gough Thomas's recent biography, *William Godwin: A Political Life* (Pluto

Press, 2019). For some reservations about the extremes of Godwin's individualism, see the review of that book by Dominic Alexander in *Counterfire* (May 16, 2019).

91 Quoted in Marshall, *Godwin*, pp. 266–8.

92 Ibid., p. 75. Interestingly, Bertrand Russell, a later student of Sidgwick's who would defend a more radical, but noncognitivist version of Sidgwick's utilitarianism, actually shared more with Godwin when it came to both education and anarchism – with his wife Dora Russell, he founded and ran a free school, the Beacon Hill School. See my "Bertrand Russell in Ethics and Politics," pp. 594–634.

93 Godwin, *The Genius of Christianity Unveiled in a Series of Essays*, in *Political Writings and Philosophical Writings of William Godwin*, vol. VII: *Religious Writings*, ed. M. Philp (Pickering and Chatto, 1993), p. 209.

94 For a comprehensive study of police violence in the US, but with implications for other countries, see Kristian Williams, *Our Enemies in Blue: Politics and Power in America*, revised edition (AK Press, 2015). Of all the utilitarians considered in this book, Godwin stands alone as the figure best able to acknowledge such realities.

95 Godwin, *The Enquirer*, p. 71.

96 Ibid., p. 67.

97 Godwin, *Enquiry*, p. 283.

98 Ibid., pp. 398–9. These remarks occur in the context of Godwin's discussion of banishment as a punishment.

99 Schultz, *The Happiness Philosophers* addresses the debates over whether Godwin should really be counted a utilitarian, but I will not repeat those arguments here. Marshall makes the case.

100 Even if Godwin can hardly be accused of favoring a steel frame of legal codification, and castigated his home country in the harshest terms, he was often prey to the same invidious, Orientalist civilizational rankings as the Mills. See his *The Lives of the Necromancers* (Cambridge University Press, 2012, originally published in 1834) on "Eastern manners and habits of mind … credulity and a love of the marvellous" (p. 206).

101 Marshall, *Godwin*, p. 3. Writing in the 1980s, Marshall suggested that Godwin speaks "directly to the new radicalism which had emerged in the last decade, which seeks a libertarian way between the bureaucratic centralism of communist states and the organized lovelessness of the capitalist world. What Locke is for liberalism and Marx is for communism, Godwin is for anarchism" (p. 3). Today, of course, "organized lovelessness" seems like the much bigger problem, and one that extends through many different economic and political systems.

2 Utilitarian Virtue?

1 Lowe, *The Intimacies of Four Continents*, p. 114. Or, as Dipesh Chakrabarty put it in *Provincializing Europe: Postcolonial Thought and Historical Difference* (Princeton University Press, 2007), the Empire's subject populations were to be left in "the waiting room of history."

2 Lowe, *The Intimacies of Four Continents*, pp. 117–18.

3 Ibid., p. 118. As Stokes suggested, James Mill did much to set the stage, for

example with his enthusiasm for forcing on the subject populations of India his policies of taxation and land reform: "Mill, in standing out for the extreme logic of his theory, had wanted the State to absorb the whole of the true rent as revenue and to prohibit the growth of a private rent property. Not only did he wish to prevent the emergence of a land-owning aristocracy or gentry, but he rejected the idea of peasant proprietorship in the ordinary sense, because he saw that once in possession of a proportion of rent, the peasant would just as readily let out his land and become an idle rent-receiver" (Stokes, *English Utilitarians*, p. 110). His view was influential, if not always accepted *in toto.*

4 Mill did not write as much about China as about India, but what he did write was also quite offensive, arguing that China was in a "stationary state" both economically and culturally, thanks in part to a low desire for accumulation and preference for leisure. See Yue Xiao, "John Stuart Mill on China's Stationary State," *History of Political Economy*, vol. 53, no. 5 (2021). Naturally, the East India Company had a century and a half of monopoly on trade with China.

5 Porter, "Where is England?" *London Review of Books*, vol. 33, no. 21 (November 3, 2011). This is a review of Julia Lovell's powerful book on the first Opium War, *The Opium War: Drugs, Dreams and the Making of China* (Picador, 2011). As Porter and Lovell demonstrate, the war was very unpopular in England, which was why its backers, such as Lord Palmerston, tried "to demote opium in the pecking order of motives for the war, putting it below Chinese 'insults', and the broader essentially ethical principle of spreading 'enlightenment' through free trade." Of course, in the case of the harsh suppression of the Indian Sepoy Rebellion of 1857–8, British casualties were around 11,000 in total, whereas the Indian deaths, from the war and resulting famines and epidemics, have been estimated as possibly closer to 800,000 (Barrow, *The East India Company*, p. 115).

6 Barrow, *The East India Company*, pp. 79–80. For an excellent account of James Mill on the subject, see Donald Winch, *James Mill and India*, Online Library of Liberty, https://oll.libertyfund.org/pages/james-mill-and-india. Winch includes excerpts from Mill's responses when questioned by a Parliamentary Committee about the opium trade, on which subject Mill was blandly reassuring about the benefits to India that came from the tax on opium falling on foreigners: "I am satisfied that the monopoly of opium has had no injurious effect on the agriculture or commerce of the country.... It has had a favourable effect on the interests of the people, in as far as they are relieved from the burthen of taxation, by the amount of revenue thus derived from foreigners.... The small amount levied on internal consumption, I have never heard objected to.... I do not consider any other mode of raising a large revenue by opium feasible" (p. 438).

7 St. John Packe, *The Life of John Stuart Mill* (Secker and Warburg, 1954), pp. 388–9. One counter to such an assessment comes from David Williams's analysis of how the younger Mill, in his less theoretical and more practical ruminations on the governance of India, was often worried and doubtful, rather than confident – see "John Stuart Mill and the Practice of Colonial Rule in India," *Journal of International Political Theory*, vol. 17, no. 3 (2021).

8 Caroline Elkins, *Legacy of Violence: A History of the British Empire* (Alfred A. Knopf, 2022), pp. 43–4, p. 13. Mahmood Mamdani would agree, arguing that for the younger Mill, "the uncivilized were not sovereign and so were at

the mercy of the civilized. Indeed, conquest was portrayed not merely as an option but as a moral responsibility. Sovereigns were obligated either to bring civilization to peoples branded uncivilized, or to save the vulnerable hostages of uncivilized societies, such as women and the enslaved – to rescue them, in today's human rights language." See Mamdani, *Neither Settler nor Native: The Making and Unmaking of Permanent Minorities* (Harvard University Press, 2020), p. 7.

9 Marwah, *Liberalism, Diversity and Domination*. Again, Marwah is concerned to demonstrate that a rehabilitated, decolonized Mill is a better source for liberalism than Kant, whether in the original or rehabilitated.

10 Ibid., p. 11.

11 Ibid., pp. 240–1. Marwah goes on to critique Rawls as well for treating "diversity as a problem to be managed and enclosed."

12 Ibid., p. 13.

13 Ibid., e.g. p. 5: "Anachronistically treating Kant, Mill or any other such historical figure as 'racist' or 'sexist' *tout court* doesn't answer many questions." To the contrary, it is more questionable to dodge such descriptions when they can aptly be applied to one's philosophical heroes and for that very reason shed light on the insidious historical forms of racism, sexism, etc., embedded in the history of "liberalism," also a contested term.

14 An insightful reviewer for the press commented that there might not be any canonical figures left to teach, after decolonization has done its work.

15 Pitts, *A Turn to Empire*, p. 112.

16 See "Dickenson and Slavery," https://housedivided.dickinson.edu/sites/slavery. As the website notes, Cooper was himself a slaveholder, and a very prominent defender of slavery. See also Daniel Kilbride, "Slavery and Utilitarianism: Thomas Cooper and the Mind of the Old South," *Journal of Southern History*, 59 (August 1993), pp. 469–86.

17 James E. Crimmins and Mark G. Spencer, *Utilitarians and Their Critics in America, 1789–1914* (Thoemmes Continuum, 2005), p. xxv. For the best treatment of Cooper, see Crimmins, *Utilitarianism in the Early American Republic* (Routledge, 2022), pp. 198–230.

18 Some parts of this section adapt parts of chapter 3 of my book *The Happiness Philosophers*.

19 John Peter DiIulio, *Completely Free: The Moral and Political Vision of John Stuart Mill* (Princeton University Press, 2022), p. 4.

20 Mill referred to Bentham often and published no less than three pieces expressly devoted to him, the most famous of which is "Bentham," in *The Collected Works of John Stuart Mill*, vol. X: *Essays on Ethics, Religion, and Society*, ed. Robson.

21 See Ben Eggleston, Dale Miller, and David Weinstein, eds., *John Stuart Mill and the Art of Life* (Oxford University Press, 2011). The potential tensions here with the ordinary understanding of Bentham and Benthamism are quite real – see DiIulio, *Completely Free*, pp. 99–108.

22 There is a deep historical irony in the fact that John Mill's Romantic Wordsworthian enthusiasms overlapped with those of an earlier generation of imperialists in India, men serving under Governor-General Wellesley in 1798–1805.

23 Ryan, *Liberal Anxieties and Liberal Education* (Hill and Wang, 1998), pp. 91–2.

24 Mill, "Inaugural Address Delivered to the University of St. Andrews" (Longmans, Green, Reader, and Dyer, 1867), pp. 42–4.

25 Mill, *The Collected Works of John Stuart Mill*, vol. I: *Autobiography*, ed. John M. Robson and J. Stillinger (University of Toronto Press, 1981), p. 24. See also *The Collected Works of John Stuart Mill*, vol. XI: *Essays on Philosophy and the Classics*, ed. John M. Robson, introduction by F. E. Sparshott (Routledge, 1978), to appreciate Mill's debt to the ancient Greeks. "Grote's Plato" conveys his respect for his fellow Philosophical Radical and underscores his view of the Socratic elenchus as largely destructive in its results.

26 Crimmins, *Utilitarian Philosophy and Politics*, pp. 54–5.

27 Ibid., p. 26.

28 Ibid., p. 109.

29 Mill, *The Collected Works of John Stuart Mill*, vol. XIII: *The Earlier Letters of John Stuart Mill, 1812–1848, Part 2*, ed. Francis E. Mineka, introduction by F. E. Hayek (University of Toronto Press, 1963), p. 601. Though Bowring himself, in his *Autobiographical Recollections*, had mostly praise for Mill senior, calling him "the great gun of the Westminster Review. His object was to crush aristocratical influence, whether Whig or Tory, and he saw little distinction between the tactics of either party. Both were equally moved by a passion for place and power, both seemed to claim an hereditary right to govern, and both concurred in the policy of absolutely excluding the middle classes and the people from any influence in the Legislature, excepting so far as that influence could be made to serve their own purposes" – see *Autobiographical Recollections of Sir James Bowring*, p. 69, https://archive.org/details/autobiographica01bowrgoog. Bowring would prove to be a case in point of a disciple who turned Bentham's views into a far more dogmatic form of colonialism, which he sought to implement in various governmental roles, not least as the Governor of British Hong Kong.

30 Macaulay, "Bentham's Defence of Mill," in Jack Lively and John Rees, eds., *Utilitarian Logic and Politics: James Mill's "Essay on Government", Macaulay's Critique, and the Ensuing Debate* (Clarendon Press, 1978), p. 101. It was not actually Bentham himself defending Mill in this exchange.

31 Ibid., pp. 176–7.

32 On this, see Sara Ahmed, *What's the Use?* (Duke University Press, 2019), ch. 3.

33 James Mill, "Education," in W. H. Burston, ed., *James Mill on Education* (Cambridge University Press, 1969), pp. 97–8.

34 Ibid., p. 63.

35 Ibid.

36 Ibid., p. 64.

37 Ibid., pp. 107–8.

38 Ibid., pp. 66–7.

39 See the seminal works of Ryan, especially *J. S. Mill* (Routledge and Kegan Paul, 1974). Also, John Skorupski, *John Stuart Mill* (Routledge, 1989), ch. 8. Bentham, for his part, would in 1789 write to a friend: "I don't care two straws about liberty and necessity at any time. I do not expect any new truths on the subject: and were I to see any lying at my feet, I should hardly think it worth while to stoop to pick them up.... I am sure you must have gone before me in regretting that a practical professional man should stand forth as an author upon subjects so purely speculative" – quoted in Cyprian Blamires,

The French Revolution and the Creation of Benthamism (Palgrave Macmillan, 2008), p. 20.

40 Ball, "Mill, James," *Stanford Encyclopedia of Philosophy*, https://plato.stanford.edu/entries/james-mill.

41 Reeves, *John Stuart Mill: Victorian Firebrand* (Atlantic Books, 2007), p. 44. The commitment to Malthus was one of the strongest links between Mill and the Benthamites, though like Place he believed in birth control as a crucial aid to the progress of the working class.

42 Mill, *Autobiography*, p. 139.

43 Ibid., p. 141. This would not have been news to Godwin: "The best motive to learn, is perception of the value of the thing learned. The worst motive ... may well be affirmed to be constraint and fear. There is a motive between these, less pure than the first, but not so displeasing as the last, which is desire, not springing from the intrinsic excellence of the object, but from the accidental attractions which the teacher may have annexed to it" (Marshall, ed., *Anarchist Writings of William Godwin*, p. 154).

44 On this, see de Lazari-Radek and Singer, *The Point of View of the Universe*. Mill, like the other classical utilitarians, may have conceived his task in terms more akin to that of Singer's *How Are We to Live? Ethics in an Age of Self-Interest* (Prometheus Books, 1995), in its attempt to achieve a convergence of egoism and rational benevolence via a kind of argumentative pincer movement. As with Bentham, Mill's aggregative concern for the greatest happiness is never advanced without a distributivist regard for the happiness of each individual.

45 Mill, *Autobiography*, p. 145.

46 See my review of Maughn Rollins Gregory and Megan Jane Laverty, eds., *Gareth B. Matthews: The Child's Philosopher* in *Teaching Philosophy*, vol. 45, no. 3 (September 2022).

47 Mill, *Autobiography*, p. 149.

48 Though Sidgwick thought the conflation of egoism and utilitarianism to be a confusion on the part of the earlier utilitarians.

49 Mill, *Autobiography*, p. 153.

50 Sterling would die at the age of 38, a victim of the tuberculosis that would take so many during this era (and that Mill and Taylor Mill also suffered from). The author of works of poetry and the novel *Arthur Coningsby*, he was, as Mill noted, very much a man of strong feeling. He was also thick with colonial entanglements, often retreating to the family sugar plantation on St. Vincent.

51 Mill, *Autobiography*, p. 147.

52 Ibid., p. 147.

53 Donner, "Morality, Virtue, and Aesthetics in Mill's Art of Life," in Eggleston et al., eds., *John Stuart Mill and the Art of Life*, p. 155, p. 157, and p. 154.

54 Carlisle, *John Stuart Mill and the Writing of Character* (University of Georgia Press, 2010), p. 127.

55 Ibid., p. 144.

56 Stephen Engelmann, *Economic Rationality* (Polity, 2022), p. 66.

57 Fred Berger's *Happiness, Justice, and Freedom: The Moral and Political Philosophy of John Stuart Mill* (University of California Press, 1984) analyzes how Mill reconciled his account of mental conditioning with his account of autonomy and valuing various ideal goods for their own sake. Joseph Raz's

work on well-being is relevant here – see Crisp, "Raz on Well-Being," *Oxford Journal of Legal Studies*, vol. 17, no. 3 (Autumn 1997). And Mill's attempt to marry hedonism and perfectionism is the target of David Brink's *Mill's Progressive Principles* (Oxford University Press, 2013), reviewed by John Skorupski in *Notre Dame Philosophical Reviews* (March 19, 2014).

58 Mill, *Utilitarianism*, p. 214.

59 DiIulio, *Completely Free*, p. 68.

60 Ibid.

61 Numerous recent works on happiness endorse some such view, albeit without the clerisy bit. See Sissela Bok, *Exploring Happiness: From Aristotle to Brain Science* (Yale University Press, 2011), and Daniel Haybron, *The Pursuit of Unhappiness* (Oxford University Press, 2010).

62 Mill, *The Subjection of Women*, in Anne P. Robson and John M. Robson, eds., *Sexual Equality: Writings by John Stuart Mill, Harriet Taylor Mill, and Helen Taylor* (University of Toronto Press, 1994), p. 396.

63 See Skorupski, *Why Read Mill Today?* (Routledge, 2006), the best short treatment of the foundational tensions in Mill's worldview. Ryan's *Liberal Anxieties and Liberal Education* situates Mill's educational views alongside those of Russell and Dewey.

64 See DiIulio, *Completely Free* (especially pp. 23–34); also Schultz, *The Happiness Philosophers*, ch. 3.

65 Marwah, *Liberalism, Diversity and Domination*, p. 135.

66 Ibid., p. 136.

67 Ibid., p. 143.

68 Ibid., pp. 139, 141.

69 Whewell, *Lectures on Systematic Morality* (John W. Parker, 1846), p. 89.

70 See J. B. Schneewind, *Sidgwick's Ethics and Victorian Moral Philosophy* (Oxford University Press, 1977), and Alan Donagan, "Sidgwick and Whewellian Intuitionism," in B. Schultz, ed., *Essays on Henry Sidgwick* (Cambridge University Press, 1992).

71 Whewell, *Of the Plurality of Worlds* (John W. Parker, 1853), p. 351.

72 Whewell, *Lectures on the History of Moral Philosophy in England* (John W. Parker, 1852), p. ix.

73 Mill, "Whewell on Moral Philosophy," p. 230.

74 As Crisp observes, both Mill and Whewell problematically conflate metaethics and first-order substantive ethics. See the relevant sections of his "Taking Stock of Utilitarianism."

75 Ibid., p. 232.

76 Mill, *Utilitarianism*, p. 305.

77 Various of Mill's admirers try to make the case that for him justification never does come to an end, that his open-mindedness and fallibilistic, empiricist epistemology were really his saving graces – redeeming features being obscured by current fixations on the colonial entanglements of liberalism. This is something of a theme in Blake's *Pleasures of Benthamism*, and it is the central theme in Menaka Philips, "JS Mill, Liberalism, and the Virtues of Uncertainty," *European Journal of Political Theory*, vol. 18, no. 1 (January 2019). But is difficult to see how his confessions of uncertainty can compensate for his complicity in the various imperial ventures.

78 Mill, *Utilitarianism*, p. 233.

79 Crisp's edition of *Utilitarianism*, along with those of de Lazari-Radek and

Singer (Norton, 2022), and Eggleston (Hackett, 2017), together yield a judicious assessment of Mill's classic in light of both its historical context and the current state of the arguments.

80 Blake, *Pleasures of Benthamism*, pp. 209–10.

81 Ibid., p. 210.

82 Ibid., p. 211.

83 For a classic work on how Oxford Idealists were a force in liberal imperialism, along with Evangelicals and other missionaries, see Richard Symonds, *Oxford and Empire: The Last Lost Cause* (Oxford University Press, 1992). Certainly Jowett, the Master of Balliol College, translator of Plato, and eager supporter of Oxford's India Institute, was clear enough in supporting the civilizing mission, writing of the Indians that "I suppose that we may begin by assuming that the natives are very like grown-up children in many ways, very apt to lie and deceive, partly from fear, and partly from want of stamina." See *The Life and Letters of Benjamin Jowett, MA*, vol. II, ed. Evelyn Abbott and Lewis Campbell (John Murray, 1897), p. 286.

84 The letter is to David Urquhart, and can be found in *The Collected Works of John Stuart Mill*, vol. XVI: *Later Letters, 1849–1873*, ed. Francis E. Mineka and Dwight L. Lindley (University of Toronto Press, 1972), pp. 1205–6. There is a follow-up letter a couple of weeks later in which he laments that there "is much in American politics that is regrettable enough, but I do not observe that there is a particle of the English upper class feeling that authority (meaning the persons in authority) must be supported at all costs; & American foreign policy is all above board & in broad daylight" (p. 1209).

85 Pitts, *A Turn to Empire*, p. 159.

86 Again, Williams argues, in "John Stuart Mill and the Practice of Colonial Rule in India," that he was more tormented over the course of his life – "Mill did justify colonial rule in India, and his argument certainly exhibited some of the 'colonial' or 'imperial' features of liberal thought more generally.... Nonetheless, a focus only on these aspects of his thought leads to a very incomplete understanding of what Mill thought about this rule.... Mill identified a very exacting set of conditions necessary if British rule was to live up to its mission; he recognized that it was hard to achieve these conditions, and he saw some very real threats to them. And certainly toward the end of his life, Mill thought Britain was not doing it at all well. Far from being the embodiment of self-confident nineteenth-century liberal imperial attitudes, Mill was actually, and increasingly, uncertain about the ability of Britain to make good on what he understood as its mission in India ... the real criticism of Mill may be not that he justified British rule in India, but that his vision of how this rule ought to be conducted was verging on utopian ... and thus that his kind of liberal justification for colonialism might in fact operate politically to mask an altogether different kind of colonialism" (pp. 424–5).

87 What follows here draws on my "Mill and Sidgwick, Imperialism and Racism" and *The Happiness Philosophers*, chs. 3–4.

88 Smits, "John Stuart Mill on the Antipodes: Settler Violence against Indigenous Peoples and the Legitimacy of Colonial Rule," *Australian Journal of Politics and History*, vol. 54, no. 1 (2008).

89 Ibid., p. 4.

90 Ibid.

91 Ibid., p. 14.

92 Quoted in J. Joseph Miller, "Chairing the Jamaica Committee: J. S. Mill and the Limits of Colonial Authority," in Schultz and Varouxakis, eds., *Utilitarianism and Empire*, p. 178.
93 See Roxanne Dunbar-Ortiz, *An Indigenous Peoples' History of the United States* (Beacon Press, 2015), and Jeffrey Ostler, *Surviving Genocide: Native Nations and the United States from the American Revolution to Bleeding Kansas* (Yale University Press, 2019). A helpful recapitulation of the salient historical facts about the defining force of various racisms early on in Anglo-American modernity is Robert P. Jones, *The Hidden Roots of White Supremacy* (Simon & Schuster, 2023).
94 Martha Nussbaum, "Mill on Happiness: The Enduring Value of a Complex Critique," in Schultz and Varouxakis, eds., *Utilitarianism and Empire*, pp. 120–3.
95 Georgios Varouxakis, *Mill on Nationality* (Routledge, 2002), p. 116.
96 Anthony Kwame Appiah, *The Ethics of Identity* (Princeton University Press, 2004), p. 144.
97 The Catherine Hall / Peter Mandler debate over the salience of the notion of race in the mid-Victorian context is important – see Catherine Hall, *Civilizing Subjects* (University of Chicago Press, 2002), p. 497, note 127. My own take on race follows Goldberg: "I am suggesting that race is a fluid, transforming, historically specific concept parasitic on theoretic and social discourses for the meaning it assumes at any given historical moment" – *Racist Culture* (Oxford University Press, 1993), p. 74. Goldberg's approach has been further developed in *The Threat of Race* and *The War on Critical Race Theory*. See also Holt, *The Problem of Race in the 21st Century*, and Sally Haslanger's contribution to *What Is Race? Four Philosophical Views* (Oxford University Press, 2019).
98 Otele, *African Europeans*, p. 49. Otele's work, like Goldberg's, is informed by and sensitive to the growing literature on "Seeing Race before Race," as a 2023 Newberry Library Exhibition in Chicago titles it, and to the shifting historical contours of racism evident in the recent attacks on Critical Race Theory, attacks that reflect a pretended "colorblindness" that simply results in a perverse "racisms without racism" and an inability to even conceptualize enduring systemic or structural racism. Otele's brilliant work is extremely good on both the history of the racisms shaping the identity of modern Europe and the ways in which they play out in the UK today.
99 Goldberg, *Are We All Postracial Yet?* (Polity, 2015), p. 23.
100 Uday Mehta, *Liberalism and Empire: A Study in Nineteenth-Century British Liberal Thought* (University of Chicago Press, 1999), pp. 195–6.
101 Ibid., p. 15.
102 David Theo Goldberg, "Liberalism's Limits: Carlyle and Mill on 'the negro question,'" *Nineteenth-Century Contexts*, vol. 22, no. 2 (2000), reprinted in Schultz and Varouxakis, eds., *Utilitarianism and Empire*, pp. 125–36, pp. 133–4.
103 Carlyle and Mill, *The Nigger Question: The Negro Question*, ed. Eugene R. August (Appleton-Century-Crofts, 1971). See also *The Collected Works of John Stuart Mill*, vol. XXI: *Essays on Equality, Law, and Education*, ed. John M. Robson (University of Toronto Press, 1984), including the introduction by Stefan Collini.
104 Carlyle, *The Nigger Question*, p. 40.

105 Goldberg, "Liberalism's Limits," p. 129.
106 Miller, "Chairing the Jamaica Committee," p. 163.
107 Goldberg, "Liberalism's Limits," p. 130.
108 Ibid., p. 134.
109 Witness his none-too-coded reference to the Black District Attorney of Fulton County, Georgia, Fani Willis, as one of the "riggers." See Vivian Ho, "First Thing: Trump Prosecutor Faces Racist Abuse following Indictment," *The Guardian*, August 17, 2023.
110 Goldberg, *The War on Critical Race Theory*, p. 153.
111 Anthony Bogues, "John Stuart Mill and 'The Negro Question': Race, Colonialism, and the Ladder of Civilization," in Andrew Valls, ed., *Race and Racism in Modern Philosophy* (Cornell University Press, 2005), p. 222.
112 Pitts, *A Turn to Empire*, p. 160.
113 As Bogues summarizes it, when the rebellion (largely led by Bogle and his followers) reached its peak, involving some 2,000 persons in the parish of St. Thomas, the "colonial government reacted by establishing a council of war. Arguing that this was but the tip of an island-wide conspiracy to overthrow the colonial government, and with the memory of the Haitian Revolution hovering over the colony, Governor Eyre organized a military force to brutally crush the rebellion. At the end of the day, Eyre unleashed severe repression – 439 persons were killed, hundreds were brutally flogged, thousands of houses were burnt, and many of the leaders including Bogle were hanged. Eyre held Gordon responsible for the rebellion and duly executed him" (Bogues, "John Stuart Mill," p. 224). The best accounts of the rebellion are Hall, *Civilizing Subjects*; Bernard Semmel, *Jamaican Blood and Victorian Conscience: The Governor Eyre Controversy* (Houghton Mifflin, 1962); and Gad Heuman, *The Killing Time: The Morant Bay Rebellion in Jamaica* (University of Tennessee Press, 1994). Also, Hall's essay "Competing Masculinities: Thomas Carlyle, John Stuart Mill and the Case of Governor Eyre," in Catherine Hall, ed., *White, Male, and Middle-Class: Explorations in Feminism and History* (Cambridge University Press, 1992), compares Mill's feminism to his views on race, and argues that on Mill's account, "whether there would be in the end, whatever the degree of education achieved by the blacks, a natural division of labor between the races, remains a problem" (p. 288).
114 Pitts, *A Turn to Empire*, p. 161.
115 Ibid., p. 162.
116 Ibid. Pitts's argument here is primarily concerned with the limits of English and French liberal discourse, rather than with the overall cultural and historical limitations of the "times," which could muster a good deal more. Presumably Lowe would agree, though curiously there is no discussion of Jamaica in her work.
117 Ibid., p. 241.
118 John Robson, "Civilisation and Culture as Moral Concepts," in John Skorupski, ed., *The Cambridge Companion to Mill* (Cambridge University Press, 1998), p. 353. Robson also quotes from Mill's "Remarks on Bentham's Philosophy": "For a tribe of North American Indians, improvement means, taming down their proud and solitary self-dependence: for a body of emancipated negroes, it means accustoming them to be self-dependent, instead of being merely obedient to orders: for our semi-barbarous ancestors it would

have meant softening them; for a race of enervated Asiatics it would mean hardening them" (p. 368). Robson's *The Improvement of Mankind* (University of Toronto Press, 1968) remains one of the most valuable works on Mill's progressivism. That historical progress *was* the story of the scale of civilization was the backdrop to the works of Godwin, Bentham, and the two Mills.

119 Georgios Varouxakis, "Empire, Race, Euro-centrism: John Stuart Mill and His Critics," in Schultz and Varouxakis, eds., *Utilitarianism and Empire*, p. 142.

120 Ibid., p. 144.

121 Ibid., p. 141.

122 Varouxakis simply misses the cogency of Goldberg's account of social constructions interweaving "race" and "ethnicity."

123 On Mill's political context and racism, such generally excellent works as Bell's *Reordering the World* and *Victorian Visions of Global Order*, or Casper Sylvest's *British Liberal Internationalism, 1880–1939* (Manchester University Press, 2009), simply concede, albeit grudgingly, all the crucial points argued above. Bell's more recent works, notably *Dreamworlds of Race* and the edited volume *Empire, Race, and Global Justice*, manifest a more insightful emphasis on race and racism, but mostly focus on later periods with only glancing references to Mill and the utilitarians.

124 Philip Sherlock and Hazel Bennett, *The Story of the Jamaican People* (Kingston, Jamaica, 1998), pp. 247–8; see also Semmel, *Jamaican Blood and Victorian Conscience.* Heuman also compellingly demonstrates how the Morant Bay Rebellion "was preceded by a long history of slave rebellions as well as a series of riots in the post-emancipation period. Many of the people involved in these riots continued to look to the rebellions as models of resistance," though after emancipation their agenda "included resisting any attempt at re-enslavement and regarded access to land as a measure of full freedom" (p. 42).

125 Manjapra, *Black Ghost of Empire: The Long Death of Slavery and the Failure of Emancipation* (Scribner, 2022).

126 Holt, *The Problem of Race in the 21st Century*, p. 47. See also Holt, *The Problem of Freedom: Race, Labor and Politics in Jamaica and Britain, 1832–1938* (Johns Hopkins University Press, 1991), and Bogues, "John Stuart Mill," p. 223.

127 Pitts, *A Turn to Empire*, p. 157.

128 On social constructions of whiteness and delusions of postracialism, see Goldberg, *Are We All Postracial Yet?*, and Linda Martin Alcoff, *The Future of Whiteness* (Polity, 2015).

129 George Fredrickson, *Racism: A Short History* (Princeton University Press, 2002), p. 8.

130 Ibid., pp. 3–4.

131 Ibid., p. 108. Fredrickson is too cautious on this score, but clearly, on his account, it does make very good sense to call some such colonial or imperial situations racist, when considering the functional or "polite" form of racism. And, obviously, "something that can be legitimately described as racism existed well before the twentieth century or even the late nineteenth century" (p. 100). Much earlier, in fact.

132 Mill, *The Collected Works of John Stuart Mill*, vol. XXVIII: *Public and*

Parliamentary Speeches, Pt. 1, November 1850–November 1868, ed. John M. Robson and Bruce L. Kinzer (University of Toronto Press, 1988), p. 118.

133 *The Collected Works of John Stuart Mill*, vol. XVI, ed. Mineka and Lindley, p. 1206. And in that other 1866 letter to Urquhart, Mill laments the "sympathy of officials with officials & of the classes from whom officials are selected with officials of all sorts" and "the sympathy with authority & power, generated in our higher & upper middle classes by the feeling of being specially privileged to exercise them, & by living in a constant dread of the encroachment of the class beneath which makes it one of their strongest feelings that resistance to authority must be put down per fas et nefas" (p. 1209).

134 Bruce L. Kinzer, Ann P. Robson, and John M. Robson, *A Moralist in and out of Parliament: John Stuart Mill at Westminster, 1865–1868* (University of Toronto Press, 1992), pp. 216–17.

135 When the Grand Jury threw out the charges against Eyre, *Punch* celebrated the occasion with a singularly nasty poem, the first stanza of which runs "Ye savages thirsting for bloodshed and plunder / Ye miscreants burning for rapine and prey, / By the fear of the lash and the gallows kept under, / Henceforth who shall venture to stand in your way? / Run riot, destroy, ravage, kill without pity, / Let any man how he molests you beware. / Beholding how hard the Jamaica Committee / To ruin are trying to hunt gallant EYRE." See *The White Man's Burden: An Anthology of British Poetry of the Empire*, ed. Chris Brooks and Peter Faulkner (University of Exeter Press, 1996), p. 206.

3 The Worst of the Best

1 DiIulio, *Completely Free*, pp. 99–100.

2 Ibid., pp. 105–6.

3 See Rawls's Foreword to the Hackett edition of Sidgwick's most famous work, *The Methods of Ethics*, pp. v–vi.

4 Judith Butler, *Giving an Account of Oneself* (Fordham University Press, 2005), p. 103.

5 Sidgwick, *The Methods of Ethics*, p. xviii.

6 C. D. Broad, *Five Types of Ethical Theory* (Cambridge University Press, 1930); Rawls, *A Theory of Justice*; Derek Parfit, *On What Matters*, vol. I (Oxford University Press, 2011); de Lazari-Radek and Singer, *The Point of View of the Universe*; Roger Crisp, *The Cosmos of Duty* (Oxford University Press, 2015); and David Phillips, *Sidgwick's The Methods of Ethics: A Guide* (Oxford University Press, 2022).

7 See Sidgwick, *Lectures on the Ethics of T. H. Green, Mr. Herbert Spencer, and J. Martineau*, ed. E. E. Constance Jones (Macmillan, 1902), p. 185. Sidgwick had many unsparing criticisms of Spencer's construal of classical utilitarianism: "if Mr. Spencer means to imply, as he certainly suggests to his readers, that the practical directions of Bentham and Mill are that everyone is to make universal happiness the object of direct pursuit, his misunderstanding of these authors is so complete that it can only be accounted for on the supposition of his having read their writings very partially" (p. 182). Spencer, Sidgwick urged, mistook Mill for Comte.

8 For the fullest accounts of Sidgwick's life and work, see Schultz, *Henry Sidgwick, Eye of the Universe* and *The Happiness Philosophers*.

9 Birks, *Modern Utilitarianism, or, the Systems of Paley, Bentham and Mill Examined and Compared* (Macmillan, 1874). Birks's work is virtually unknown today, but it is important for purposes of understanding how someone like Sidgwick could still consider himself a utilitarian reformer fighting the intuitionist orthodoxy.
10 Sidgwick, *The Methods of Ethics*, p. 14.
11 For a range of critical perspectives, see Donagan, "Sidgwick and Whewellian Intuitionism," T. H. Irwin, *The Development of Ethics*, vol. III (Oxford University Press, 2009), and Hurka, *British Ethical Theorists from Sidgwick to Ewing* (Oxford University Press, 2018).
12 Sidgwick's posthumous *Lectures on Green, Spencer, and Martineau* repeatedly declare his sympathies with utilitarianism: "I do not regard the verdicts of Common Sense, even when it is clearly pronounced, as final; if I find it conflicting with what appear to me clear deductions from self-evident principles – such as those which according to me lie at the basis of Utilitarianism – I venture after full consideration to dissent from it, though even so I may not think it right to proclaim my dissent" (p. 351). But he immediately goes on to explain that both analytical and historical study converge on the view that "the current civilized morality of the present age" is "merely a stage in a long process of development, in which the human mind has, I hope, been gradually moving towards a truer apprehension of what ought to be. We do not find merely change, when we trace the history of morality; we see progress through wider experience, fuller knowledge, more extended and refined sympathies" (pp. 251–2). In other work, Sidgwick even finds in suttee something of "the true intuition" that the soul "was immortal," such that "the sentiment of the Hindoo widow is noble, though its expression is cruel and exaggerated." See Sidgwick, *Philosophy: Its Scope and Relations*, ed. James Ward (Macmillan, 1902), p. 171.
13 Sidgwick, *The Methods of Ethics*, p. 27.
14 Moore, *Principia Ethica* (Cambridge University Press, 1903), pp. 69–71.
15 Anthony Skelton, "Review of David Phillips, *Sidgwick's The Methods of Ethics: A Guide*," *Notre Dame Philosophical Reviews* (October 6, 2022), p. 8.
16 In my 1992 *Essays on Henry Sidgwick*, I criticized Sidgwick's hedonism and rational intuitionism, but since that time both of those views have received sophisticated philosophical defenses. See the previously cited works: de Lazari-Radek and Singer, *Eye of the Universe*; Crisp, *Cosmos*; Phillips, *A Guide*; and Parfit, *On What Matters*.
17 See Phillips, *A Guide*, pp. 53–7, and Crisp, *Cosmos*, pp. 32–56.
18 See, for example, Schneewind, *Sidgwick's Ethics and Victorian Moral Philosophy*; M. Nakano-Okuno, *Sidgwick and Contemporary Utilitarianism* (Palgrave Macmillan, 2007); Phillips, *A Guide*.
19 See his important posthumous work, *Lectures on the Philosophy of Kant*, ed. James Ward (Macmillan, 1905).
20 Which is to say that the foundationalism in Sidgwick's epistemology can often seem more aspirational than actual, and that the multiple criteria allow for a more holistic, dialogical, and social epistemological approach, as is evident from the broader expanse of Sidgwick's work. As the *Lectures on Green, Spencer, and Martineau* explain: "reflection shows us in the morality of earlier stages an element of what we now agree to regard as confusion and error. Therefore it seems to me reasonable to suppose that similar defects are

likely to lurk in our own current and accepted morality; even if observation and analysis of this morality had not led us – as they have in fact led me – to see such defects in it. How to eliminate, if possible, these elements of error, confusion, and uncertainty is, in my view, the fundamental question of ethics" (p. 352).

21 Sidgwick, *The Methods of Ethics*, p. 414.

22 Sidgwick, *The Methods of Ethics*, 1st edition (Macmillan, 1874), p. 473.

23 Sidgwick, *Lectures on Green, Spencer, and Martineau*, p. 188.

24 Ibid., p. 186.

25 Phillips, *A Guide*, p. 231.

26 Some even argue that Sidgwick is better viewed not as the last great classical utilitarian, but as the philosophical godfather of a new school of metaethical philosophy that would blossom in the first decades of the twentieth century (see Hurka, *British Ethical Theorists*), with ongoing relevance today. With Moore and others, such as Hastings Rashdall, utilitarianism sometimes became 'ideal' utilitarianism, the demand that a plurality of ultimate or intrinsic goods be maximized. But the metaethical school that Hurka traces back to Sidgwick is related to such philosophers as W. D. Ross, a deontological pluralist rather than a utilitarian, but one in line with Sidgwick's minimalist metaethics, even while arguing that there is a better way to patch up dogmatic intuitionism – namely, by appealing to the notion of prima facie duty, duty as defeasible, to address apparent conflicts. This approach also enjoys a considerable current academic following, and has importantly shaped the views of Parfit, Crisp, Stratton-Lake, and other Sidgwick enthusiasts.

27 Sidgwick, *The Methods of Ethics*, pp. 414–15.

28 Parfit, *Reasons and Persons*, Part Four.

29 See McMahan et al., eds., *Ethics and Existence*, for an extensive collection of essays elaborating on these challenges.

30 Sidgwick, *The Methods of Ethics*, p. 489.

31 See Schultz, *Henry Sidgwick, Eye of the Universe*, for a detailed account.

32 See Williams, "The Point of View of the Universe: Sidgwick and the Ambitions of Ethics," in his *The Sense of the Past: Essays in the History of Philosophy* (Princeton University Press, 2006), pp. 277–96.

33 See Parfit, *Reasons and Persons* and *On What Matters*, and de Lazari-Radek and Singer, *The Point of View of the Universe*, but also Crisp, "Partial Attachments," in McMahan, Campbell, Goodrich, and Ramakrishnan, eds., *Principles and Persons*, pp. 151–65.

34 But it is worth noting that Sidgwick's *The Principles of Political Economy* (Macmillan, 1883) contains his most extensive discussion of distributive justice and goes well beyond Mill and the earlier utilitarians in heavily qualifying any case for economic individualism and laissez-faire. As his analytical table of contents concisely puts it: "The egoistic influences of the individualistic organization of industry need to be counteracted: hence the moral value of Cooperation," and "Political economy has exploded the fallacy that the luxurious expenditure of the rich benefits the poor; but it has also drawn attention to the dangers of almsgiving" (p. xxiv). The work concludes: "there is reason to hope that, in minds of a nobler stamp, the full perception of the difficulties and risks attending the voluntary redistribution of wealth will only act as a spur to the sustained intellectual activity required for the successful accomplishment of this duty" (p. 595). But his labors with the

London and Cambridge Charity Organization Societies could cast him in a rather Dickensian light, given his eager attempts to sort the deserving from the undeserving poor.

35 See, again, Karuna Mantena, *Alibis of Empire: Henry Maine and the Ends of Liberal Imperialism* (Princeton University Press, 2010), which stresses how, over the course of the nineteenth century, "the central tenets of liberal imperialism were challenged as different forms of rebellion, resistance, and instability in the colonies instigated a more general crisis about the nature and purpose of imperial rule, a crisis that precipitated the waning of ethical justifications of empire.... In place of the universalist project of civilization, which at its core believed in the possibility of assimilating and modernizing native peoples, a new emphasis on the potentially insurmountable difference between peoples came to the fore" (pp. 17–18). In this context, Sidgwick is an oddly mixed bag of reactions, lamenting both the past and the present.

36 Sir John Seeley, *The Expansion of England: Two Courses of Lectures* (Macmillan, 1883), p. 10. Seeley urged England to get over the self-image of being "in a great pool, a swan's nest," and embrace the reality of Greater Britain and the related ethical/political duties.

37 See the important writings of Stefan Collini on Sidgwick's political theory and practice – "My Roles and Their Duties: Sidgwick as Philosopher, Professor, and Public Moralist," in Ross Harrison, ed., *Henry Sidgwick* (Oxford University Press / The British Academy, 2001), pp. 37–8. Also his contributions to Stefan Collini, Donald Winch, and John Burrow, eds., *That Noble Science of Politics* (Cambridge University Press, 1983), which track the long shadow Sidgwick's *Elements* cast over the Cambridge curriculum. As Collini claims, by the 1890s, Sidgwick actually did seem to think of himself as the Point of View of the Government, or at least the governmental perspective of Arthur Balfour.

38 In a letter from March 27, 1883 to his colleague Oscar Browning, Sidgwick agreed with Browning about the unsatisfactory state of the Indian Civil Service, but allowed "I should be very sorry if Cambridge retired from the competition and left the whole business of training Indian Civil servants in the hands of Oxford. I think such a step would tend to place us in a distinctly inferior position, and would injure us materially in indirect ways." See the letters to Browning included in *The Complete Works and Select Correspondence of Henry Sidgwick*, general ed. Bart Schultz, 2nd edition (InteLex, 1998).

39 A. Sidgwick and E. M. Sidgwick, *Henry Sidgwick: A Memoir* (Macmillan, 1906), p. 445.

40 Elkins, *Legacy of Violence*, p. 66. But, for many of the nuts-and-bolts details about imperial militaries and conflicts, V. G. Kiernan's works – for example *European Empires from Conquest to Collapse, 1815–1960* (Leicester University Press, 1982) – remain a valuable resource.

41 See the insightful article by David Miller, "The Political Philosophy of Henry Sidgwick," *Utilitas*, vol. 32 (2020), pp. 261–75. Miller rightly puzzles over how Sidgwick's work could skirt such core issues as political legitimacy.

42 Bell, *Dreamworlds of Race*, p. 307. Although Bell does not explore the possibility that Sidgwick, for all his dry anti-utopianism, belongs in the company of H. G. Wells or Jules Verne when it comes to spinning out "dreamworlds of race," or potential material for "steampunk" appropriations of the Victorian

world, there is a very real sense in which he did contribute to such developments, not least in his psychical research, which was markedly Orientalist in Said's sense. But "dreamworlds" does not seem like the right term, given all the anxiety and dread that Sidgwick harbored about the racializations of the future.

43 Sidgwick, *Principles of Political Economy*, p. 49. This was a favorite point that Sidgwick repeats nearly verbatim in a number of his works to illustrate how historical methods are a necessary supplement to analytical or deductive ones. Needless to say, Maine was not celebrating what he regarded as "primitive" communal property arrangements.

44 Included in *The Complete Works and Select Correspondence of Henry Sidgwick*, general ed. Schultz.

45 Sidgwick, *The Elements of Politics*, 4th edition (Macmillan, 1919), p. 312.

46 Ibid., p. 311.

47 Ibid., p. 313.

48 Ibid., pp. 345–6.

49 Ibid., pp. 382–4.

50 Ibid., pp. 213–14.

51 See Schultz, "A More Reasonable Ghost: Further Reflections on Henry Sidgwick and the Irrationality of the Universe," *Rounded Globe*, February 15, 2016, https://roundedglobe.com/books/4477156a-7bc9-4fb6-94f1-10901a557723/A%20More%20Reasonable%20Ghost:%20Further%20Reflections%20on%20Henry%20Sidgwick%20and%20the%20Irrationality%20of%20the%20Universe.

52 See Rita McWilliams Tullberg, *Women at Cambridge*, 2nd edition (Cambridge University Press, 1998).

53 On the practical ethics, see A. Skelton, "Utilitarian Practical Ethics: Sidgwick and Singer," in Placido Bucolo, Roger Crisp, and Bart Schultz, eds., *Henry Sidgwick: Ethics, Psychics, and Politics* (University of Catania, 2011).

54 Seeley, *Expansion of England*, p. 355.

55 Muirhead, "What Imperialism Means," reprinted in David Boucher, ed., *The British Idealists* (Cambridge University Press, 1997), p. 250. Curiously enough, this sympathetic account of British imperialism strikingly anticipates the arguments of Mehta and Pitts, zeroing in on John Stuart Mill as the higher-minded and more ardent utilitarian imperialist who saw in Empire "a guarantee of peace and free trade," as well as a force "to strengthen the moral influence in the counsels of Europe" (pp. 240–1). Mill recognized that "civilised nations owed each other sacred duties which were not owed to the lower races" (p. 241). And like Mehta and Pitts, Muirhead claims that Burke had a keener and wiser appreciation of difference.

56 As in the previous chapter, some of the material here concerning the racism of Mill and Sidgwick draws heavily on my earlier publications.

57 See, for another example, his correspondence with James Bryce, included in *The Complete Works and Select Correspondence of Henry Sidgwick*, general ed. Schultz. As elaborated below, Sidgwick's exchanges with Bryce are singularly revealing, not least because Bryce wrote more fully and explicitly about the subject of race, as in his 1902 Romanes Lecture, "The Relations of the Advanced and the Backward Races of Mankind" (Oxford at the Clarendon Press, 1902), which deals at length with questions of whether to allow legal intermarriage and "race-mixing." And Bryce considers such legal and

political implications even while admitting, in terms Sidgwick would have accepted, that "We may pass by the question of what constitutes racial differences, merely observing that stress must not be laid upon linguistic affinities; nor need we inquire how far the present backwardness of a race indicates inferior natural capacity, being content to take the existing state of things as we find it. Let us go to straight to the facts and problems which the contact of diverse races brings into being" (p. 9).

58 Sidgwick, *The Elements of Politics*, pp. 327–8.

59 Ibid., p. 327.

60 Quoted in Geoffrey Dutton, *The Hero as Murderer: The Life of Edward John Eyre, Australian Explorer and Governor of Jamaica, 1815–1901* (Collins, 1967), p. 250; Dutton's biography celebrates Eyre and Carlyle, bringing out how the Carlyleans cast the Governor as a "hero."

61 Sidgwick to Mary Sidgwick, Jan. 21, 1867 (Sidgwick Papers, Trinity College Library, Cambridge University).

62 Mill, *The Collected Works of John Stuart Mill*, vol. II: *The Principles of Political Economy Pt. 1*, ed. John M. Robson, Introduction by V. W. Bladen (University of Toronto Press, 1965), pp. 104–5. Mill's remarks about "the state of mind of the negroes" betray weaker versions of the same Carlylean stereotypes of Blacks as "lazy," "docile," and "sensuous," etc. In his *Principles of Political Economy*, Sidgwick expresses similar views, suggesting that an increase in wages for Indian railroad laborers might enable them to maintain their standard of living "with less energetic work" and "unsalutary indulgences"; he cites Lord Brassey on how the "Hindoo workman knows no other want than his daily portion of rice, and the torrid climate renders watertight habitations and ample clothing alike unnecessary. The labourer, therefore, desists from work as soon as he has provided for the necessities of the day" (p. 318, note 1).

63 Hall, *Civilizing Subjects*, p. 31. Hall also stresses the importance of Sidgwick's colleague Seeley as a continuing influence: "Empires, forgotten in the wake of decolonization as an embarrassment and source of guilt, re-emerge as it becomes clear that neo-colonialism is alive and well, and that imperial histories are playing a part in postcolonial politics.... Seeley's categories – race, nation and empire – remain central to reconfiguring those histories in postcolonial terms" (p. 3).

64 Fredrickson, *Racism*, p. 91. And here Sidgwick's deep indebtedness to Kantianism might multiply the problems.

65 As in the work of Bryce – see note 57, above.

66 As noted, even the well-researched work of Bell (see *The Idea of Greater Britain: Empire and the Future of World Order, 1860–1900* [Princeton University Press, 2011]) and his sometimes collaborator Casper Sylvest on late Victorian colonialism and imperialism seems to miss the point. Thus, Sylvest, quoting me, writes: "There is some truth in the statement that 'To gloss over the racism of the past is to perpetuate it', but to castigate Sidgwick for 'swimming in rather than examining the various prejudices of his times' seems too obvious an instance of the intellectual historian longing to be a time-travelling moralist" (*British Liberal Internationalism*, p. 136). But Sylvest actually concedes all of my major points, and seems only to object to my "schoolmaster" tone; also, my "time-travelling" involved nothing more than expressing objections that in substance might well have

been made by Bentham and others in the relevant historical contexts (indeed, even by Whewell). In fact, Bell himself writes of E. A. Freeman's "virulently racist" views (see p. 191 of his *Reordering the World*), and now highlights the significance of race and racism more forcefully, though with some curious lapses, missing the influential Sir Charles P. Lucas's *Greater Rome and Greater Britain*, first published in 1912 and often treated in comparison with Bryce's work.

67 Henry Sidgwick, *Miscellaneous Essays and Addresses*, ed. E. M. Sidgwick and A. Sidgwick (Macmillan, 1904), p. 219.

68 Pearson, *National Life and Character: A Forecast* (Macmillan, 1893), pp. 337–8. This work *is* included in Burton and Hofmeyr, eds., *Ten Books that Shaped the British Empire*, in an excellent chapter by Marilyn Lake, "'The Day Will Come': Charles H. Pearson's *National Life and Character: A Forecast*," pp. 90–111. As Lake argues, Pearson's claims were actually regarded as too restrained, too neutrally empirical, by some critics. It is surprising that Pearson makes no appearance in Lowe's *The Intimacies of Four Continents*, given his extensive accounts of the possible futures of various racialized groups. For an excellent history of anti-Asian prejudice in the US, see Iris Chang, *The Chinese in America: A Narrative History* (Penguin Books, 2004). The recent hate crimes against Asian populations are part of a long and horrific history of Anglo-American racism taking violent form, as in the two Opium Wars. It seems only fitting that the instigation of the second of those, from 1856 to 1860, has often been blamed on none other than Bentham's literary executor, disciple, and editor John Bowring, who was then serving as the British Governor of Hong Kong. See the *Autobiographical Recollections of Sir John Bowring*.

69 Pearson, *National Life and Character*, p. 342.

70 Ibid, pp. 343–4.

71 Ibid., p. 31. Pearson's claims about historical evolution bear some comparison to Kant's on cosmopolitan history, though with a more pessimistic conclusion – Kant thought that history would inexorably work toward the triumph of his race. Again, see Marwah, *Liberalism, Diversity and Domination*, and Robert Bernasconi's "Will the Real Kant Please Stand Up?" *Radical Philosophy*, vol. 117 (Jan.–Feb. 2003); also Huaping Lu-Adler, *Kant, Race, and Racism* (Oxford University Press, 2023).

72 Pearson, *National Life and Character*, pp. 84–5.

73 W. Stebbing, ed., *Charles Henry Pearson: Memorials by Himself, His Wife, and His Friends* (London: Longmans Green, 1900), p. 186.

74 Ibid.

75 Sidgwick to Pearson, Feb. 8, 1893, Bodleian MS.Eng.Lett.d.190, 175.

76 "Of course if it should become clear that the social amalgamation of two races would be debasing to the superior race, or otherwise demonstrably opposed to the interests of humanity at large, every effort ought to be made to carry into effect some drastic and permanent measures of separation": Sidgwick, *Elements*, p. 326, footnote 2. Sidgwick does express relief that proof of this "danger" has not yet been forthcoming.

77 Sidgwick, *Lectures on Green, Spencer, and Martineau,* p. 236. Eyre would have agreed.

78 Balfour, "Decadence," in W. Short, ed., *The Mind of Arthur James Balfour* (George H. Doran, 1918), p. 92. It seems obvious enough what Balfour would

have considered a "superior" breed of humanity. Ironically, Balfour was here delivering one of the Sidgwick Memorial Lectures at Newnham College. And as it transpired, another US president, none other than the Bull Moose Progressive Teddy Roosevelt, found the piece inspiring and wrote to Balfour: "It is equally to the interest of the British empire and of the United States that there should be no immigration in mass from Asia to Australia or North America." It was possibly in response to this fan letter that Balfour wrote to Roosevelt to propose an Anglo-Saxon Confederation, arguing that disarmament was a pipedream and peace would come "only when these powers have divided the world between them" (Short, ed., *The Mind of Arthur James Balfour*, pp. 274–84). That was a white "dreamworld" of race – or, rather, racism.

79 Otele, *African Europeans*, pp. 202–3.

80 Symonds, *Oxford and Empire*, especially chs. 4 and 9. And as Symonds notes, "During the high period of Empire between 1880 and 1914 the Prime Minister and Foreign Secretary were usually Oxford men; in the Indian Civil Service and Sudan Political Service Oxford men outnumbered Cambridge men by almost two to one. Over the whole period of British rule in India 15 Governors-General or Viceroys came from Oxford compared with five from Cambridge. Between 1888 and 1905 three Viceroys in succession were Balliol men. In the other direction the unique institution of the Rhodes Scholarships brought to Oxford hundreds of young men who had been selected as potential leaders from the colonies of settlement" (p. 2).

81 Chakrabarty, *The Crisis of Civilization: Exploring Global and Planetary Histories* (Oxford University Press, 2019).

82 For a still very useful summary of the state of the art at this stage, see J. J. C. Smart and Bernard Williams, *Utilitarianism For & Against* (Cambridge University Press, 1973), particularly the bibliography.

83 See his autobiography in Jeffrey A. Schaler, ed., *Peter Singer under Fire: The Moral Iconoclast Faces His Critics* (Open Court, 2009), p. 13.

84 Ibid., p. 74.

85 See Singer, "Famine, Affluence, and Morality", *Philosophy and Public Affairs*, vol. 1 (1972), pp. 229–43.

86 As one of the press reviewers of the manuscript of this book observed, we should note here that there is a considerable argumentative gap between "saving lives" and "promoting the greatest happiness," since the former may or may not accomplish the latter, and Singer does not always try to fill in the argument.

87 Singer, *One World Now*, pp. 9–10.

88 The book is available for free on the website The Life You Can Save, www.thelifeyoucansave.org.

89 Thomas Nagel, "What Peter Singer Wants of You," *New York Review of Books*, 25 (March 2010).

90 "Animal Liberation," *New York Review of Books* (April 1973).

91 This book has been completely revised and updated – see Singer, *Animal Liberation Now*.

92 This passage is from the first edition of Singer, *Animal Liberation: A New Ethics for Our Treatment of Animals* (HarperCollins, 1975), p. 20.

93 Singer, *Democracy and Disobedience* (Oxford University Press, 1973).

94 Singer, *Rethinking Life and Death* (Oxford University Press, 1994), pp. 187–206.

95 Singer, *The Expanding Circle*, 2nd edition (Princeton University Press, 2010), pp. 38–9.
96 Ibid., p. 199.
97 Ibid., p. 202.
98 For an exceptionally concise and insightful short account of Parfit's metaethical development, see Crisp, "Derek Parfit's Non-naturalist Cognitivism," in Paul Bloomfield and David Copp, eds., *The Oxford Handbook of Moral Realism* (Oxford University Press, 2023).
99 See *Does Anything Really Matter?* Also of special importance is the essay, with de Lazari-Radek, "Parfit on Act Consequentialism," in *Principles and Persons*, pp. 233–46.
100 Quoted in Singer, *One World Now*, p. 177, this passage is from *The Methods of Ethics*, p. 246.
101 Singer, *One World Now*, p. 185.
102 Ibid., pp. 186–7.
103 De Lazari-Radek and Singer, *The Point of View of the Universe*, pp. 310–14.
104 *One World Now*, p. 191.
105 Ibid., p. 197.
106 Ibid., p. 165.
107 Singer and Shih Chao-Hwei, *The Buddhist and the Ethicist* (Shambhala, 2023), is an extremely important work that takes some of the scattered remarks of both Singer and Parfit about the congeniality of their views with Buddhism to a much deeper level.
108 De Lazari-Radek and Singer, *The Point of View of the Universe*, pp. 310–14.
109 Sidgwick, *Practical Ethics*, ed. S. Bok (Oxford University Press, 1998), pp. 20–1.

4 Different Places, Different Voices, Different Virtues

1 Charles W. Mills, *Black Rights/White Wrongs: The Critique of Racial Liberalism* (Oxford University Press, 2017), p. 94.
2 Ibid., p. 71.
3 "Charles W. Mills Obituary," *New York Times*, Sept. 27, 2021.
4 Ibid.
5 Graeber and Wengrow, *The Dawn of Everything*, p. 17.
6 Ibid., p. 47.
7 Ibid., p. 52.
8 That cooperative arrangements have been more the norm than the exception in human history is not a point that has been front and center with most utilitarian economists. Elinor Ostrom won the Nobel Prize in Economics in 2009 for her work nudging economists to a belated recognition that the "tragedy of the commons" was less historical fact than ideological fancy. And on fear of the state, see James C. Scott on "Zomia" in *The Art of Not Being Governed: An Anarchist History of Upland Southeast Asia* (Yale University Press, 2010); Scott supports the case made by Graeber and Wengrow about the broad, global historical importance of "baseline communism."
9 As *The Red Deal* explains: "Under current US law, Indigenous sovereignty provides limited recourse. Tribes themselves represent a third sovereignty next to states and federal authorities. The imperialist foundation of federal Indian law, however, severely limits the exercise of tribal self-government. Racist

and colonial legal doctrines that make up the foundation of federal Indian law – such as the Doctrine of Discovery, domestic dependent nation status, and plenary power – and oversight by the Bureau of Indian Affairs, reveal that Indigenous–US relations are colonial to the core and remain centered on the acquisition of land. The successive stages of federal Indian law – allotment, citizenship, tribal enrollment, termination, and self-determination (our current era) – have also, in various ways, presented colonial domination as a form of empowerment, to enable Indigenous consent for their own dispossession": The Red Nation, *The Red Deal*, p. 28.

10 As movingly demonstrated by the 2023 movie *The Bones of Crows*, directed by Marie Clements and based on the true life story of Cree elder Aline Spears, who survived the horrors of the residential schools.

11 Nick Estes, Melanie Yazzie, Jennifer Nez Denetdale, and David Correia, *Red Nation Rising* (PM Press, 2021), p. 88.

12 The limit of plausible generalization is just about reached by Carolyn Smith-Morris in her *Indigenous Communalism: Belonging, Healthy Communities, and Decolonizing the Collective* (Rutgers University Press, 2019), which emphasizes the relational and communal ethics of many Indigenous peoples.

13 Ritchie, *Practicing New Worlds: Abolition and Emergent Strategies* (AK Press, 2023).

14 Kimmerer, *Braiding Sweetgrass* (Milkweed Editions, 2013), p. 123.

15 Ibid., pp. 56–7.

16 Kimmerer, "Nature Needs a New Pronoun: To Stop the Age of Extinction, Let's Start by Ditching 'It.'" *Yes! Magazine*, March 30, 2015.

17 Kimmerer, *Braiding Sweetgrass*, p. 55.

18 Ibid., p. 30.

19 Ibid., p. 58.

20 Ibid., p. 179.

21 Ibid., p. 28.

22 Ibid., p. 384.

23 The most extensive defense and elaboration of Leopold's Land Ethic is in J. Baird Callicott's *Thinking Like a Planet: The Land Ethic and the Earth Ethic* (Oxford University Press, 2014). Callicott's reading fleshes out the Land Ethic with a Humean metaethic and updated ecological framework. But he worries that the local nature of the Land Ethic unfits it for serving as an Earth Ethic.

24 See the Aldo Leopold Foundation (www.aldoleopold.org) for a short account of the Land Ethic.

25 Whyte, "Kinship," in the series *Kinship: Belonging in a World of Relations*, vol. V: *Practice* (Center for Humans and Nature, 2021), pp. 37–8. The notion of reciprocity at work here was not captured in that anthropological standard by Marcel Mauss, *The Gift*, since it is quite different from competitive status-seeking or self-interested tit-for-tat practices. Reciprocity as positive regard for the relational partner dissolves the rigid binary between altruism and self-interest.

26 See Savoy, *Trace: Memory, History, Race, and the American Landscape* (Counterpoint, 2016). Savoy, a geologist, does an extraordinary job of exposing how racism is inscribed in place names and geological formations, and she provides an important complement to Kimmerer on linguistic imperialism.

27 B. McKibben, *American Earth: Environmental Writing since Thoreau* (Library of America, 2008).

28 The Red Nation, *The Red Deal*, p. 27, citing Dina Gilio-Whitaker's poignant *As Long as Grass Grows* (Beacon Press, 2020). Under Trump, "millions of acres of this land were opened to oil and gas extraction, threatening Indigenous sacred sites and surrounding communities" (ibid.).
29 Grant, *The Passing of the Great Race; Or, the Racial Basis of European History* (Charles Scribner's Sons, 1916).
30 Spiro, *Defending the Master Race* (University of Vermont Press, 2009), p. 365. Arguably, it was only the opposition to Germany in World War II that kept the US from emulating many of the Nazi policies.
31 Hourdequin, *Environmental Ethics: From Theory to Practice* (Bloomsbury, 2015), p. 58.
32 Jamieson, "Animal Liberation Is an Environmental Ethic," in his collection *Morality's Progress* (Oxford University Press, 2008), p. 201.
33 Ibid., pp. 204–5. Samuel Scheffler's article on "Valuing," in his *Equality and Tradition: Questions of Value in Moral and Political Theory* (Oxford University Press, 2010), pp. 15–49, fleshes out the analytical issues involved in "valuing" as a process and how it differs from merely preferring or desiring. It is seriously ridiculous to think that "I value world peace" is equivalent to "I prefer world peace."
34 Jamieson, "Animal Liberation Is an Environmental Ethic," pp. 204–7. For Jamieson, the concept of "sentience" is far from simple, despite the deceptive, apparent clarity of a term like "pain." For him, sentience is entangled with other things, such that the "agency" of beings seems to play a role in ethical considerability as well. See, for an accessible account, his "Sentience Is More Complicated than You Think" (February 17, 2022), online video clip, www3.youtube.com/watch?v=iGIeyqY1RGo. He also notes that Buddhist traditions have been far more committed to the term "sentient creatures" than other cultural or religious traditions.
35 Jamieson, "Animal Liberation Is an Environmental Ethic," p. 210.
36 Ibid., p. 212.
37 Compare Tom Regan's *The Case for Animal Rights* (University of California Press, 1983) and Christine Korsgaard's *Fellow Creatures: Our Obligations to the Other Animals* (Oxford University Press, 2018) to Claire Palmer's relational or care-ethical alternative in *Animal Ethics in Context* (Columbia University Press, 2010).
38 The Red Nation, *The Red Deal*, p. 143.
39 Coulthard, *Red Skin, White Masks*, pp. 9–10.
40 Jamieson, "When Utilitarians Should Be Virtue Theorists," *Utilitas*, vol. 19, no. 2 (June 2007).
41 Ibid. That "the problem" is indeed *the Big problem* hardly needs additional support here, but for the record, the following works should convert anyone: David Attenborough, *A Life On Our Planet: My Witness Statement and a Vision for the Future* (Grand Central Publishing, 2022), and Rockström and Gaffney, *Breaking Boundaries*. *Kiss the Ground* (https://kisstheground.com) is an effective plea for regenerative agriculture, another cause that should be a priority for Effective Altruists.
42 But Jamieson misses an important gambit here by not pointing out how any sensible moral theory (even Whewell's) finds some role for universal benevolence, even if a subordinate one.
43 Jamieson, "When Utilitarians Should Be Virtue Theorists," pp. 161–2.

44 Ibid., p. 163.
45 Ibid., p. 169.
46 Ibid., p. 170. Of course, Parfit's "Triple Theory" was not so hostile to contractualism and Kantianism, though it did "consequentialize" them.
47 Ibid., pp. 165–6.
48 Ibid., p. 172.
49 Ibid., pp. 181–2. For a wealth of supportive perspectives, see K. D. Moore and M. P Nelson, eds., *Moral Ground: Ethical Action for a Planet in Peril* (Trinity University Press, 2010).
50 Jamieson, "When Utilitarians Should Be Virtue Theorists," p. 180.
51 Ibid., pp. 177–8.
52 See the *Manifesto of the Dark Mountain Project*, dark-mountain.net/about/manifesto.
53 Jamieson and Di Paola, "Climate Change, Liberalism, and the Public/Private Distinction," in Mark Budolfson, Tristram McPherson, and David Plunkett, eds., *Philosophy and Climate* (Oxford University Press, 2021).
54 Jamieson, *Reason in a Dark Time*, pp. 188–9.
55 Ibid., pp. 192–3. There are important criticisms of the now widespread use of the term "Anthropocene." As The Red Nation, *The Red Deal*, urges, "Framing this as a panhuman problem or a problem of the species – such as the term 'the Anthropocene,' the geological age of the fossil fuel economy – misses the point. A select few are hoarding the life rafts while also shooting holes in a sinking ship.... The immiseration of billions sustains the gilded lives of the few. The upper one-tenth of humanity is responsible for half of the carbon emissions from consumption" (*The Red Deal*, p. 19).
56 Here too, a vast landscape of scholarly literature opens up – on the green virtues and virtue ethics, see such works as Ronald L. Sandler, *Character and Environment: A Virtue-Oriented Approach to Environmental Ethics* (Columbia University Press, 2007), which objects to Jamieson's utilitarian glossing of the green virtues: "rather than implying that utilitarians should be virtue theorists locally for this issue, virtue-oriented ethical theory's capacity to respond to collective action problems, including those where an individual agent's actions are nearly inconsequential to causing or resolving the problem, favors it over utilitarianism generally" (p. 166).
57 Jennings, *Paradise Now* (Random House, 2016), pp. 84–5. For the rich history of cooperative experiments in the US, see John Curl, *For All the People: Uncovering the Hidden History of Cooperation, Cooperative Movements, and Communalism in America*, 2nd edition (PM Press, 2012). So many of those involved in these experiments in living took themselves to be promoting happiness, or justice as the public face of love, that no concise summary is possible.
58 Graeber and Wengrow, *The Dawn of Everything*, pp. 19–20. This is the kind of security that really matters.
59 Sandler, *Character and Environment*, presents an elaborate typology of possible green virtues, with one category specifically featuring those related to environmental activism: cooperativeness, commitment, perseverance, creativity, and optimism (see p. 82). The list is nice as far as it goes, but it is drawn from a very limited menu of sources. And it is very odd to omit courage in this context. Compare Ritchie's *Practicing New Worlds* on the pleasures of resistance.

60 The Red Nation, *The Red Deal*, pp. 24–5. Across the world, environmental activists are at high risk. For an all-too-typical story about the murder of two activists in Honduras, see www.wbur.org/hereandnow/2023/01/16/honduras-environmental-activist-deaths.

61 On the variable foci of justice, which can parallel the variable foci of charity, see Roger Crisp and Theron Pummer, "Effective Justice," *Journal of Moral Philosophy* (August 13, 2020).

62 Dungy, ed., *Black Nature* (University of Georgia Press, 2009); Dunning, *Black to Nature* (University Press of Mississippi, 2021); Glave, *Rooted in the Earth* (Lawrence Hill Books, 2010).

63 Bullard, *Dumping in Dixie* (Westview Press, 2000, first published 1990).

64 Smith, *African American Environmental Thought* (University Press of Kansas, 2007), p. 195.

65 Pellow, *Total Liberation: The Power and Promise of Animal Rights and the Radical Earth Movement* (University of Minnesota Press, 2014), pp. 255–6.

66 See Luke W. Cole and Sheila R. Foster, *From the Ground Up: Environmental Racism and the Rise of the Environmental Justice Movement* (New York University Press, 2001), p. 26.

67 The Red Nation, *The Red Deal*, p. 5.

68 Pellow, *What Is Critical Environmental Justice?* (Polity, 2018), pp. 152–3. The language of the so-called "Rights of Nature," as recognized by such countries as Ecuador and New Zealand, is not the most coherent one, though a focus on stopping "ecocide" may prove valuable – see Stop Ecocide (www.stopecocide.earth). Legal standing is distinct from political/ethical standing.

69 See Mary Christina Wood, *Nature's Trust: Environmental Law for a New Ecological Age* (Cambridge University Press, 2014), an informed critique of regulatory agencies, laws, and policies supposedly concerned with environmental protection. Wood defends a revisionary, trust-based framework for environmental law and policy.

70 Kimmerer, *Braiding Sweetgrass*, p. 322. The Onondaga Nation lost that case, but in due course were successful in their "Land Back" efforts, being granted by the State of New York control of most of Lake Onondaga – see Joseph Winters, "Major Land Back Victory in New York State," *Grist* (July 5, 2022).

71 The Red Nation, *The Red Deal*, pp. 34, 98. Also Winona LaDuke, "Love Your Mother Deeply," *The Progressive* (October/November 2023).

72 The Red Nation, *The Red Deal*, p. 8.

73 Ibid., p. 141.

74 Simpson, *As We Have Always Done*, p. 78.

75 Ibid., p. 91.

76 Ibid., p. 162. On schooling in Native American communities, see the NPR *Codeswitch* story "A New Movement on Standing Rock" (www.npr.org/sections/codeswitch/2022/04/04/1090825396/a-new-movement-on-standing-rock. Mní Wičhóni Nakíčižiŋ Wóuŋspe, or the Defenders of the Water School, is located near the site of the historic Standing Rock protest community formed to oppose the Dakota Access pipeline and reflects the ongoing impact of that movement.

77 Simpson, *As We Have Always Done*, pp. 164–5.

78 For more on this, see Edgar Villanueva, *Decolonizing Wealth: Indigenous Wisdom to Heal Divides and Restore Balance*, 2nd edition (Berrett-Koehler Publishers, 2021).

79 Ord would insist that unaligned AI is the most serious threat at this point, but the lifestyle of the green virtues can also help people distance themselves from the tech world.
80 Consider the remarkable Davi Kopenawa Yanomami, whose book *The Falling Sky: Words of a Yanomami Shaman* (Belknap Press of Harvard University Press, 2013) conveys a starker image of the realities of extractivist capitalism than anything emanating from mainstream academic social sciences.
81 See Driver, *Consequentialism* (Routledge, 2012) and *Uneasy Virtue* (Cambridge University Press, 2001).
82 Whyte, "White Allies, Let's Be Honest about Decolonization," *Yes! Magazine: The Decolonization Issue* (April 3, 2018).
83 Ibid.
84 Carol J. Adams, Alice Crary, and Lori Gruen, *The Good It Promises, the Harm It Does: Critical Essays on Effective Altruism* (Oxford University Press, 2023). Critical utilitarians can agree with the claims of many of the activists featured in this work.
85 Ibid., pp. 27–8.
86 Ibid., p. xi.
87 Paul Vallely, *Philanthropy, from Aristotle to Zuckerberg* (Bloomsbury Continuum, 2020) is the most comprehensive treatment of Western philanthropy.
88 The echoes in this work of opposition to the Benthamite and Millian perspectives are obvious. See Jerry Mander and Victoria Tauli-Corpuz, *Paradigm Wars: Indigenous Peoples' Resistance to Economic Globalization* (International Forum on Globalization, 2002), and Abhijit V. Banerjee and Esther Duflo, *Poor Economics: A Radical Rethinking of the Way to Fight Global Poverty* (PublicAffairs, 2012); also Mander, *The Capitalism Papers: Fatal Flaws of an Obsolete System* (Counterpoint, 2013).
89 The book is available for free at The Life You Can Save, www.thelifeyoucansave .org.
90 Singer, *Life*, pp. 19–20.
91 Charles Camosy has argued that, despite Singer's Benthamite hostility to the major religions (excepting Buddhism), there is scarcely any daylight between them on Good Samaritanism – see Camosy, *Peter Singer and Christian Ethics: Beyond Polarization* (Cambridge University Press, 2012), p. 259.
92 Ibid., pp. 22–3.
93 Ibid., p. 24.
94 Consider the problem of homelessness in the UK, where it affects over 300,000 people, with many others in positions of precarity. The numbers in the US are nearly double that. Food insecurity is an even more pervasive problem, with around 25 percent of the US population and 9 percent of the UK population suffering from it. Given the widespread associated feelings of insecurity and anxiety, and however "relative" the poverty in question may be, EA can seem like a very hard sell. As Anthony B. Atkinson has long argued, the challenge is not just inequality, but also, and even by mainstream economic standards, the ways in which anti-poverty programs continue to fail and ever greater numbers of people are getting left behind in the "affluent" world. See his *Inequality: What Can Be Done?* (Harvard University Press, 2015); also Deaton, *Economics in America*.
95 Elizabeth Ashford, "Severe Poverty as an Unjust Emergency," in Paul

Woodruff, ed., *The Ethics of Giving: Philosophers' Perspectives on Philanthropy* (Oxford University Press, 2018), especially pp. 134–6. Ashford worries that "Act consequentialism focuses on the impact of the various choices available to individual agents, taking as given the background social structures… However, structural harms can be seen only by looking at the combined effects of the ongoing patterns of behavior of a vast number of agents" (p. 130). She argues, however, that EA "can be presented in a way that is compatible with acknowledging the need for structural reform…. If affluent agents' duties to donate to NGOs are understood as backup duties, which arise because the primary duties imposed by the human right to subsistence have been violated, it is built into this way of framing the duties to donate to NGOs that the status quo is fundamentally unjust" (p. 123).

96 The Life You Can Save, www.thelifeyoucansave.org, pp. 43–4.

97 For an up-to-date review, see Larry S. Temkin, *Being Good in a World of Need* (Oxford University Press, 2023), especially chs. 11–14. See also his appendix A, on "How Expected Utility Theory Can Drive Us off the Rails," for a concise statement of the type of critique noted in my earlier chapters. On Deaton's argument that Singer and EA might be "doing more harm than good," he judiciously concludes: "I don't believe that we have all the evidence we need, about the direct and indirect short-term and long-term consequences of aid efforts, to definitively conclude whether past aid efforts have done more good than harm, or whether future aid efforts are likely to do so" (p. 280). He also points up the problem that, even if as individuals we might be obligated to support aid agencies, we might, as collectives, bring about "morally undesirable outcomes" by doing so, leaving it unclear how to reconcile the individual and collective perspectives.

98 Singer, *Life*, p. 89.

99 Ibid., pp. 109–10. The "warm glow" that comes from giving is quite real, though it can only be achieved indirectly, not by giving with the direct aim of getting the warm glow. But whatever the allure of reasons of pure impartiality, Singer, like Sidgwick, has always hedged his bets by casting in an attractive light an other-minded vision of "self-interest," albeit with a streak of anti-consumerism (not to mention veganism) and disgust with the lifestyles of the rich and famous that everyone from Gandhi to Arne Naess to Freya Mathews could appreciate. This fact comes as a jolt to many with fixed prejudices about the meaning of utilitarianism.

100 Ibid., p. 165.

101 Ibid., pp. 165–7.

102 Ibid., pp. 163–4.

103 Ibid., pp. 164–5. But see Ratik Asokan, "The Long Struggle of India's Sanitation Workers," and the other articles on Modi's reactionary and authoritarian policies in India, in the August 24, 2023 *New York Review of Books.*

104 Singer, *Doing the Most Good: How Effective Altruism Is Changing Ideas about Living Ethically* (Yale University Press, 2015), p. 7. He allows that most EAs "think that other values are good because they are essential for the building of communities in which people can live better lives, lives free of oppression, and have greater self-respect and freedom to do what they want as well as experience less suffering and premature death" (p. 9). Temkin's *Being Good in a World of Need* discusses distance and intermediary actors (and corruption), showing that Singer's pond example is not so clear-cut. His chapter 10

provides a somewhat abstract account of how worries about continuing the legacy of colonialism apply in the case of EA.

105 Singer, *Doing the Most Good*, p. 142.

106 Ibid., pp. 146–7. On the environmental philosophy side, it is puzzling that Singer so rarely mentions other examples of ecocentrism.

107 De Lazari-Radek and Singer, *The Point of View of the Universe*, pp. 373–4.

108 And recall Jamieson's confession that "About all one can do in defending a normative theory, in my opinion, is to appeal to its intrinsic plausibility, and then demonstrate that it suffers from fewer and less severe infirmities and failures than alternative views" – a perspective sharing much with Bentham and Mill. And his account of moral progress is more open to particularity and context: "Still in the end it is difficult to live at a level as general and abstract even as the American fight for civil rights and animal rights. Ultimately, most of us live short lives compared to human history, and in small neighborhoods compared to the global community. It is from this point of view that our lives are lived and our motivation is gathered. Small moments of success should be savoured" (*Morality's Progress*, p. 15 and p. 26). Such an outlook seems congenially place-based and bioregional.

109 Mathews, "Deep Ecology," in Jamieson, ed., *A Companion to Environmental Philosophy* (Blackwell Publishers, 2001), pp. 228–9.

110 Kimmerer, *Braiding Sweetgrass*, p. 338.

111 Ibid., p. 236.

112 Guha, "Postscript," in Nina Witoszek and Andrew Brennan, eds., *Philosophical Dialogues: Arne Naess and the Progress of Ecosophy* (Rowman & Littlefield, 1999), p. 478. Guha's original article criticized the American Deep Ecologists (but not Naess), and in Naess's response to it he noted that in Europe "the term 'free nature' is more important than 'wilderness,' and it is increasingly used when discussing very large parts of the Third World. The difference between the two terms is that 'free nature' is compatible with human habitation, provided that this habitation is in no way dominant. Thus delimited, it is of course a rather vague and ambiguous term – but it is a term which implies a context-dependent compromise between the human and natural habitus" (p. 327).

113 Ibid., pp. 475–6.

114 Although he does not make the connection, Erik Linstrum, in *Age of Emergency: Living with Violence at the End of the British Empire* (Oxford University Press, 2023), paints a vivid picture of the context in which the World Wildlife Fund came to be. Looking at the denial that shaped the British outlook, denial with respect to the actual brutality and violence for which they were responsible, Linstrum notes that "moral language was ubiquitous in the age of counterinsurgency. Christians described ongoing struggles between good and evil while humanitarians spoke of the urgent obligation to help human beings in need. Although both kinds of language promised moral clarity, they actually led to endless moral compromise.... Aid workers conceded the barest definition of humanity to the empire's enemies, then denied their political legitimacy and their claim to be treated justly. Appealing to morality proved far more effective at rationalizing behavior than changing it" (p. 143).

115 Val Plumwood added: "We need a concept of the other as interconnected with self, but as also a separate being in their own right, accepting the 'uncontrollable, tenacious otherness' of the world as a condition of freedom and

identity for both self and other. Feminist theory can help us here because it has developed logical and philosophical frameworks based on maintaining the tension between Same and Different rather than generally eliminating difference in favour of sameness or vice versa": Plumwood, *Environmental Culture: The Ecological Crisis of Reason* (Routledge, 2002), p. 201.

116 Veganism alone is of tremendous importance – see Singer, *Why Vegan? Eating Ethically* (Liveright Publishing Corp. / W. W. Norton and Co., 2020).

117 Anthony J. Nocella II et al., eds., *A Historical Scholarly Collection of Writings on the Earth Liberation Front* (Peter Lang Publishing, Inc., 2019), p. 55.

118 Jamieson, *Morality's Progress*, p. 15 and p. 26.

119 Quoted in Gruen's "The Change We Need," in Adams, Crary, and Gruen, eds., *The Good It Promises, the Harm It Does*, p. 248. Speth is a very sober radical – see his *They Knew: The U.S. Federal Government's Fifty-Year Role in Causing the Climate Crisis* (MIT Press, 2022).

120 MacAskill, *What We Owe the Future* (Basic Books, 2023), p. 232.

121 Though Douglas Tompkins, the founder of North Face who went on to found the Deep Ecology Foundation, is a suggestive example – see www.discoverthenetworks.org/organizations/foundation-for-deep-ecology-fde.

122 MacAskill, *What We Owe the Future*.

123 Ibid., p. 260.

124 Ibid., p. 99.

125 Ibid., p. 100.

126 MacAskill denies that EA/Longtermism entails utilitarianism or vice versa, but he admits that he personally favors it and sees no inconsistency with EA.

127 Dale Jamieson and Bonnie Nadzam, *Love in the Anthropocene* (OR Books, 2015), pp. 204–7. Compare Ritchie, *Practicing New Worlds*.

128 Jamieson and Nadzam, *Love in the Anthropocene*, pp. 209–14.

Index